LAW, LAWYERS, AND LAYMEN

LAW, LAWYERS, AND LAYMEN

Making Sense of the American Legal System

BERTRAM HARNETT

HARCOURT BRACE JOVANOVICH, PUBLISHERS

SAN DIEGO   NEW YORK   LONDON

Copyright © 1984 by Bertram Harnett

Library of Congress Cataloging in Publication Data
Harnett, Bertram.
    Law, lawyers, and laymen.
    Includes index.
    1. Lawyers—United States. 2. Practice of law—United
States. 3. Judges—United States. I. Title.
KF297.H33   1983   340'.023'73   83-10779
ISBN 0-15-149102-x

Designed by Dalia Hartman

Printed in the United States of America

B C D E

To Ruth—FOR EVERYTHING AND ALWAYS.

ACKNOWLEDGMENTS

If it is true that behind every successful man stands a loyal woman, and if that notion is contagious, this book should be a smashing success—three loyal women stand behind it.

My wife, Ruth, read and reread manuscript through every draft. In addition to her editorial comment, she supplied candid, intelligent criticism. In a more classic uxorial role, she endured endless hours of writing and put up with me in the loving manner she has in such abundance. Marie Arana-Ward, a highly talented woman and my editor, became a fast friend during the editorial process. Marie was indispensable to the paring and shaping of the book. I am grateful to her for her understanding and sagacity and the gentle but firm way in which she guided the edition of this work. Janet Trama, my longtime assistant, secretary, and friend, was responsible for the physical production of the manuscript. Her ability and her continued willingness to allow me to impose on her loyalty and good nature secure her place in this triad of women to whom I owe so much.

I am grateful to William and Peter Jovanovich for their early confidence in *Law, Lawyers, and Laymen,* my first book for the general reader. With no shortage of self-interest, I hope history resoundingly vindicates their judgment.

Many of my colleagues in the profession—judges, practicing lawyers, and professors—reviewed parts of my manuscript. While their help was vital to me, I am reluctant to list them here lest they be associated with positions of mine which they neither agree with nor care to acknowledge publicly. Unfortunately, candor in the established legal profession goes a long way—most of it the wrong way.

My father, fellow lawyer, and ever-staunch supporter, the late Sydney G. Harnett, still lives vividly in my mind and on the pages of this book. The Colonel, as he was known to many with respect and with affection, inspired me to enter the legal profession, and he constantly urged me in my every effort to become a better lawyer. The Colonel would have loved every word of this book if only because I wrote it. He was a father to have.

New York City   BERTRAM HARNETT
January 1984

CONTENTS

ACKNOWLEDGMENTS   vii

BY WAY OF INTRODUCTION   1

1.

THE RULE OF LAW(YERS)   9

It Is Only People Who Rule   11
Doing Injustice by Law   13
The Formal Shapes of Law   16
Uncertainty and Complication of the Law   19
Hierarchy of Legal Redress   22
Law Is What the Lawyers Say It Is   23

2.

THE BAR, ITS PEOPLE, AND HOW THEY GET THERE   27

Law School   29
Meaning of the Bar   35
Some of the Numbers   37
Some of the Definitions   38
The Geography of Law Practice   40
Meaning of "Practicing Law"   42
Constitutional Restraints On Admission Requirements   45
The Bar Examination   47
More Open Admission   49
Common Characteristics of Lawyers   50

3.

HOW LAWYERS KNOW THE LAW   57

Reliance upon General Knowledge   59
Research in Law Libraries   60
Common Law: Weighing Cases as Precedent   64
Construing Statutes   67
Citations   69
Getting into the Problem   72
The March of Experience   77

4.

LEGAL ETHICS 79

Ethics and the Legal Monopoly 82
The Model Rules of Professional Conduct 84
The Advertising and Solicitation Bugaboos 87
Confidentiality 91
Candor toward the Tribunal 93
Harassing the Other Side 95
Social Imperative 96
Can a Decent Person Be a Lawyer? 97

5.

THE ECONOMICS OF LAWYERING 99

Legal Fees 102
Disbursements 117
Making Partner 118
Getting Business and Holding On to It 119
The Bottom Line 122

6.

PAYING FOR THE CASE 125

Contingent-Fee Practices 127
Conflicts of Interest by Contingent Fee 129
Is Contingent-Fee Practice Desirable? 130
Safeguards in Contingent-Fee Lawyering 134
"No Fault" Automobile Liability 137
Should the Loser Pay the Winner's Fee? 140
Fixing the Loser's Legal Costs 142
Legal Adventures with Private Fee Responsibility 144

7.

HAVING YOUR "DAY IN COURT" 147

The Federal Courts 150
State Courts 151
Trials 152
Appeals 163

Essential Uncertainties of Proof   167
Choice of Trial Lawyer   170
The Competency of Trial Lawyers   171
Certifying Trial Lawyer Specialists   175
You Never Know What a Jury Will Do   179

8.

TO BE A CLIENT   183

The Basics of Choosing a Lawyer   186
Conflicts of Interest   190
Political Pull   193
Cost   194
Is a Lawyer Necessary?   196
Settlement Decisions   200
The Litigating Wife   201
Lawyer Wariness of Clients   205
Client Misconceptions   206
Client Handling   208

9.

SELECTING JUDGES   213

Selection of State Judges   216
Judicial Campaigning   217
Political "Appointment"   221
The Federal System   223
Bar Association Role in Judicial Selection   226
Merit Selection   228
Blocks to Judicial Quality   231
Career Judges   235

10.

VIEW FROM THE BENCH   239

Order in the Court   241
How Judges Decide Cases: The Moving Hypothesis   244
The Power and Person of Judges   248
Witnesses   251

The Slow Pace of Trials   257
The Judge as a Person   259
Efficiency versus Justice   263
Judges Settling Cases   265
Trusting Juries   269
Are Judges Soft on Criminals?   272
Sentencing   276
Bail   278
In Requiem   279

11.
EQUAL/LEGAL/SOCIAL/JUSTICE   281

Supremacy of Social Justice   284
Lawyers in Politics   285
Need for Supermajority Consensus   287
Public Responsibilities of Lawyers   289
Social Conscience in Lawyering   292
Inequality   296
Prepaid Legal Services   300
Agenda for Legal-System Reform   301
Overload of Social Utility   303
Paying the Price   305

READING MATERIALS   309

INDEX   315

—BY WAY OF INTRODUCTION—

In our society, where iconoclasm flourishes, law continues to maintain misleading holds on popular imagination. Law is perceived as an objective force for fairness and justice, or a set of fixed standards by which everyone's conduct can be measured. But neither is the case. Perhaps the need to believe feeds the belief itself; stability and protection are eagerly sought in uncertain times of rising feelings of individual vulnerability. Whatever the reason, these popular perceptions are wildly inaccurate, principally because they fail to take into account the actual nature of the legal process and the critical effect of lawyering in projecting the law. The ideals are illusion; the law is what the lawyers say it is.

Lawyers are reasonably obvious features of our legal system. But how many people know what the law really is and what lawyers really do? What makes the members of this vocational group, who function not only in their profession but also as leaders in government, business, and nonprofit institutional sectors, think as they think and do as they do? There are compelling reasons to seek better understanding, because the working of law is a public monopoly, an exclusive franchise for the "guild" of lawyers, a great social grant by the many to the few. Despite the immense social significance of lawyers, not much is told, in the endless ranks of moldering tomes in our libraries, to laymen of lawyers.

I mean *truly* told. I do not mean works that appear on bestseller lists, which abound with glossy versions of sensational cases of famous people, the celebration of social causes, even the "kiss and tell" memoirs, embroidered by publicly recognized lawyers, bootstrapping themselves on their more well-known clients—lawyers whose confessed virtues plainly exclude modesty. The legal affairs of the mighty and the exotic and the doings of the notorious may satisfy our appetite for legal drama, perhaps cater to our taste for gossip and peeping; but their narration seldom illuminates the ways of lawyers that underlie our legal system. Nor does it tell of the workaday lawyer and his live-a-day client, of the legal array in the operating senses that bear daily on society and every man's expectations.

As you will find out for yourself, if you persist, there is no attempt here either to idealize lawyers or to derogate them. There are no "cheap shots" or pious exercises. My basic thesis is that lawyering is an inseparable part of the law itself. To understand law in this country, people must understand its lawyers; for their better or for their worse.

Now, quite obviously, law has more elements than simply lawyers. There are principles of morality; the necessity for regulated, civilized conduct; and the common feeling of what is "right"—every society has its customs and usages. There are intellectual and logical bases to each rule and statute, but many rules are nothing more than entrenched ruminations about proper conduct. The wielding of legal thought is as critical as its idealized content. There are the laymen-become-clients to whom the entire process is addressed, whose purses and demands make it all necessary and possible. In the broadest sense, the layman is the material of the law. The trinity of law, lawyers, and laymen—the interrelationship between the elements—reveals the essence of American law.

According to the fashion of its times, a Bar Association program in New York was once entitled "Is Law Dead?" The more appropriate question is whether it ever lived. Law has no existence apart from people. The stubbornly held belief that ours is a government of law, not men, presupposes some law energy source that can be tapped for regulatory force much in the same way as electricity. But law is neither a physical nor a metaphysical phenomenon. It is a process, a mode of human conduct.

An understanding of the working law is based on an acceptance of three premises.

The law is not a body of rules; the rules are only a medium for the working of a greater process. The common misunderstanding is that law is a series of precisely drawn, written, or readily located rules that cover all eventualities. This is a computer version of the law; one implying that the answer to a question can be programmed and printed out at the touch of a juridical button. The judge is merely a recorded announcement. This is nonsense; there is no organized or easily understandable body of American law. There is a vast and malleable assortment of felt principles of human conduct, as well as oral and written rules and usages, which human beings must process. In their application, "rules" of law filter through human sieves that, by force of personality, and under social pressure, alter their contents and consistency. That law works differently for different, or even similar, people, in different places at different times is a fundamental observation.

The process of law is an art form crafted by human beings called lawyers. Judges, prosecutors, private practitioners, hosts of legislators, and a heavy proportion of important governmental officials are lawyers. Undeniably, the stuff of American law fits squarely in the hands of lawyers. What is done in law is done by them. Rules of law are as perceived and declared by lawyers; they are what lawyers say they are. And they are "applied" to the case at hand by lawyers. Law is a process; in truth, it is an art form. The rules are the medium. One way or another, by the mouth and the hand of the lawyer—figuratively fashioned as a ruler, a spoon, a fan, a brush, a palette knife, a scalpel, a baseball bat, or a shovel—the medium of law is worked around and laid on.

Shaped "legal rights" are valued only in relation to the practicality of asserting them. Legal rights are meaningless where they are unobtainable. To become meaningful, rights must be shaped and recognized; supporting facts must be provable, enforcement of those rights must be practicable, and economic means must be available to bear the cost of pursuing them.

However unconventional, the message of these three premises is crucial. Those who go to law, or rely on it, or would change it for whatever reason will do so deficiently if they do not comprehend it.

The public lives with its lawyers in a love-hate relationship; the lawyer is both hero and villain. One lawyer who stalks the popular imagination is wise and kind, puffing his pipe while dispensing pearls of wisdom to the comfort of all. This lawyer relieves the distressed and is admired for his dignity, knowledge, skill, and dedication, not to mention his high social prestige. Another lawyer is pictured as a sorcerer, breaking contracts, and pulling legal rabbits from hats, on cue and with proper payment. He may be disputatious, rapacious, conniving, greedily sucking in fees, and thoroughly unprincipled—a hired gun.

The unpopularity of lawyers is understandable. In being oppressed, people often associate the opposing lawyer with their oppressor. The lawyer spells danger; he is a mysterious figure who magically negotiates the costly perils of courts and legal maneuver. Many are already in trouble when they deal with lawyers, and the prospect of legal expense is doubly disturbing. Lawyers are simply bad news.

President Harry Truman minced no words in paying his lack of respect: "Lawyers with Ha-Vud [Harvard] accents . . . seemed they didn't make any bones about telling lies. Dress a man up in a fancy suit with a fancy accent and people think he's telling the truth. . . . Those lawyers with Ha-Vud accents are always thinking up new ways to take advantage of people. . . ."

Literary figures through the ages have delighted in tweaking the legal beak. Boswell reports in his *Life of Johnson,* "He did not care to speak ill of any man behind his back, but he believed the gentleman was an attorney." In *Anatomy of Melancholy, Democritus to the Recorder* (1621), Robert Burton suggested, "We may justly tax our wrangling lawyers. They do grow old in lawsuits, are so litigious and busy here on earth, that I think they will plead their clients' causes hereafter, some of them in hell."

In *Utopia,* Thomas More found "they have no lawyers among them, for they consider them as a sort of people whose profession it is to disguise matters." Jonathan Swift in *Gulliver's Travels* was very much in accord: "There was a society of men among us, bred up from their youth in the art of proving, by words multiplied for the purpose, that white is black and black is white, according as they are paid." A particular hurt was to learn that gentle poet John Milton said in "Of Education," "Some allude to the trade of law, grounding their purposes not on the prudent and heavenly contemplation of justice and equity, which was never taught them, but on the promising and pleasing thoughts of litigious terms, fat contentions, and flowing fees."

Lawyers come to grief even in scripture: "And [Jesus] said, Woe unto you also, ye lawyers! for ye lade men with burdens grievous to be borne, and ye yourselves touch not the burdens with one of your fingers" (Luke 11:46).

While the older literary masters tended to deal harshly with the lawyer, he seems to fare rather better in modern arts, especially in television and film. The villainous lawyer (normally a slightly seedy and cynical type) may consort with his co-villainous principals to some initial but temporary advantage. In the end the day belongs to our real legal hero, whether he be magnificently maned old Judge

Turner (the family lawyer forever) dishing out soap-opera advice to the teary clients who receive his counsel with mobile, expressive faces, or the square-jawed, no-nonsense district attorney, the breezy but earnest "for the defense" lawyer, or the young firebrand (in shirt sleeves) at society's barricades with legal armaments from his neighborhood storefront office's law library.

Popular taste for legal entertainment runs high. There are always best-selling books and well-patronized performances, live or filmed, featuring some legal legerdemain. I suppose I will always remember the old scene in which the suave fictional defense lawyer sums up for the jury with a vial of dark fluid conspicuously in his hand. His words are, roughly, "Poison, they say. The prosecution rests its case on its contention that this vial contains poison. *This* is our case." He proceeds to drink the entire vial in one swallow, and sits down as the jury gasps in horror. Court is recessed, and the lawyer walks gravely out of the courtroom, past clamoring reporters, and into a hotel room across the street where his associates await with a stomach pump. Thus disencumbered, he returns to the courtroom in time to receive without a flicker of the eye or pyloric spasm the joyous verdict of "not guilty." Truly, a dramatic tour de force, not recommended in today's era of courthouse delays, unpredictable elevators, and traffic congestion.

Undeniably, there is media magnetism in sensational murder trials and lurid matrimonial litigation. Military courts-martial, labor strife, official misconduct, kidnappings, grisly injuries—all such cases can become popular drama depending on the journalistic concoctions that accompany them. Much of the curiosity about such cases may be morbid, even gossipy, or titillating, but the lawyers themselves become public figures by association. Through highly publicized court adventures, some lawyers become celebrities, and cater to their success while feeding either their egos or their pocketbooks, or both. Their dress, speech, and appearance become more and more flamboyant; they write books on their legal derring-do; they foster attention with pungent newspaper quotations freely dispersed—sometimes with professional assistance—and they may even cultivate various conspicuous idiosyncrasies.

But these are the exceptions, the rare ones. Beyond family, friends, clients, the narrowly publicized scope of community activity, and immediate legal circles, the lawyer is not well known. His work is obscured in confidential office practice, or in court cases significant only to the participants. In urban centers where legal economic success flourishes, the biggest fee earners, the best result getters, the happiest lawyers, usually labor in relative obscurity. There are countless lawyers with annual incomes well in excess of $250,000 who are unknown to the public. Some earn over a million dollars a year. And although many lawyers do become known as politicians or officeholders, their legal track records rarely rise to public view.

This book is meant to address the layman's misconceptions of law and lawyers, and the monumental gap between legal theory and the practice of law. The layman's critical error is in separating an idealized concept of law from the controversial person of the lawyer. The cynicism with which the lawyer is viewed neglects the reality that the lawyer is intimately connected with the essential regulation of society's affairs.

That I will not dwell in the text at length on analysis of specific economic, racial, ethnic, and religious weights in law applications does not mean that any of these are unimportant. Quite to the contrary, they are critically important. The recognition of these weights is crucial in the realization that human application swamps the printed rule, and that everything that affects a person going to law affects law. That law works differently for different, or even similar, people is a basic premise of this book.

Legal writing is a discipline of its own. Briefs and memoranda of law, as well as court opinions, communicate measured facts with reasoned conclusions and citations from supporting legal documents. But this is not a lawbook, and does not follow that example. For an old legal hand, the delivery of a meaningful message about law without lapsing into supporting footnotes and citations of cases, statutes, or the writings of others is a tight exercise. To quell the urge, even to cool the fever of unease, I employ the occasional authoritative text reference to augment my personal observations and ratiocinations. It is hard for a dyed-in-the-wool legalist to describe legal import in naked prose, unadorned with the comforting dressings of the supportive authorities customarily invoked to add to the weight of conclusion, and to protect from charges of legal adventurism. The temptation to pull that wool up higher, or to hedge, or maybe to find the back door is always there. If, now and then, a minuet of legal letters is paced out before you, be understanding, if not forgiving. But, irrepressible as a lawyer must be, allow me to double back and observe that law is not easy. There are those who would have us believe that everything can be made simple. In actuality, many legal involvements are complex, and forces of change are constantly at work, shaping and reshaping legal conclusion.

Another caution (a caveat, as we lawyers are wont to say) is in order, a kind of truth-in-legal-packaging. References to rules of law are made here only in general terms, to carry a point. They are not to be translated to specific problems. In the legal process, tidy principles cannot be meted out wholesale for specific application; constant qualification and reservation—the handmaidens of legal conclusion, annoying though they may be—must attach to every single one of them. Appealing though "pat" rules and principles may be, they are not the way of the law.

This introduction closes on a necessary gender note. Throughout the text, the references are to "he" even though "she" shares equally in legal involvement. Because of the limitations of the English language in impersonal singular reference, I thought of using "s/he" but eventually opted against it, both for awkwardness and the fear of overburdening the unconventionality of much of my substantive message. Consequently, I now reflect, at times the lesser includes the greater.

1

THE
RULE OF
LAW(YERS)

May 1 of every year is proclaimed by Congress as "Law Day." Although it is not exactly a holiday that closes the banks or precipitates picnics, it does provide an opportunity to reflect on things legal. In places where lawyers congregate, formal observances are held, sometimes with food and drink, but always with speeches.

The standard forensic fare of Law Day tends to sonorous exaltation of the "Rule of Law." It may surface as in the phrase "We have a government of laws, not men"; or as a courthouse wall in Ohio reads: "The Rule of Law Is Preferable to the Rule of the Individual." Rule of law, however loftily characterized, presumes equal treatment of all persons by objectively applied standards.

——IT IS ONLY PEOPLE WHO RULE——

If "rule of law" implies a government of laws, not people, then the phrase is rich in naïveté. There is no such thing as a government of laws. People are ruled by people, not by laws.

We have a government of people who apply law, whatever that may be. It cannot be otherwise. Law is an abstraction, and no abstraction is self-executing. A critical interaction of people with the given word is at the heart of our legal process. A balance of rule and personality is built into administering, legislating, judging, and practicing law.

Professor Marshall McLuhan taught us that the form of communication is a part of the message itself. Accordingly, the mental and emotional capabilities or idiosyncrasies of the person applying the law become part and parcel of the law he perceives and applies.

We have no cohesive or defined body of law. In no one place is there stated the whole of our law, or even a major portion of it. We do have vast aggregates of statutes, reported court cases, administrative rules, textbooks, treatises, texts, oral traditions, and accumulated learning. When a lawyer seeks to apply law, he recollects, reads, reflects, and reasons from these aggregates, all the while filtering them through his own mental and emotional processes, consciously and unconsciously.

The facts of a case are critical elements of any legal conclusion that may follow. To apply law, the lawyer must first nail down the situation under question, and this can be an elusive target. It is well known that there are at least two sides to every case. Indeed, seasoned lawyers are heard to say that there are three sides to every case: what each of the two parties claim and what *really* happened.

While some "determination" of facts must precede legal conclusion in any specific case, fact finding remains a derived process. It may or may not yield an accurate conclusion as to what actually took place. I say "derived process" because the lawyers and judges do not typically see or hear the facts firsthand. The lawyer mainly hears the facts from his client, who has a questionably subjective perspective. The judge or jury must determine the facts from conflicting testimonies of uneven witnesses in an adversary trial, in which opposing lawyers of varying capabilities strain to give color to their clients' versions, and to distort any truth that threatens their clients' positions.

In essence, "determination" of facts means "assumption" of facts. When a lawyer renders an opinion on facts, he assumes they are true. In court, determination of facts still means assumption, because if the judge and jury accept one version of the facts, they are really making an assumption only from their personal perception of the evidence. Many an injustice is attributed to faulty rules, when the loser simply was not believed. Many a wrong legal move has been made because a lawyer and his client have not communicated the pertinent facts to one another.

With facts assumed, the legal decision involves any associated practicalities, any applicable affective moral and social precepts, any subjectivities of the one "applying the law." These factors together with perceived rules produce the result, the decision in the case, the advice given, the counsel taken . . . the law.

Realistically, the law is not a thing, or even a rule. It is a process that enables society to function by regularizing and coordinating the relations of its participants. Finding, choosing, advising, counseling, and applying law are creative acts of individuals; and wielding the mass of written and oral components of law can be characterized as an art form.

My notion is that law is not what is "on the books." Law is what comes out of them. The process of law involves human application of perceived rules to perceived happenings.

Under the rule of law, we hear, people are supposed to act, be governed, and be adjudicated according to the letter or principle of objectively invoked rules of law uniformly recognized. The reality that I have seen in over three decades of legal multipractice is that law application cannot be purely objective or impersonal. I have seen that lawyers (including judges, who are a kind of "lawyer") vary in intellect and in nimbleness of rule manipulation. They vary in competence and financial means. They include, along with those of sterling traits, the stupid, lazy, error prone, impatient, vain, fearful, sympathetic, avaricious, vengeful, dishonest, envious, greedy, bigoted, disturbed, and more. In the hands of these people, the law is vulnerable to all kinds of personal preferences and perspectives. One individual's personal standards can wreak havoc on even the clearest rule. The potential for deviation from any rule is limitless.

It is, then, a fundamental error to regard legal application as a mechanical process. Lawyers and judges are not cogs in a computer mechanism. They are thinking, unthinking beings with all the frailties of the human condition.

This concept is essential to anyone who would seek to understand law as it exists in this country. True, "words" of rules must be known. They are important and comfortable, for they ostensibly represent some consensus of how particular causes are to be determined. But which line of rules to pick? How much willingness to stretch a point? How clear are the facts; can they be looked at differently? How different are the law appliers? What personal, political, or economic factors are afoot? Between the underlying event and the final decision—that ambiguous ideal called "justice"—lies a critical mass of the subjective, the practical, and the fortuitous.

——DOING INJUSTICE BY LAW——

Law and justice are not always or even necessarily synonymous, although they theoretically—and often—converge. It is unrealistic to expect that every rule of law will be universally considered justice in every individual case. By the very nature of a process where one person gains at the expense of another, or where one suffers sanctions, it is a bit much to expect everyone to agree always that justice has been done.

Law and injustice link classically where there are mistakes of law, failures to establish the actual happening, or incidences of corrupt official conduct. In these cases, a result or decision is wrongly applied, and the "proper" legal action is thwarted. The classic story is of the lawyer who telegraphed his victorious client a two-word telegram: "Justice triumphed." Responded the client by return wire: "Appeal at once."

Law and justice too often diverge when people cannot afford to seek legal remedy or defense. These instances may not arise from a lack of funds, but because the transgressions are minor. How many will sue for the price of a defective mail-order pen if it cost only one dollar? This does not mean that the rules of law dealing with defective products apply to products worth thousands but not to one-dollar products. Yet it works out that way almost every time. Justice is also frustrated by economics where the burden of a rule presses more heavily on the poor than on the rich: the rules of bail, for those who cannot afford to post bail, are meaningless.

What of the manufacturing companies polluting the rivers with massive amounts of chemical wastes? How many lone citizens, even those with means, can afford full litigation, involving huge numbers of legal environmental challenges with technical applications, particularly if their powerful corporate adversaries are fighting for big dollars?

A salutary change in recent years has come in the form of financial subsidies for disadvantaged plaintiffs who seek to challenge wrongdoers. Law offices that furnish legal assistance to the poor are increasing in number, as are "public interest" law firms. Pro-consumer procedures and environmental protection laws are on the rise. Developments such as these have come about because of acknowledged difficulties in asserting one's rights and affording legal assistance.

And there is the "unjust" law. Law and morality do not necessarily equate, and individual moral codes vary greatly. A law may be regarded as unjust by an individual, in the way military conscription is by a conscientious objector, or liquor restrictions are by thirsty citizens of a dry area, or antiabortion laws are by pregnant women who do not wish to bear children. Among people there are individual differences, often deeply held, on what is "just" in these moral issues.

Until it is upset, however, the legal rule prevails by some previous consensus. Some, for instance, may deplore the possession of marijuana; others may favor it. Whether marijuana possession is to be prohibited by law is a social judgment; if the populace wishes it, its elected legislature, by statute, will render marijuana sale criminal. If sufficient consensus develops to change the statute, marijuana use will become legalized. But as long as they are denied possession by law, marijuana users will feel that the laws inhibiting them are unjust. Any law may be plain enough and acceptable to most, but to some it may be implacably unjust.

Sometimes a principle of general social utility prevails over individual happenstance. To illustrate, there is a legal rule that a contract for a sale of a house must be in writing; an oral agreement is not enforceable. Suppose Ames orally agreed to sell his house to Burton and they shook hands on the transaction. Burton went out immediately and ordered new furniture and sold her old place. Then Ames reneged before any contract was drawn because someone else offered him more money. Burton, who has plainly suffered damage, cannot compel Ames to sell her the house or even collect any money damages. The rule of law limiting the enforcement of contracts for real estate sales to written ones is meant to protect the security of real estate titles. The requirement of written contracts presumably promotes certainty. The legal rule unabashedly favors this general purpose at the expense of the occasional individual injustice.

Statutory rape is a crime in which a man engages in sexual relations with a young woman below a defined age. Whether he has her consent or not is immaterial. Statutory rape laws are on the books to protect young women from imposition and, perhaps, from themselves. Let us assume that the age of consent is seventeen years. If a maturely developed female of sixteen years of age, who looks to be in her twenties, sexually encourages a man, and he responds, he has committed statutory rape. Whether or not he thinks this is unjust— whether or not he was seduced—he is guilty. The deterrent force of the statute remains all-important, and as an example to others he is punished.

Consider, too, a written contract—freely entered into and fair when made—that later turns out to be a very bad bargain. The holder of the short end and eventual loser in a lawsuit may feel very put upon, even disadvantaged by the result, but stable society relies on the enforceability of contracts. In these instances, it is assumed that individual injustice must be subordinated to preemptive social regularization.

Some lawyers would argue that the right application of the law, by definition, produces justice. They would separate the law from principles of morality, holding that the law correctly applied represents a justice even though it may be unfair to the affected individual. Are they right? Or do they toy with semantics? I think the latter. "Justice," in the legal sense, holds a narrower, more parochial meaning than that broader justice which encircles political, moral, social, and economic fairness.

——THE FORMAL SHAPES OF LAW——

Laws, strictly stated, are usually one of three varieties: statutes enacted by legislatures, rules and regulations of administrators of the executive branches, and the results of court cases, called "decisions" or "opinions." There are overlaps because court cases may interpret, uphold, or strike down statutes or rules and regulations. The body of court cases, taken together, is generally known as the "common law." Legal rights that do not emanate from statute or executive regulation are known as "common-law rights."

Statutes are pronouncements by legislatures; they are declarations of law. Legislatures acting as a body make law; individual legislators do not. Historically, English common law was *the* law, with relatively infrequent statutory insertion. But where statutes were proclaimed, they took precedence over cases. In this country, particularly in modern times, statutes are more and more the facts of legal life, and with them grow the administrative infrastructures. A legislative enactment on a subject preempts common-law case rules except where courts strike down or limit statutes, usually on grounds of unconstitutionality. Where statutes are incomplete or ambiguous, the courts step in with interpretative authority, which, in truth, often results in a rewriting of the statutes.

Administrative units of government issue rules and regulations to implement their mandating legislation. But whereas legislative action takes hegemony over case law, the courts assert primacy in adjudicating whether the administrative rules and regulations are properly taken in implementation of the pertinent statutes. The line between enforcing the legislature's policy and interposition by a court of its own policy judgment is uncertain, and one that is the subject of ongoing debate.

In theory, court decisions are not general declarations of law at all. Each is based on the specific facts of the case before the court. Presumably, if an identical case were to reappear in that court, the same result would follow. However, identical cases do not occur with any frequency. In similar cases—a more usual occurrence—the common-law judge may, by logical deduction, extend the principle of the prior case to the present one. The rule of the prior case becomes the "precedent" (an example to follow)—a key word in common law. Decided cases form a body of precedent from which other judges decide cases, and, in turn, lawyers predict the court outcome of fact situations placed before them.

From this emanates the fiction that judges under our common-law system only "discover" or "find" the law; they do not make law. Theoretically, making law is for legislatures, but statutory gaps, ambiguities, and constitutionality give ample rein to judicial creativity. The belief that judges never make law is absurd.

The power of judges to make law has been dramatically illustrated in the last two decades by such federal court directives as those involving school desegregation (school busing), prisoners' rights, mental institutions, and housing or employment discrimination cases. Professor David S. Clark pointed out in a 1981 *Southern California Law Review* article that public-law litigation emerged from the new social structure and climate of the country following World War II, culminating in a large increase in the 1960's in federal civil filings. In many of the cases, federal judges prescribed the conduct of local officials, even to the point of supervising school districts. While many lawyers and others believe the federal courts have gone too far, it is beyond doubt that they have been making law with relish and without apology. In his *America in Search of Itself* (1982), Theodore White wrote, "What concerns us here is the role of the federal courts in changing the system and thus the elemental forces in American politics. For the courts were now spraying the United States Constitution into every nook and cranny of national life, draping it about matters best left to state legislatures, or about trivia which in other times might have been left to city halls or town councils." In an amusing quotation, White further offers that the United States Supreme Court is "always an institution of political judgment masquerading as a council of priests."

While the courts wallow in the comfortable assumption that they only decide each case before them, they will be quick to concede that its principles should govern similar cases. Actually, courts do make case law (as opposed merely to finding the result in the library) in at least four principal respects: in overruling a prior precedent, in considering the fact situation of a case not previously recorded, in distinguishing cases from one another, and, most subtly, in their ability to choose between precedents.

The choice of line of precedents is inherently a personal value judgment. When faced with a contractual clause barring blacks, for example, is civil liberty or freedom of contract the guiding star? Must the polluter desist from contaminating the air, or is he simply a property owner exercising his legal rights? The choice need not be one of grand concept. A fine point under the Social Service Assistance Laws in New York states that damage to a mattress by insect infestation is not a fortuitous event, and reimbursement for destroyed property is not called for. Nevertheless, another provision allows for payment if emergency need can be proved. In one particular case, payment for a new mattress was demanded because the owner claimed an emergency need for bedding infested by insects. By selecting the "emergency" principle rather than the "requirement of a fortuitous event for property destruction reimbursement," payment for a new mattress was secured.

Vague (weasel) phrases such as acting "reasonably," "in good faith," "in the best interest of the child," and "under due process" are often used to imply that governing precedent does not exist. Claiming that a defendant acted "reasonably" in facts close to, yet distinguishable from, a case where an earlier defendant was held to have acted "unreasonably" may really be a way of simply not following the prior result. The processes of recognizing such vague language, of rationalizing precedent to form a new result, of distinguishing cases, and of ignoring them in style are all part of the judge's art, and that of all lawyers who must figure out what to tell a client.

There are, nonetheless, substantial advantages in the use of precedent in deciding cases. Whereas statutes proclaim law in established terms, precedent serves to establish and clarify common law. If every law case were to start from ground zero, without precedents, social order would become chaotic. Cases that conclude in lawyers' offices, and many in court as well, tend to follow existing uncontroversial precedent or clear senses of proper conduct. Our society is long-lived and does not lack for previous example. Precedent is work-efficient; there is no need to reinvent the wheel every time. Prior cases are also educative; they make available the accumulated wisdom of previous judges who may have been confronted with resembling situations.

—UNCERTAINTY AND COMPLICATION— OF THE LAW

The primary and most meaningful assurance of legal justice in the courtroom lies in the person of the judge. How different is this actuality from the lay concept that a prefabricated legal rule exists for every happening and that an automaton judge dispenses it. In the real legal world, the only certainty is the lack of certainty.

People criticize lawyers—in part fairly—for complicating the law. They believe that if it were not for lawyers, law would be certain. Judge Jerome Frank wrote a fascinating book, *Law and the Modern Mind*, which first appeared in 1931, legal light-years ahead of its time. Judge Frank characterized the notion that law can be made stationary and certain as a "Basic Myth." He also offered a Freudian explanation for the layman's quest to derive certainty from law: he saw the search as an effort to find in law a father substitute of authority, certainty, and infallibility. However passé Freud may seem today, Judge Frank's 1931 invocation of Freudian theory at least deserves high marks for insight and courageous willingness to make the point to a legal establishment still encrusted in ancient theory.

Lawyers are partially to blame for their own image as complicators of the law. Poor methods of communicating with clients are endemic to lawyers. Clients listen to legal verbiage, to complicated explanations that trace the language of statutes or cases, and shake their heads. Many lawyers are not even aware that laymen may not understand them. Because many lawyers speak only in the precise language they believe necessary to their craft, they ignore the lay point of view and fail to communicate any message at all.

Lawyers who counsel are particularly responsible for communicating effectively with their clients. In the end, the client makes his decision not on what his lawyer actually told him, but on what he thinks his lawyer told him. Unhappily, in addition to the poor communicators, there are those lawyers who see complication as part of their mystique, and feel that the more the client believes in the lawyer's unique expertise, the more dependent he becomes.

Too many lawyers try to give the impression that the law is certain and that they will assuredly take care of everything. They may themselves believe it. But complications in adversarial or government proceedings are inevitable, and their end effects are confusing. If the client persists in believing those original assurances, it is the lawyer for the other side who becomes the complicating factor, a thought rarely discouraged by his own lawyer.

Many legal matters are complex to begin with; this is a point generally lost. Cases that cannot be adjusted amicably between the parties themselves—that persist even after discussions between representing lawyers—tend by adverse selection to be the more troublesome ones. These are the situations that come to court, and the more unyielding of these rise to higher appellate courts, which issue the opinions that become general precedent.

People find ingenious means of complicating the law. They figure out complex compliances, evasions, and ways of doing things. As government regulation enlarges its spheres, sophisticated devices and new methods are generated. The country is brimming with tax shelters, sales and leaseback of realty, new white-collar crimes, reckless securities sellers, alternative manners of credit extension, and innovative patterns of the distribution of goods and services. There are always the latest ways to tap social assistance, and change landlord-tenant control regulations. Why should anyone think all this can be reduced to simplicity? Was there ever any constitutional promise of a legal rose garden?

Let us say a decision has been reached in a trial court, then reversed by an intermediate appellate court, and later modified by a higher court. The same facts held throughout the proceeding, without any pertinent intervening new cases or statutes. In New York, for example, it is possible for many judges to differ in opinion on the very same case. The trial judge may rule one way, then the Appellate Division may reverse in a split decision, with three judges favoring reversal and only two judges favoring affirmation. In this hypothetical case, we now have three judges holding one opinion and three others with an opposing view. Suppose the Court of Appeals decides, on further appeal, to reverse the Appellate Division, modify the trial court ruling, and remand the case back to the trial court. We can see a four-to-three split of the maximum judicial complement of that court. The New York Judges, thirteen in all, will have divided seven to six on a single case; and yet that case will ultimately go down in the books as a single document of authority for subsequent cases. It would seem there is unease in a system where every other judge finds the law to be different on a given set of facts. More subtly, there is no assurance that even more judges would help the resolution; the issues could become even more clouded.

There are also the diachronic changes. Take the United States Supreme Court cases of the past two decades on school desegregation, obscenity, abortion, and sex discrimination. Past precedent was totally redefined each time. But why? Were the decisions wrong the first time? Or are judicial decisions, and the understanding of "law" that follows in their wake, each a sometime thing, subject to the caprices of prevailing social and political attitude? This is one of the most difficult questions of the law, and I suppose the answer is that much law is indeed a social and political response, and laws relate to the societal matrix that gives them reason to exist in the first place. A delicate stability between discernible preexisting rules and changing morals and mores must be maintained; the line of living law, predictable yet acceptable, is not easy to draw. It lives perilously close to rigidity on one side and uncertainty on the other. Yet law must be known to be followed.

Ironically, some uncertainty in law is good—not bad. The flexibility of the common law accommodates changes in social policy and revised social expectation. It leaves room for human compassion and mercy; it enables anticipation of the unanticipated. Since the purpose of law is to serve the ends of the society which sponsors it, an ability to respond to special or changed circumstances, or to correct past errors, is indispensable.

Judge Frank pointed out that United States Supreme Court Justice Oliver Wendell Holmes, Jr., "has been telling us for 50 years that in effect the Golden Rule is that there is no Golden Rule." It was Holmes himself who uttered one of the classic maxims of the law when he said, "The life of the law has not been logic; it has been experience." The sentence following that one in his book *The Common Law* (1881) is not so well known, but is equally instructive: "The felt necessities of the time, the prevalent moral and political theories, intuitions of public policy, avowed or unconscious, even the prejudices which judges share with their fellow-men, have a good deal more to do than the syllogism in determining the rules by which man shall be governed."

Holmes said long ago that laws are essentially predictions of what judges would do if presented with a fact situation. That has to be augmented with the observation that lawyers must now guess what administrative officials will do, as well. Indeed, lawyers must be alert to what legislatures might do, let alone to what they have already done.

—HIERARCHY OF LEGAL REDRESS—

As a structure, legal redress is pyramidal. At its wide base, most people behave passably well towards each other. They simply assume that their grievances are among life's events; they forget them or hold grudges. If they do have disputes, they settle them, or not, quickly and among themselves. Most disputes never surface in a lawyer's office or in court. People will accept wrongdoing to them without going to court because too often they are unwilling to undertake the legal expenses or suffer the unpleasantries. Anyone persisting in seeking legal remedy goes to a lawyer's office, where he becomes a "client" with a "case." If left unsettled even after representative lawyers have discussed the matter, the case proceeds to a trial court for adjudication. Some cases may go on to an intermediate appeal. Of these, only a small number step up to the highest appellate court, the top of the legal pyramid.

The first legal person to field a dispute for one side or the other is a lawyer. The lawyer may review his client's complaint and tell him to drop it, settle it by some form of compromise, or pay up. Here, the lawyer applies the law and the client accepts it. The lawyer's understanding and proclamation of the law and its practicalities dispose of the matter so far as the client is concerned. Criminal charges may be dropped when a defense lawyer consults with enforcement authorities. Or a plea bargain—a criminal-case compromise—may be struck, making later court appearance no more than a formality. If the district attorney declines to prosecute, it is he who is applying the law. So is a government official when he declares whether there is or is not a violation, and when he levies a fine. Many government officials uttering suspiciously legal things are neither lawyers nor judges, but inspectors, accountants, economists, policemen, or even clerks.

The trial judge steps in only when the case goes to court. He makes the initial judicial decision, sometimes with, sometimes without, a jury. The judge decides only the disputes or prosecutions that come before him; he does not counsel, he does not represent either side—he decides. He may, however, insert himself between the parties to try to reach a compromise in the case.

The concept of a pyramidal hierarchy should be reemphasized here. Most disputes unresolved by the participants are settled between their lawyers some time before trial. In comparison, cases decided in open court are relatively few. With each successive level of appeal—and there are normally two—the pyramid narrows. The higher the court in the judicial hierarchy, the fewer cases it hears, and the greater general effect its proclamations carry. Higher-court decisions tend to become published and known, and thus feed back into the system of personal, then lawyer, then judicial, applications of law.

——LAW IS WHAT THE LAWYERS—— SAY IT IS

People apply the law themselves in an endless variety of situations. We are fond of criticizing those who take the law into their own hands. Although we generally reserve censure for drastic retributions such as lynching, the fact is that Americans usually do take the law in their own hands. Most people commonly resolve their legal problems by working it out without a lawyer and outside the court. Our concern here, however, is not with informal lay resolution. It is, rather, with the formal encounters between people and the law, where law ostensibly rules and outsiders call the legal tune.

The role of a judge, who is a kind of lawyer, is generally understood. The most emphatic example of the law being what the lawyers say it is occurs when a decision is reached in court. The law of that case is exactly what the lawyer-turned-judge (but always a lawyer) declares it to be. If the case is reversed on appeal, other lawyers will do the declaring. Most shrouded in mystique is the practicing lawyer, really the pivotal person of the legal process, the relater of the people to the courts, the front receiving line of society's law business, and the licensed holder of a franchise in the state-constituted law monopoly.

If a client comes to a lawyer with a supposed claim, and then declines—by virtue of the lawyer's advice—to take his claim to court, the lawyer fixes the law. The "law application" in that claim for that client was made for him by a lawyer in the privacy of his own law office.

Actually, civil (not criminal) lawyers, more than they appear in disputed court cases, give advice (perhaps on taxes or tenant's rights), or they represent personal or corporate interests in transactions (as in negotiating agreements or buying a house or an apartment), or they execute single-party transactions (a will, a trust). Very often the functions of counseling, negotiating, and drafting combine, as, for instance, where a client intends to purchase a business. The lawyer may outline legal problems and advise a plan of best procedure for the purchase offer, considering tax factors. He may then negotiate the terms of the purchase with the other side, and finally draw up the contracts, leases, deeds, and corporate papers necessary to implement the transaction. Where the lawyer is counselor, advocate, or draftsman of legal documentation, his way to proceed is the way the client proceeds.

If a client acts on the advice, or accepts the work product, of a lawyer, he is accepting the lawyer's conception of the law as the governing law. For better or worse, and very definitely for richer or poorer, the lawyer has called the law. The lawyer's articulation of the law *is* law so far as that occasion is concerned for that client.

People hire lawyers and pay them a great deal of money. They entrust lawyers with their most important affairs. They listen to lawyers with fear or gladness, reassurance or worry—always at a time important to them. There is a signal relationship here—but one so little understood.

The nervous man in the grey suit stood before the stern-faced judge, who glared down at him.

"Young man, you broke the law. What do you have to say for yourself?"

"But, your honor, I did not know I was breaking the law."

"Ignorance of the law is no excuse!"

"Really? I didn't know that."

2

THE BAR,
ITS PEOPLE,
AND HOW
THEY GET THERE

All states, the District of Columbia, the territories, and the federal courts, separately, require of lawyers an official license to "practice law." This licensing procedure is most popularly known as "admission to the bar" or "being admitted."

Today's lawyer enters law school after two to four years of undergraduate work. As prerequisite to admission, the better-regarded law schools now require a four-year college degree. In law school, the lawyer completes a three-year course leading to an LL.B. (Bachelor of Laws) or J.D. (Juris Doctor) degree. My LL.B. degree was granted by Columbia University Law School in 1948. Some twenty-five years later, for an uncomplicated $25 payment, I received a new diploma proclaiming me a Juris Doctor, which is the law school diploma now generally awarded. Years ago it was feasible to qualify for bar admission with only law office work experience, and with no law school attendance. While that method, called "reading law," only continues vestigially nowadays, lawyers who came into law that way still practice.

A qualifying test known as the "bar examination" must be passed, perhaps a residency requirement met, and character and fitness must be screened by some agency, before formal induction to practice.

LAW SCHOOL

Law school admission is really the basic screening device in determining who will become lawyers. It has been estimated that about half of those seeking law school admission (with varying degrees of resolution and scope, to be sure) fail to get in, and never become lawyers because of that early but fatal rejection. Yet this does not remotely compare with the Japanese experience, where only one-half of 1 percent of the would-be-lawyer applicants are able to get into the one national law school necessary to become a lawyer.

In 1982, there were 171 law schools approved by the American Bar Association (ABA), of which 139 were also members of the Association of American Law Schools (AALS). Every state recognizes graduation from an ABA-approved school as satisfying the legal education requirement for bar admission. There are a handful of law schools accredited by neither ABA nor AALS, and their graduates generally can qualify for bar admission only in the state of the school's location. The principal effect of AALS accreditation is in the transferring of credits between law schools. All the better-regarded law schools hold AALS accreditation.

The LSAT, or Law School Admissions Test, is, in general, the single most important tool in law school admission, although it is most often used in tandem with undergraduate college grade averages. Inclusion within the top twenty percentile keeps in the running applicants with superior college grades from highly regarded undergraduate schools. Theoretically, the raw scores are fitted to a scale that makes LSAT scores comparable to all given since 1948, the time of the test's introduction. However, the competitive scores are now so high that many old-timers (vintage forty and beyond) cannot quite make up their minds whether the students are smarter or the grading is easier today. Reasonable adjustment to today's world urges belief in the latter, although the suspicion of the former tugs uneasily.

There are many private study courses and LSAT tutorings available. It is good to take one of the reputable courses, for it provides the disciplined regimen to do the test samples that most students require. It may build confidence; fear is itself disqualifying to some.

Many students find themselves dissatisfied with their LSAT scores and wish to try again. There is considered to be a thirty-point marginal variation, up or down, in any individual student's test performance the second time. If the first performance is merely creditable, the student should consider the risk of retesting. While some improve markedly, they are not many, and almost an equal number do worse. To mean anything, improvement must break out of the thirty-point anticipated margin. Some observers of the scene believe an improvement,.to be meaningful, should exceed by as much as sixty points.

A particularly troublesome aspect of the LSAT lies in the very skills and capacities it is designed to measure. The quick reader holds an obvious advantage, and although fast reading is a useful faculty for lawyering and law studying, it is only a desirable but not necessary trait of successful lawyering. In practice and study situations, there is time for reading. Comprehension is the key, not within a short time, but within a reasonable time. The candidate with a quick mind has the testing edge over his more deliberate and plodding —yet perhaps in the end more perspicacious—colleague. The LSAT puts a premium on skills that are more germane to some branches of the law than others: one is the ability to hold variables in mental solution, and to interplay them. This sort of conceptualization plays a heavier role in a tax scheme or corporate reorganization, perhaps in an estate plan, or complicated contractual negotiation of many terms and principles and subcategories, than it does in the more commonplace lawyering instances of buying a house or evicting a tenant for nonpayment of rent. Many important legal activities stress entirely different attributes. The patience of the matrimonial counselor, the reactivity of the trial lawyer, and the judgment of the wise counselor are traits not evaluated on any LSAT.

While the LSAT and college grades are flawed as omnipotent indices, they do say something. Before we chase blind ambition—or, worse, the ambition of another—we must first be honest with ourselves. Those who do poorly there must ask themselves, "Is the law for me?"

Surprisingly, most people, even many students, fail to appreciate qualitative differences between law schools. A lawyer is a lawyer and that is that. But that is not that. Initial law school training may be pivotal in a lawyer's whole career. It sets his sights, imprints initial legal work habits, establishes a durable attitude to the law, and creates opportunities. Although it is certainly true that many graduates of lesser-known and often lightly regarded law schools go on to become superb lawyers, and some graduates of the ranking schools become lawyers of low capability, the probabilities do not go that way. Given equality of talent, the superior schools tend to produce better-trained prospects, and offer greater opportunities for employment in varied directions.

Harvard, controversy of fading glory or no, still stands, by reputation, at the national law school summit, closely followed by Yale and then Columbia. These three have traditionally stood apart in legal regard, although Stanford has now joined their company in the eyes of most in the East and by all in the West. In the next rank stand the law schools of the universities of California at Berkeley (sometimes called "Boalt"), Chicago, Michigan, New York University, Pennsylvania, Texas, and Virginia, in alphabetic order. A third rank might include California at Los Angeles, Cornell, Duke, and

Northwestern. Even another rank might include Hastings and Illinois, Minnesota, North Carolina, and Wisconsin. While there are numerous other law schools offering good legal education and surroundings, the ones mentioned do have solid reputations, established by successful alumni, strong oral traditions, individual and aggregate faculty renown, widely published scholarship, extensive law libraries, adequate physical facilities, and regard in legal hiring circles.

The major law schools, particularly in the first ranks, doubtless cover themselves with a mantle of elitism. But nonetheless there is substance in their aspirations and their ways. Their view is that they are training not simply lawyers, but people to be leaders in society. It was once said of Harvard that it was teaching students to practice law in the grand manner. The essence is instruction not so much in the rules of law as in their meaning and theory and their policy fit in the more general schemes. Since the understanding of why the rules are what they are, and of the ends they are meant to serve, is critical to social adaptability and thrusting to institutional reform, the well-trained lawyer is an asset to society.

Good performance in a ranking law school ensures greater access to the most desirable jobs. In general, degrees from recognized but lower-ranking schools are interchangeable in the job market, except for a general preference by law firms for schools in their regional area. At preferred schools, job recruiters come in throngs to review the crop and make offers. Second-year students are often engaged for the summer at handsome salaries in hopes that they might come back upon graduation. Often a preference for particular schools results from the school ties felt by alumni partners in a firm. The relationships between top schools and top law firms are reciprocal: big firms hire new graduates from schools that reflect their practices, and law school curricula are geared to practices of big firms.

The most important things to learn before going to law school are reading and writing. This statement is neither comedy nor flippancy. Many law students and even full-fledged lawyers are simply unable to read and write the language. English, literature, and composition are thus the most important law school prerequisites. Of the social sciences, political science and history, for governmental structure and practices, and economics, for theory and patterns of wealth and distribution, are particularly helpful. Studies in statistics and computer sciences are increasingly invaluable. Speech courses are excellent, as are basic college courses in accounting. College courses in law are usually worthless, as too little too early, although they do no lasting damage and perhaps satisfy the nagging (but false) sense that some preparation is being done which ought to be done. Since bad writing is often a manifestation of bad thinking, mathematical and philosophical training are pluses. Disciplined study habits are most important of all.

Lectures are most useful in huge classes, and are used universally in most local law schools. The professor conducts a monologue, stating the rule with connecting principles. He may answer questions, usually when he asks for them. The subject is put forth in relatively absolute terms, which tend to impart improper ideas of the definiteness of legal application. Nevertheless, students usually like this kind of presentation for its simplicity; it gives them the "cold dope."

The case method, widely used in national law schools, originated at Harvard in the nineteenth century. It is essentially the Socratic method, of the ancient Greek philosopher Socrates. It involves the presentation of course material through a series of appellate decisions, which recite their own facts, presented in casebooks (as opposed to textbooks). Instead of laying out the information as the lecturer does, the case-method teacher builds up his subject from the cases by asking his students questions about their principles, policy factors, language, and results. He may encourage cross-discussion among students to develop, eventually, the basic propositions of the course. With its ceaseless challenging of factual and policy assumptions, the case method is superbly tuned to the essential uncertainty of legal application. The method can be maddening, however, for students. The teacher normally answers a question with a question, seeking by logical association to bring out the latent ideas. Some law teachers even practice Socratic irony, pretending ignorance to promote thinking.

In practice, rigid adherence to the case method, which is traditional to law teaching at the top, is withering. Part of this is due to the increasing importance of statutes, administrative rules and regulations, and new subjects that do not lend themselves to Socrates's ways. It would also appear that the number of teachers who can effectively project the case method is not expanding with the growth of the law-teaching profession. Case-method teaching is also harder and more time-consuming. As law teachers tend more and more to lecture to cover their expanding material on time, and to revert to the case method only at preferred times, the case and lecture methods are coming together. Casebooks themselves now feature considerable textual annotations.

The modern national law school organizes itself around the searching case method, supplements it with lectures, with seminars and activities to promote research and writing, leavens it with clinical and moot court activities, and for voluntary text and assignments maintains a well-stocked library of thousands of volumes of case reports, statutes, regulations, treatises, textbooks, and literary sources of great variety.

There have been proposals to shorten law school by a year or two and to add law office experience instead. I am opposed to this. I believe in law school as a learning period that is none too long considering what there is to know. Law school is the time for learning in the abstract, for mastering method, and for footing. Law office supervision is spotty, unmonitored, and subject to all the exigencies of practice, which can distort the experience of a limited time. The cheapness of the labor of apprentice students can lead to exploitation, as was the considerable experience of old-time practices of legal apprenticeships.

This leads to perceptions of university education versus trade schooling. Law school, to be sure, has its heavy trade connotations even in a university context, yet the traits of intellect and humanity that are university objects should also apply to the law school part of the university. The university-trained lawyer should be much more than a skilled tradesman. He should be a functioning intelligent being, able to draw intellectual challenge and social concern not only from his avocational activities but also from within the confines of his lawyering itself. In an absorbing article some years ago, Professor Frances A. Allen, a past president of AALS and a law professor at the University of Michigan, deplored the ignorance of the underlying "dialogue of values" that "goes forward in law school classrooms every day. . . ." While most students go to law schools to become practicing lawyers, it would appear to me a university obligation to seek to install philosophic habits of thought.

Studies in sociology, economics, and political science have values and relevancies important to social infinity, but if one is to be an effective practicing lawyer, there are fundamental things one simply must know, skills one must have. True, every item from law school cannot be held in memory, but basic notions of legal subjects, which are foundations to build upon in real practice, can be ingrained. A working lawyer requires a framework of knowledge around which he does his research. After the client says "How do you do," you cannot excuse yourself and run to the library and speak to him from there by intercom between long pauses for research. You are expected to be reasonably conversant, in your office, at your desk, in meetings, in court, with basic legal subjects, and a budding lawyer had better know that at the outset. Paying clients expect lawyers to know what to do with the problems and tasks they pose, regardless of how mundane they may be to the social scientist.

Whatever the motive in going to law school, if there is the intent to work as a lawyer, for the dollar, or, for something else, it seems most sensible to use the time to learn to become a lawyer. No one has to go to law school to be a social organizer, a fighter for causes, or a community leader. Law school attendance is a specific effort to equip the student with a lawyer's skills for the tasks ahead. Otherwise, why bother? Those who would do legal battle must have the ability to contend with skilled lawyers on difficult subjects and often on terms not their own, which may include balky judges. Cases are won by skill and by preparation, not by wishful thinking or by good intentions. Those dedicated to establishment challenge must know that their adversaries field the best legal talent they can afford and they may be relentless in their efforts. They have very deep pockets. Fighting them at law is no job for unskilled lawyers. The law student must exhaust every opportunity in law school to acquire the equipment to think, work, write, speak, and know like a lawyer. Law school is the time for that.

MEANING OF THE BAR

The American lawyer is a member of the "bar." Lawyers stand before the "bar of justice"; they are called to the "bar." Judges and lawyers taken together form "the bench and the bar." Indeed, the word "bar" often connotes the body of the legal profession itself, as in statements made to the press by "local bar representatives." The word "bar" also holds fraternal imputations; as when lawyers occasionally refer to "my brother at the bar."

The word "bar" probably referred initially to courtroom railings, usually wooden, about three feet high, which separate the judge from the parties, lawyers, and witnesses. When lawyers address the judge, they are, presumably, physically barred from passing beyond the railing without permission of the judge. The word "barrister," the classic English trial lawyer, is associated with his customary arguing position at the railing bar. Even more traditionally, in the old English Inns of Court, the "bar" was a wooden barrier that separated the students' seats from the barristers when a learning session was in progress.

In England, it is only barristers who are members of the bar. English solicitors, the office lawyers as we know them—those who have only limited access to lower or specialty courts—are more prosaically known as "solicitors of the court." In the United States, however, no such distinctions are made, and all lawyers holding at least one license to practice law are members of the bar.

Lawyers are formally admitted to practice by being sworn, usually as part of a group, in a courtroom ceremony called an "induction." The courtroom is likely to display on one of its walls a huge official seal or some other representation symbolizing justice, showing a blindfolded woman holding both a sword and a set of scales. (One contributor to the New York Law Journal, Andrew Simmonds, wrote of his fascination, during a vacation visit to the Old Bailey in London, on seeing that its statue of the woman of justice had no blindfold. Similarly, there is no blindfold on the statue at the International Court of Justice in The Hague.)

The goddess of justice is of early origin. She was known for the clarity of her sight in both Greek and Roman lore. The blindfold, as Mr. Simmonds tells it, originated in Germany about 1494, in a woodcut illustration for a poem, Ship of Fools, by Sebastian Brant, showing a jester tying a blindfold over her eyes. Its purpose was to ridicule courts; in Renaissance allegory a blindfold implied absence of judgment. It is suggested that in the sixteenth century the English church encouraged the blindfold practice to undermine the secular courts then taking hold. Over a period of time, however, the blindfold became a symbol of impartiality. No further explanations appear for either the sword, which seems the enforcing power of the state, or the scales, which obviously weigh the merits. Yet it must be observed that with her blindfold in place the lady cannot see to use either effectively.

————SOME OF THE NUMBERS————

By statistical average, today's American lawyer tends to be white, male, older rather than younger, conservative, city dwelling, and in plenty of company. Lawyers themselves form a sizable work force; and, in concert with the economic activities of many others, they foot the current American growth industry that offers the law product.

From best estimates, there are more than 600,000 practicing lawyers in this country. Predictably, the heaviest concentrations follow the population clusters of the major cities. Lawyers in metropolitan areas that exceed half a million in population make up about 40 percent of all practicing lawyers in the United States. Roughly, two-thirds of all practicing lawyers are in cities with populations exceeding 100,000.

The American ratio of lawyers is believed to approximate one lawyer for 575 people, although in a heavily lawyer-populated area like New York City the ratio is about one for 230. New York City is plainly the nation's lawyering capital, followed by Washington, D.C., Chicago, and Los Angeles.

A revealing commentary on the American numbers may be found in comparisons with other countries. In Japan, the ratio is about one practicing lawyer for each 14,000 of population. European lawyering ratios are less dramatic but still much thinner than the American score. Generally, the ratio of population to one lawyer in Great Britain is 1,500, in Italy 1,500, and in France 6,000.

The vast proportion of current American lawyers is male, with women a small minority in the nation overall. However, the numbers of women practicing law are in for sharp escalation in years and decades to come, given the fact that most law schools are currently reporting female enrollments constituting between 25 percent and 50 percent of their first-year classes. Women are projected to make up one-third of the bar by the end of this century. This is a long way from the day in 1950 when venerable Harvard Law School admitted its first woman to regular classes. Actually, the very first woman law school graduate arrived on the scene in 1872, from a predecessor of Northwestern University Law School. Belle Mansfield was the first woman admitted to a state bar, Iowa's, in 1869. It was not until this century that women were permitted to practice law in most American jurisdictions.

The enrollment figures of "minority group" students are informative. There are, according to one study, about 5,200 black Americans in law school, less than 5 percent of the total. Mexican Americans, or Chicanos, number 1,300, or about 1⅓ percent; and Hispanic Americans, including Puerto Ricans, the same. Asian Americans lag slightly behind at about 1 percent, and American Indians make up about .3 percent. Since the modern trend is to greater representation in law school, the existing minority bar-membership percentages must be smaller.

————SOME OF THE DEFINITIONS————

Generally speaking, it is assumed that a lawyer has been admitted to a bar. In usual parlance, one who simply graduated from law school but was never admitted to any bar is not called a lawyer. A "practicing lawyer" is one who works at it. A lawyer who practices by himself or with a law firm is deemed to be in "private practice"; he is not employed principally by a business corporation or any branch of a government.

Lawyers in this country are essentially of one category and rank, regardless of their specialization, their degrees, or their training. American lawyers may do very different kinds of work in different places, but they are simply "lawyers." They may call themselves "tax lawyers" or "trial lawyers" or "criminal lawyers" or "corporate lawyers," and limit their field of activity to their indicated specialty. Such usage is largely informal and self-assessed, even in those states that purport to certify some legal specialties.

Lawyers may be called "lawyer" or "attorney" or "counselor," among the more polite phrasings. Law schools like to feel they are producing "lawyers," and that is what most traditional practitioners call themselves. My own preference is for "lawyer," since for me that ancient word embraces the whole range of the working function.

But the title "attorney" enjoys high legal popularity, predicated, I believe, on some assumption of additional toniness. Technically, the status of "attorney," as meaning a representative or actor for someone else, may not require bar membership; as, for instance, one holding a "power of attorney." A layman may act for someone as his "attorney in fact," which means as a designated alter ego. In some communities, a lawyer may be referred to as "Attorney" Smith, similar to the reference to a physician as "Dr. Smith."

The word "counselor" has come to have a bit of a humorous reference in greetings. Irascible judges tend to bark "counselor" at a troublesome lawyer. ("Now what do you say to that, counselor?") "Counselor" often carries an edge of impatience or sarcasm; nonetheless, it is a traditionally accepted legal title and traces the significant legal function of advising, which is counseling. In fact, many lawyers refer to themselves in their listings as "attorney" *and* "counselor at law," thus describing both their representation and advisory roles. A modern practice, particularly among larger better-known law firms, is to omit all reference to the profession on stationery and on calling cards.

The word "Esquire," usually abbreviated and appended to a name (Richard Roe, Esq.), is a customary respectful formality in addressing lawyers. The usage derives from the English "squire," who was a citizen of local gentry status and indubitably male. The rush of women lawyers has not routed the "Esquire"; it has simply made the title heterogeneous.

There are two unflattering references to lawyers so common they have come to be part of our language: "shyster" and "Philadelphia lawyer." The word "shyster" is of obscure origin. The Random House dictionary indicates derivation from the old English word "shy," which was a slang expression for "shady" or "disreputable." The Oxford English Dictionary lists "shuyster" as an alternate spelling. Webster's Third New International Dictionary indicates the word is "probably after Scheuster (about 1840)—American attorney frequently rebuked in a New York court for pettifoggery." But whether shy, shuyster, or Scheuster, it never amounts to flattery. The word always suggests a person devoid of moral scruples.

"Philadelphia lawyer" is an interesting expression of clear-cut birth that connotes a sharp lawyer of doubtful ethicality. It is an outgrowth of the famed John Peter Zenger case in New York in 1735. Zenger, a pioneer newspaper editor in the prerevolutionary struggle for a free press, printed fierce criticism of local crown officials. For his pains, he was arrested, and his trial, which was to become a landmark in American legal annals, ensued amidst great public controversy. Immediately after the trial began, Zenger's two New York lawyers were disbarred. On the very day the trial convened, August 4, 1735, Andrew Hamilton, an octogenarian and a distinguished lawyer from Philadelphia, stood up and walked forward to volunteer to represent Zenger. His impassioned plea to the jury, expounding broad principles of individual liberty, earned Zenger a jury acquittal after only ten minutes of deliberation. Hamilton left for Philadelphia to a hero's ovation, including a gun salute from ships in the harbor. However, a minor part of his legacy stemmed from constant disparaging references during the trial itself by the crown counsel to Hamilton as a "Philadelphia lawyer." The phrase came to stand for both praise and criticism, though the praise of it has faded over the years and the pejorative remains.

It simply would not be right to ignore the classic "ambulance chaser." This unsubtle characterization refers to the ignoble lawyer who pursues an ambulance going down the street to persuade its flattened occupant to affix his signature to a retainer agreement. Some go so far as to say that there are lawyers successful enough to own their own ambulances. Ambulance chasing as a figurative device extends beyond personal-injury litigation to all excessive zeal in pursuing clients, and has lived to enter the American lexicon.

THE GEOGRAPHY OF LAW PRACTICE

Ordinarily, a lawyer is admitted in one state, where he establishes his office. Beyond that, the average lawyer may, on the basis of his state admission, be separately admitted to appear in the federal District

Court (the basic federal trial court) of his home-base area, the Circuit Court of Appeals, which is the intermediate federal appellate court of his multistate region, and possibly the United States Supreme Court. The Supreme Court is the nation's highest, and relatively few lawyers ever appear there on a case. An admission certificate to practice before the United States Supreme Court hanging on the wall in the average law office is really a professional token.

Various special federal tribunals have their own licensing requirements. A basic law license will qualify a lawyer to practice before these, although nonlawyers with special qualifications may also be admitted. The Tax Court, for instance, will admit qualified accountants, and the Interstate Commerce Commission licenses client representatives who have taken certain courses and passed an examination.

Most legal service takes place outside a courtroom, and may be conducted across state lines. Many an urban lawyer lives in a suburban municipality outside the state of his practice, and has friends and acquaintances in his residential community who may become his clients. New York, Chicago, and Washington, D.C., all share this multistate metropolitan aspect. A client's business, too, may be conducted interstate, if not internationally. For these reasons many lawyers seek admission to more than one state or country.

Admission to the bar is basically by state. Federal admission in that state is generally automatic. The principal federal direct-admission authority is in the District of Columbia. Lawyers from one state can be admitted to another state by going through the regular admission process, which includes taking the other state's bar examination. Sometimes an experienced lawyer can be admitted in another state without examination if there is reciprocity between the state in which he has a license and the state for which he seeks a license. Lawyers do not, however, always require separate licensing in every state to which their legal travels take them, if they stay out of court there, maintain no separate office presence, and conduct their activities in a circumspect way. Where the lawyer's business is done principally from an office in a state where he is licensed, activity in unlicensed places is usually regarded as ancillary. A court (often a federal one) may permit an attorney licensed only elsewhere to appear in that court for a single case. As a rule only lawyers licensed in a jurisdiction may regularly appear in its courts.

Many law firms maintain offices in more than one state or country. Law firm stationery usually lists all places of business, and identifies—sometimes with asterisk notations where appropriate—the geographic limitations on each lawyer's authorized practice. The assumption that each lawyer practices only where licensed is, in reality, fictional, since every lawyer may function through the collective licensing of the firm. In theory, the public is protected by the office that houses locally licensed lawyers who are subject to local regulation and discipline.

Law practices are branching out; we now hear of "national" law firms. Multiple state offices were once considered unsuitable establishments for gentlemen lawyers, but modern business notions have taken hold, and law has followed social and commercial expansion across state lines. The District of Columbia itself has burgeoned with out-of-town firms. Some firms acquire interstate and foreign identities by merging with existing firms in the desired localities. The population migration to the Sun Belt has jolted a number of firms into movement, with the realization that they may lose their clients' estates to undeserving lawyers down beyond. Florida particularly is witnessing an invasion of big northeastern law firms, who either merge with a local office or have one of their regular partners procure admittance to the Florida bar.

—MEANING OF "PRACTICING LAW"—

My son James was admitted to the New York bar in the fall of 1978 in the impressive Brooklyn courtroom of the Appellate Division, Second Department, of the New York State Supreme Court. A large crowd clustered about the new lawyers after the induction ceremony. A father, apparently one of a practical bent, shook his son's hand vigorously and said, "Congratulations, you now have a license to charge for anything except the practice of medicine." But I knew better. I had learned long ago that some of a lawyer's compensable activity, in fact, invades the province of the psychiatrist—a career my other son, David, chose.

What are legal services? Lawyers unquestionably share a monopoly of certain services—but what are they? Working appearances in court are the most clear-cut indications of practicing law. Conducting trials and preparing the pleadings and affidavits that go with them are indubitably legal services. So are the classic instances of drawing wills, trusts, formal contracts, and security instruments. Advising people as to their legal rights and duties might seem a clear enough legal instance, but this is not always so. Many activities regularly performed by nonlawyers have legal components and involve the lawful conveyance of legal information. Some examples come to mind: the accountant tells his client it is a crime to cheat on income taxes; the auto-driving instructor tells the pupil he must drive within prescribed speed limits and advises on the rules of the road; the building contractor informs his customer about the building code. No one conceives the unlawful practice of law in these instances. Quite obviously, some rule of reason sets in, enabling nonlawyers to advise others of generally known legal requirements. Giving general legal advice is acceptable, then, if it is truly incidental to another legitimate business activity. Giving specific legal advice by itself is practicing law, and this requires a license. Incidentally, the unlawful giving of legal advice is not excused by failing to charge for it.

But applying the theory to reality is easier said than done. The unlawful practice of law, however unintentional, is likely to generate problems, for instance, in the tax field for accountants, and in wills and trusts for insurance sellers and bankers. There are legal things to say in selling insurance, or mutual funds, or pensions, in establishing estate plans, in giving tax advice, and in preparing for the contingencies of death or the financial imprudence or inexperience of loved ones. Some professionals seek to solve their problems by dual licensing, to be licensed as both lawyers and insurance agents, for example. This may solve the licensing dilemma, but it sometimes produces added ethical complications.

Unfortunately, the unlawful-practice problem is often ignored: there are those accountants, insurance salesmen, and bank employees who sidestep the difficulty by simply getting on with it. Discretion enables careful operatives to thrive in this grey area of legal practice. Sometimes a pious "see your lawyer" is tucked in orally or in writing, but this caution is usually obscure or issued after the action is committed.

The whole matter is rendered more complex by the fact that practices vary according to locale. In California, for instance, insurance companies execute the closing of real estate titles, while in New York this is exclusively a lawyer's domain, with a title closer only in helpful attendance. In some Southern states, bankers may draw wills. It is an interesting social commentary that much doubtful "practice of law" by banks, insurers, and securities sellers never meets with lawyers' complaints, since the moving parties may generate legal business for lawyers in other contexts. Often, these extralegal efforts—even if they generate offending incidents of unauthorized law practice—may benefit the lawyer, since he may get the balance of the legal work to be done. An insurance agent may work up an entire estate plan for his client, normally an activity for lawyers, but a lawyer is called in to draw the will and the trust and maybe to effect corporate revisions. Many lawyers would conclude that were it not for the bird-dog efforts of the insurance agent, none of the legal work would have arisen at all. Other lawyers might not wish to offend those whom their clients trust, particularly if, in so doing, the lawyer can be painted as obstructive or unknowing. Banks, with their massive economic power and constant deployment of lawyers, are not lightly assaulted by the legal profession.

To further complicate the situation, lawyers often are paid for services that cannot be described strictly as lawyering. These services include assembling financings, promoting real estate syndicates (and keeping a share), and other services that are essentially business activities and that require no lawyer's license.

There are also those matters that bear on millions of people but do not fill the average lawyer's cash register. I have in mind the welter of advice on such affairs as Social Security assistance, social-welfare assistance, small income tax returns, Medicare, and low-rent tenancy rights. Plainly, advice is needed; government regulations can be complex, and important to those affected. Most lawyers actually do not know many of the hard answers, and care little because these problems do not involve new clients who can afford significant fees. The bulk of advice here comes from lay people. Some are government employees, some work for unions, some are politicians, or volunteers, or friends, some are generally knowledgeable from other activities in insurance, real estate, or accountancy. Social workers and voluntary social-service organizations with trained workers help fill this advisory void. Some unlicensed individuals charge for their assistance. Much of the advice sought and given in these instances is legal advice by every definition. Nevertheless, the "unauthorized" practice of law is silently authorized by the general disinterest of lawyers. The need for sound legal advice or action in these areas has produced limited law programs for the poor. In these, lawyers are employed by government or nonprofit organizations to furnish regular legal services at little or no cost to the consumer.

Paralegals are not lawyers. As the prefix "para" indicates, paralegals are accessories—lawyers' helpers—who are not normally licensed. Some get institutional training, ranging from sixty days to nine months; others learn on the job. Paralegals are indispensable in busy law offices, and do everything from full legal work to fetching the coffee (according to the inclinations of their employers). Working under the supervision of lawyers, they may draft simple litigation papers, real estate closing statements, uncomplicated tax returns, and estate accountings. Advanced and trusted paralegals do research; some interview clients and witnesses and assemble needed facts. They may watch the court calendar, serve papers, or make appearances in places where a simple talking presence is required. The difficult economics of paying fully qualified lawyers for all law office tasks and passing the charges through to clients are increasing the use of paralegals as assistants in busy law offices.

——CONSTITUTIONAL RESTRAINTS—— ON ADMISSION REQUIREMENTS

Each state exercises regulatory power over the admission of lawyers and over their ongoing conduct. But the United States Supreme Court holds the final word over the states' broad power to regulate professional admissions and practice. It has held that states must uphold the constitutional rights of "due process" and "equal protection of the law." A state cannot act arbitrarily; there must be a demonstrable basis for preventing a person from becoming a lawyer within its borders.

States can require oaths that lawyers support the federal and state constitutions. They cannot exclude applicants for admission to legal practice because of unpopular political activity, race, or religion. Applicants have the burden, however, of establishing their own good character, and can be turned down if they refuse to furnish reasonably relevant information. The mere fact that an applicant was a member of a Communist Party has been ruled not grounds for rejection unless there is a reasonable basis for a belief that the applicant desires overthrowing the government by force.

The key features of legal admission are education and the bar examination. Screenings by character and fitness committees tend to be formalities largely based on brief interviews with established lawyers of local standing, picked by court or Bar Association officials on mixed blue-ribbon, political, and old-boy-networking basis. But these committees do not really deal in rejections; they serve only the ritualistic function of impressing new lawyers with the discipline and responsibility of the profession. Given the Supreme Court's views on constitutional rights, just about the only effective moral grounds for exclusion are recent conviction for serious crime or some outrageous conduct defying acceptability.

It was not always that way. Historically, character and fitness requirements were used in many places to preclude the socially unpopular and to keep down the underdogs. In this way the political and moral preferences of the established order were preserved. Radical political or religious beliefs, skin color, religion, sexual habits, alcoholism, psychiatric treatment, and conviction for minor offenses were enough to exclude a candidate. But old habits die hard. Not long ago, a Virginia Bar committee refused to issue a certificate of good character to a female applicant—a government lawyer who wished to take the bar examination—on the grounds that she was living with a man to whom she was not married. In light of modern acceptance of such states of affairs, the Virginia Supreme Court overruled the committee and permitted the putative sinner to take the bar examination.

————THE BAR EXAMINATION————

The bar examination is a written test given by all but five states as an absolute prerequisite for admission. Actually, the bar examination, the final real obstacle to practicing law, is, in the long view of things, a relatively recent feature. The earliest American written bar examinations were given in 1855 in Massachusetts and in 1877 in New York. By 1917, most states had them. Only Mississippi, Montana, South Dakota, West Virginia, and Wisconsin waive this requirement; but only for their own state university law graduates. In Wisconsin one private university also enjoys this "diploma privilege" for admission to the bar.

In 1981, all states but Indiana, Iowa, Louisiana, and Washington gave a uniform short-answer test known as the "multistate" bar examination (MBE). The test is a long exercise currently consisting of many multiple-choice questions, administered twice each year. This is supplemented with one or two days of essay questions, which are chosen at the discretion of each state. In testing idiom, the essay portion is deemed "subjective," and the short-answer portion "objective." Those states not using the MBE utilize their own short-answer and essay combinations.

The great increase in law applicants triggered the multistate-examination approach. Many states were strained in their examination facilities, and they welcomed the grading, the national standardization, and the professional expertise in formulating the central examination. However, there is opposition to MBE in that it reflects no local composition, that it is pedagogically unsound (a standard but unproven objection to short-answer questions generally), and that it is unfair to minority students. The last objection is a curious one, since some states, including New York, employ the MBE to avoid minority bias. But all current testing modes face some minority challenge—on the basis of cultural differences and the relevancy of testing to the competent practice of the law.

Except for the gifted few, bar examinations are not simple. Certainly, the two- or three-day test periods cause physical and emotional strain. In my view, bar examinations are formidable, but entirely manageable by the educated student who takes a "cram" course to refresh himself, particularly on those subjects covered in early law school. Many law schools with national pretensions deal with law generally, and do not dwell on the law of any one state. Local procedural laws, which cover time limits within which to file papers and responses, forms of pleadings, and legal technique relevant to processing a case for trial and appeal, usually take special cramming because of their specificity and the scant treatment given them in law school.

Success on the bar examination is no index to ultimate legal competency, except that if you persist in failing, you will never have a chance to perform as a lawyer. High objective test scores tend to identify the knowledge, comprehension, and reading skills associated with the best lawyers. To the extent that reasoning and analysis are isolated by short-answer and essay test performance, an intellect for lawyering is assessed, but no test can assess the qualities of character, diligence, common sense, cunning, energy, perspective, and judgment that are critical to competent lawyering.

There is some redemption, I have found, in the intensive preparatory study for the bar. The ordinary course of learning is spread over three years, with varying imminency. A four- to six-week course of study before the bar examination serves to synthesize the whole of law. My own experience is that the exercise helped fix mental patterns which to this day form the basis for some of my legal impressions.

Some see a ritualistic value in the trial by ordeal—a thought that is alien to me. With the increased emphasis on educational prerequisite, there is questionable validity in allowing a single test to disqualify a graduate of a three-year course at an accredited university. States that automatically admit graduates of authorized law schools by diploma privilege have the right idea, to my mind. If someone can successfully weather the course of study at a proper law school, failure in the bar examination can only mean that the applicant—for some reason unrelated to his training—did not test well. No law student who has passed an extended course of study and has been screened by proper academic authority deserves discreditation.

Surprisingly, law school people are among the principal opponents of the diploma privilege. There is the fear that the official linkage of law schools to law practice admission will eventually lead to political control (or judicial, which is seen as the same thing) of law school curricula. There is also a fear that the diploma privilege can favor local people in admission, and prejudice outsiders with stiff examinations. Finally, a view persists that the bar examination is a necessary credential to weed out inept people who slip through uneven law school processes. More assured law school quality is plainly the key.

MORE OPEN ADMISSION

There are those who favor more "open" admission approaches to the bar, who feel that there should be greater encouragement to admission in the form of relaxed educational standards and elimination of the bar examination. Supporters of this view argue that the issue is one of political representation, and, therefore, of democracy. They believe that more lawyers (rather than fewer) will relate more people to the legal and governing processes.

The question of open admission to the bar produces division. On the one hand, there is a need for professional standards; on the other hand, open admission would minimize discrimination. Of course there are the many "mainstream" students who do not test well or who lag in demonstrable reading or writing skills, notwithstanding sufficient intelligence levels, who can go on to become adequate and useful lawyers. But the issue is particularly pertinent to minority students who may have difficulty negotiating a law school course and a bar examination that is culturally distinctive. Some believe that minority lawyers would add a net value to society that is greater than any feared sacrifice in lawyer quality.

It seems to me a clear social advantage to have more lawyers in disadvantaged communities. Qualifications relating only to conventional standards do not serve well. If a lawyer from a disadvantaged background can establish an adequate ability to do legal work, he should be encouraged. To fail in this encouragement may be to have no lawyer at all. White middle-class lawyers simply cannot function as well in a black community as a black lawyer who has empathy with his clients and understanding of their particular problems.

California has experimented with an alternative to the bar examination: a "clinical" test, which purports to minimize cultural bias by testing the skills involved in interviewing clients, oral argument, examining witnesses, and writing briefs. Based on early results, it was claimed that the test reduced the numbers of qualified candidates who tended to fail in conventional tests. One difficulty is that large numbers of applicants cannot be processed in this way on any objective basis.

There are many arguments for restricting the number of lawyers that actually stem from desires to protect the economic interests of existing lawyers. In a competitive democratic society, the guild protection of lawyering has no real place. While many divisions of the bar are not really competitive with one another, competition—where it exists—is salutary.

In the end, the true purpose of licensure to practice law is to ensure minimum levels of legal competence and preclude unacceptable character defect. The profession of law is too vital for its activity to become insufficiently regulated. In any desire to accommodate social policy, we must not overlook the fact that incompetent lawyers can cause harm across the whole social spectrum—from loss of liberty to loss of significant property rights.

——COMMON CHARACTERISTICS—— OF LAWYERS

The process of becoming a lawyer is an experience all lawyers share, notwithstanding their differences in economic standing and intellectual capability. Lawyers share problems in coping with clients; and most have some similar burns and scars. In a room of laymen, their language and their insights are often unique. Even though they may be adversaries, they are fellow performers, and each curiously watches the other—always wary of the other's potential.

Lawyers are by and large establishment people, with more than the population average of respect for and understanding of stable process. It is true that some lawyers do gravitate to institutional challenge by violence, picketing, disruption, or excitation, either from deep conviction, emotional instability, or sense of showmanship, or some combination, but they are not many. In fact, lawyers are more often accused of wanting to preserve the status quo. Indeed, with their training steeped in precedent, and their livelihood intertwined with existing rules they know and accept, the charge has more truth than is comfortably recognized in many legal precincts. Nevertheless, it is a simplistic accusation. Among the lawyers who clutch the past, there are a few who reach out to social change.

Airs of dignity and assurance are common to experienced lawyers. I suppose it is inevitable that successful lawyers who thrive on respect and confidence will eschew eccentric personal habits. Choice of language and telltale phrasing will give away the ingrained professional lawyer. He leans to logical oral presentation, even in social situations. He may punctuate an explanation by the verbal use of outline form, with points A, B, and C, and subpoints 1, 2, and 3. Phrases like "making undertakings," "fair consideration," "invoking remedies," "exercising rights," and "holding one's self out" tell us there is a lawyer in the house. Who can fail to be alerted by "I submit that . . ." or "not a scintilla of proof!" *Res ipsa loquitur*, anyone? Or it is just that the venerable expression "It takes one to know one" is applicable here?

More than in many other working fields, lawyering is an activity congenial to older people. Apart from extended trial work, which may exact immediate physical toll, or heavy traveling, or highly pressured corporate dealings, legal practice inclines to the sedentary. It tolerates physical infirmity or weakness in that the sensible lawyer can pace his work. With a sufficiently proportioned case or client load, an organized lawyer can forestall deadlines and unnecessary late night work. So long as the lawyer remains mentally clear, he can work effectively. His experience becomes increasingly important, and palliates diminished physical stamina. It is not surprising, then, that great numbers of older people practice law. The lawyer in his late sixties is often in his prime, while his corporate-executive friends may already be consigned to compulsory retirement. It is now believed that almost half the lawyers in the United States are over fifty years of age, and, of these, a quarter are over sixty-five years of age.

The wide and deep imprints of lawyers in politics, in government, in university and foundation leadership, in giant corporations, and in community and public drives tell us some things. There is common denomination to be drawn from the omnipresence of lawyers in society's major formations and institutions. Concededly, many lawyers are economically motivated to mingle where they can meet potential clients and expose their talents. Moreover, strategic positions may be filled by lawyers because the roles call for applying law; the regularity with which much public disputation winds up in court reflects a heavy legal component in our public affairs. We see this particularly in environmental controversies, in class actions against fraudulent merchants or bad-acting corporate executives, in suits to resolve zoning distress, in taxpayers' suits, and in efforts to quell arbitrary official action. The ubiquitous Alexis de Tocqueville, the nineteenth-century French commentator on the Americans, observed, "There is hardly a political question in the United States, which does not, sooner or later, turn into a judicial one."

Beyond all this stand the dimensions of talent and training of lawyers for discharging social functions. Here is where we find a common characterization among the able lawyers who figure so heavily in society's stewardship. Note, I have now slipped into discussion of the "able" lawyer. This is worthwhile, I believe, notwithstanding the low level of ability demonstrated by more lawyers than is decent, since it is the outstanding who are the achievers and establish the ideals of professional characteristics. Few lawyers combine all these characteristics, but the able ones share most of them. Aside from some popular irritabilities engendered by negativeness, technicality, or downright combativeness thought to be inherent in lawyers (and often correctly so), the qualities that lift the able lawyer in the eyes of public groups tend in varying degrees to be the same qualities that characterize his class of professional peers. These are the ability to organize thoughts and a talent for self-expression, maintenance of perspective among the rules and the ability to weigh and apply them, and the ability to listen patiently to the thoughts of others and to use and understand them.

The lawyer's bread-and-butter work is part of society's rule book. The lawyer knows how an institution is organized, he knows the levers of response. He is a professional in problems of social organization and redress. The lawyer in private practice is not limited to any one transaction, one job, one client, one field of industry, or any one governmental institution. The able practicing lawyer takes on all comers, not on his own terms, or necessarily in his own place. The lawyer goes not only to his own familiar office, he goes, as well, to any number of courts, to his diverse clients, to governmental agencies, to the adversary or to that person's lawyer. He sets up on strange and often hostile grounds. He carries with him his own brand of thinking and doing, that of the professional lawyer.

A basic ingredient is intelligence. The increasing competition of law school admission, with its emphasis on college grades and test scores, is driving steadily upward the testable raw-intelligence factor found in emerging lawyers. Some digression is necessary here, for intelligence is a deceptive conception. We are now talking neither of cultural nor intellectual virtuosity, nor even of the other vital traits that go into total lawyering. It has been my own observation that too many lawyers languish in professional insularity and restrict their interests and activities to things narrow to the law or their economic or political survival; too few sample richly of life's social, humanistic, intellectual, and artistic choices. However they may tilt themselves, able lawyers tend to be a cerebral group. They test well, have comprehension in reading, and can reason out complex problems.

It is therefore surprising to some laymen to find lawyers of moderate intelligence who do well economically and help their clients. The keys to such success as may be encountered by these lawyers lie in the nature of what they do. It is constantly emphasized in the course of this book that different lawyers do different things. The faculties needed to cope with intricate litigation, large estates and trusts, securities, and the tax, corporate, commercial, patent, copyright, and technical fields, which require much knowledge and mental dexterity, not to mention handling the high-flown, sophisticated clients inhabiting them, differ markedly from those required in less complicated practices. Lawyers can get rich settling accident cases with insurance-company adjusters, and as journeymen lawyers dealing with unsophisticated clients. There are lawyers who deal repetitively in well-defined areas, such as the buying and selling of one-family homes or land, unsophisticated matrimonial and accident cases, and others of social importance, who become adept at their work by experience and determination. I am not by this saying these lawyers are stupid, or that many lawyers in these forms of practice are not brilliant; I am merely suggesting that intelligence levels vary, and even those lagging well behind their more clever colleagues can do very well for themselves and their clients.

You may say that other professions—medicine, architecture, science—nurture people at least as intelligent as lawyers, perhaps more so. This is true. Here is another point then. The person of high intelligence who is a lawyer is more likely equipped with the important reading, writing, and speaking skills, which are often neglected in more technical pursuits; he is a ready entrant into the social milieu. The lawyer learns from the outset that he must function within the dynamics of pairs and clusters of people and societal groups and institutions. He knows he will have to persuade, argue, plead, and reconcile competing forces.

Whether it is that competitive types are attracted to the law or that people become competitive types from their law training, the lawyer emerges, in fact, as a professional bloodless fighter. Whether the socially or politically ambitious gravitate to the law or become that way in its service does not alter the way they appear. The lawyer achieves goals with or despite other people, and often over their objection.

The "legal mind" is a controversial term. It is used at once to denote either a keen or a limited analytical ability. The negative interpretation of the legal mind sees the lawyer as focusing excessively on rules and details, and disregarding the broader considerations of humanity or social policy. Insistence on technicality is part of this. So is the excessive caution endemic to the legal craft, the harboring of a presumption not to do. Often, the process of legal analysis can distort and deny reality itself. This is the legal mind at its worst.

The key traits of the legal mind in its most positive senses are the able lawyer's ability to analyze events, to develop facts and separate fancy, and to assign governing rules or consequences to the facts. Here is the heart of the professional lawyer's talent: the ability to think through to the central issue, to the core of the matter. The lawyer holds principles in solution, and analyzes each component part separately and together. He grasps the problem, breaks it down, aligns the pluses and minuses of alternate choices of conduct, and then acts or recommends action.

Lawyers must learn to distinguish cases and situations—to discern the aspects of a case that make it similar to or different from another, and therefore subject or not subject to the same rule. They must learn to read cases for what they really mean, the exact facts and the issues that turn on them. A legal mind, if there is such a thing, is orderly, analytical, dispassionate, and able to establish the relationship of principles and actions, not only to the case at hand, but also to its place in a larger scheme. The legal mind is oriented to legal consequence: whether the conduct under study does or may give rise to liability or the impairment of rights.

I am reminded of one incident which serves as a commentary upon a legal mind in formation. A first-year law student acquaintance of mine came charging out of the library into the crowded law school lobby. Her pen was still in her hand, pointed well forward. Her immediate thought was to retract her pen, for if it stuck into someone she would be personally liable for damages. A subsequent thought disturbed her—because it intruded only hours later: she might well have hurt someone.

Lawyers are notoriously skeptical; some call them cynics. They see the seamy underside of life as a daily matter. Their view of life is framed by more disputation than any other in society. They get an intimate look at human motives and frailties. Lawyers know how things can go wrong. It is this compelling sense of realism coupled with analytical ability that makes them valuable to society. Unfortunately, these traits can become warped if a lawyer's world view remains entrenched in worst-possible contingencies. Lawyers tend to look for the worst; laymen look for the best. The question "But what if . . ." has caused much harmful overlawyering, for its answer is predicated on the occurrence of the "if" and so assumes a non-legal conclusion. Since much practical harm is done by assuming un-likely occurrences in theoretical contexts, the client must be alert to his lawyer's chain of "what if"s. It is the client, after all, who must live with the result.

3

HOW
LAWYERS
KNOW THE LAW

Just how do lawyers know the law they declare? Much of it is known out of hand by virtue of their education and experience. But when they consult the sources, the process is known as legal research.

Researching the law varies with individual capabilities and limitations. Some lawyers and judges are simply more thorough than others; some brighter, better educated, more imaginative, more energetic, more interested. Some work within different time frames, and with different resources. Incentives to work fluctuate, as do the pressures of higher-priority items.

Not surprisingly, personal philosophical attitudes may affect the research. Those who oppose divorce are easily attracted to theories that block divorce; the sexually frustrated find the means to punish transgressors severely; the politically conservative magnify property rights.

The search for legal conclusion once again allows for the influence of personality in law. Nevertheless, the methodology of legal research is a basic tool of lawyering, and despite the variations that may arise from human application, there are standard tools and measures for determining the law.

Education and early work experience have much to do with how a lawyer goes about finding the law. These are the times when a lawyer, as apprentice, learns the basics of his craft. The sources are the same for all lawyers, either on their office shelves or in central libraries. The art is in knowing where and how to dig, when to accept a conclusion, how to distinguish the essential differences in cases that seem in point, how to construe a statute, and how to use collateral approaches to establish, fortify, or attack a conclusion.

——————RELIANCE UPON——————
GENERAL KNOWLEDGE

Most questions put to lawyers in everyday practice require little or no legal research. Many of these questions do not call for special knowledge—they are simply ministerial or to seek out reassurance. Some questions are answered by common sense or business sense. Numerous inquiries fall into areas of common professional knowledge or transactions: buying or selling vacant lots, or evicting a store tenant for nonpayment of rent. Negligence cases, in their nonspecific aspects, turn on well-known rules of law. To an experienced matrimonial lawyer, most divorce questions are predictable and readily answerable. Specialists respond with immediate knowledge in their field more readily than do responsible general practitioners who operate in more diverse legal terrain.

Specified questions are often posed prematurely, and they are parried with generality until their resolution becomes critical. Law cases may be settled well before they reach an advanced trial-preparation stage, and therefore costly preliminary comprehensive forays into the printed authorities may be unnecessary.

——RESEARCH IN LAW LIBRARIES——

But let us assume the lawyer does not know the answer. Let us suppose he must give an opinion to a client, or file a brief (a legal memorandum typically given to a judge), or submit the legal analysis of a problem to a senior partner.

The basic legal research implements are the books. In aggregate they constitute a "law library"—raw material necessary to the process of law.

Lawyers aspiring to professional competence must be reasonably good at legal research, and, more important, must be willing to do it. In professional jargon, lawyers "read up" on a point, implying that one is purely making current an already sound base of knowledge. A lawyer confronted with a research problem will say, "I'll look it up," meaning that he will consult sources in lawbooks to find his answer. Too many clients are critical of such a response—they feel the lawyer should know the answer automatically. It is good, not bad, that a lawyer wants to "look it up." A client should be wary of the lawyer who is in the habit of "winging it." Legal advice that is fortified by research is bound to be more satisfactory than that which is guessed and "off the cuff." Quick judgments are often referred to among lawyers as "horseback" opinions.

Much is made of dazzling courtroom oratory and complex

negotiations that close big deals. But the heart of law work is in the library. The thorough preparation that is the trademark of proper legal representation takes place there. The ability to perform and direct exhaustive legal research and to analyze its fruits characterizes lawyers of high competence.

The critical first step in legal research is to have a firm grasp of the factual background involved. The well-stocked law library is a bottomless pit, and a trap for the inexpert. There is legal authority for almost every proposition—much of it apparently contradictory—and the trails lead everywhere. Precise knowledge of the facts narrows the problem, and enables legal research to be reduced to the areas of pertinency. Part of the art of lawyering is in determining what is pertinent. Pertinency is important not only to avoid the right answer to the wrong problem, but also to curtail the work—an expense that otherwise may or may not be passed to the client.

Too many lawyers have the bad habit of relying on information from other lawyers. Except where the specialties are concerned, this practice is the mark of the unskilled lawyer, one who lacks confidence. Answers gathered in this loose manner are, however, so widespread that they have a general name, "curbstone opinions."

Most lawyers and law firms have some kind of in-house library facility. A typical library of an established urban firm would contain published reports of law cases of the state of primary practice, as well as all federal cases. These cases are usually of a trial court, an intermediate appellate court, and the highest appellate court. In the federal system, the last court is the United States Supreme Court. There are, in addition, collections of federal and state statutes. Specialized published services may appear on the shelves, covering such federal administrative subjects as taxation, securities, and governmental agencies. These services usually annotate statutes with references to administrative regulations, legislative history, and interpretative court cases. Finally, there are miscellaneous government publications, such as regulations and releases, legal encyclopedias, treatises, textbooks, and periodicals known as Law Reviews or Law Journals.

In sizable communities, larger central libraries, operated by governments, universities, or Bar Associations provide a central source for a much larger scope of search than afforded even in a fine office library. They are open, typically, to all lawyers. These central libraries carry the basic books of the law office library, but include the out-of-state court reports. The numbers of statutes, services, and commentary books are greatly expanded. Full records on appeal may be maintained, to supply data missing from published opinions. Often books on economic theory, descriptions of varying governmental activities, and social-policy matters—once tangential but now important to professional technique—are represented.

The history of legislation or administrative rules is often found in documents collected in central libraries. These may be transcripts of debate, committee hearings, committee reports, or memoranda of governmental agencies or their counsel. Legislative history is important in supplying meaning to gaps in statutory expression. The application of statutes or rules often turns on the intent of the drafters, particularly where the stated meaning is either unclear or its application unlikely in the face of greater principle. But the cases and the statutes (including their implementing administrative regulations) themselves are the basic tools of legal research. Books of commentary and specialized services are useful in organizing and summarizing general principles, and in highlighting pitfalls.

I do not mean to slight the use of textbooks, encyclopedias, and other reference works; indeed, I am grateful when one of mine is purchased. Texts are standard sources, particularly when the author's reputation is established. All lawyers who look up the law use these secondary sources, but too many use them too often. The overview of a subject is the most important contribution of textbooks, since each common-law case by itself is limited in overall doctrinal guidance. Actually, when a judge, in a common-law opinion, recites principles or situations beyond those strictly necessary to his own case, he is essentially operating as a text writer does. The actual citations of case authority conveniently presented in textbooks enable a researcher to check the author's conclusions, and form a way into the cases themselves. Some legal authors have such reputations that their works are cited as authority for sought conclusions, particularly in the absence of actual relevant cases. These writers—typically law professors, such as Williston or Corbin on Contracts, Wigmore on Evidence, Weinstein on Federal Rules of Evidence, Prosser on Torts, and Loss on Securities Regulation—are familiar to all informed lawyers.

The textbook genre is exemplified by the famous series of more or less elementary (for professional lawyers, that is) textbooks from time to time published by West Publishing Company on specific legal subjects. The series name, Hornbook, has come to be part of the legal language. An obvious proposition—one that is stated without any supporting authority—is often referred to as "Hornbook law." The adjective "Hornbook" signifies that the proposition is so settled or elementary that no supporting cases need be cited at all.

Law cases are "reported," published in book form, usually by an official "reporter," sometimes by private publishers, and sometimes by both in contemporaneous publication. Reported cases are usually products of appellate courts, but do include significant trial court opinions. They consist of the name of the case ("the caption")—for instance, *John J. Francis v. Donald Peter Orange*—followed by the decision date and court docket identification number. A "headnote" normally prefaces an opinion. This headnote is an informal summary of the principal points of the case as prepared by the reporter for the guidance of the reader. The researcher should not rely on headnotes, since these are simply the reporter's interpretations of the cases, and are not necessarily accurate. The reporter therefore has a critical role, not only in ensuring an accurate printed text and in deciding which cases to print, but also in headnote writing. There is probably no practicing lawyer alive who has not cut a corner at least once by employing the headnote indications in a case.

The names of the lawyers, and sometimes a summary of their arguments and cases, generally follow the headnotes. Usually, the first words in an opinion identify the writing judge by name. (To this day, I feel a twinge of pleasure to run across a reported New York case starting with "Harnett, J.") The "J" stands for judge or justice, depending on the title the particular court uses. The titles are interchangeable and the nomenclature is of no significance. Variations of "J" include "JJ," to signify the plural, more than one judge. A "C" in front of the "J" stands for "Chief," "P" for "Presiding."

Since appellate courts sit with varying numbers of judges, three to nine typically, there may be more than one decision written in a single case. Most often, there is a single opinion, written by and attributed to one judge, expressing the views of the participating judges. However, other judges sitting on the same appellate court may disagree with the result and file dissenting opinions. A "strong" dissent is a cogent, well-reasoned one, often identified as strong because the identifier personally agrees with it. Alternatively, a fellow judge may agree with the majority but this agreement is based on different grounds, in which case he may file a "concurring opinion." This can result, particularly in the United States Supreme Court, in three or more opinions on the same issue. Indeed, a determination may be forged by an alliance of those judges subscribing to the majority opinion with the concurring judges, so that an important result may be established even though there was no actual majority accord as to the reasons for it. An example is the sex discrimination case of *Frontiero* v. *Richardson*, 411 U.S. 667 (1972), in which a married woman Air Force officer was granted the same dependency benefit treatment for her husband that males received for their wives, correcting a prior discriminatory practice. Justice Brennan filed the court's judgment in an opinion that was joined in by Justices Douglas, Marshall, and White. Justice Stewart concurred on separate grounds. Justice Powell concurred on further separate grounds, and he was joined in his concurrence by Chief Justice Burger and Justice Blackmun. Justice Rehnquist dissented. There was no five-judge majority on the reasons for the decision.

Appellate opinions usually end with terse uniform appellate verbiage: "affirmance" (confirmed on appeal); "reversal" (the higher court reverses the decision of the lower court); "overruling" (changes of principle in later case that leaves the result of the original case intact). "Remand" (sent back to the court below); or "modified" (result changed in part)—perhaps a summary description of the result, and some order directed to the participants.

—COMMON LAW: WEIGHING CASES— AS PRECEDENT

Locating the pertinent cases is only the beginning; they must be synthesized into a cogent whole. One must determine what is important and what is not, when to keep and when to discard. The judicial response to precise facts offered in a case is called the "holding" of the case. A holding is a conclusion of law, which must be found for the result to be reached: it is an essential element of the decision. A holding is the foremost judicial authority.

On the other hand, judges tend to run on in their decisions, quite like the authors of books on legal subjects, and say things, or declare principles, interesting enough, but not essential to reach the particular decision in the case at hand. A nonessential statement is a "dictum" ("dicta" in plural)—one of the law's vestigial Latin remnants. Sometimes the excess is more fancifully referred to as "obiter dictum." Dicta are not important to the holding, and are less important judicial pronouncements generally, but they are sometimes indications of value, and serve as predictions of what that judge or the court may do under different circumstances.

The common law is an aggregate of rules derived from court holdings that facilitate decisions in later cases with factual similarities. It is a use of past judicial behavior to lay down rules of conduct, and predict future judicial behavior. Customarily, a lawyer will refer to cases of his own state and to federal cases, although where interstate activities are involved there may be complex rules as to which law governs.

Cases, it must be impressed, do not carry the authority of law found in a statute, which is a legislative prescription. Cases are supposed to respond only to the litigants and the facts before the court. A case has precedent value only if a conclusion can logically extend from it to another case. There should be no difference in analogizing treatment of a contract for the sale of a brown horse to that of a black one. Incidentally, situations that are significantly identical in their facts are called "black horse cases." Sometimes they are referred to as "on all fours." But to continue the argument, if there is no difference between a contract for the sale of a brown horse and that of a black horse, what about a contract for the sale of a distinctive multicolor horse, a female horse in foal, a sale while the barn is burning, a carriage, an automobile, and on and on?

"Find me a case!" The search for precedent is the sounding cry of common-law research. When lawyers report their legal findings, whether by intraoffice memorandum, opinion letter, brief, or court opinion, "authority" is cited to support nonobvious points. Authority includes precedent but is greater in attainable scope, since it goes beyond cases themselves and includes statutes, rules, regulations, text writers, and other sources. The discussion and citation of authority are the essential parts of communicated legal findings.

The search for precedent builds in a predilection for enshrining the past. The value of precedent is inculcated in lawyers from professional birth. Mark this point well in considering lawyers. The doctrine of *stare decisis* (a Latin phrase meaning "let the decision stand") lends weight to existing precedent as the accumulated reasoned experiential judgment of the past and discourages change for the sake of change. In these modern times, the term has adopted the connotation of reflexive resistance to change, and signifies the dangers in a precedential calcification that is unwilling to depart from the status quo.

Precedent is said to be "binding" on a court, which means that a court, usually a lower one in lineal descendancy than the higher court that renders a decision, is obliged to accept the results of that higher court in its own deliberation. Of course, it is critical in determining bindingness whether the earlier case is really in point and whether significant distinctions or policies can be demonstrated that justify a divergent result. Again, the individual capacities and traits of lawyers (including judges) come into play. The degrees of acceptance or distinction of precedent may be functions of personality, of discernment, or merely of greater capacity for disputation.

Precedent as a concept is difficult for laymen to comprehend. After all, there are the decisions of New York, California, Illinois, Texas, Virginia, and all other states, and various court levels within each jurisdiction. The federal courts have their own actions. Which case is precedent to which? Certainly the high-court decisions of the state where the case takes place are precedent that is binding on every inferior court in that state. Accordingly, a decision of the New York Court of Appeals is binding on the intermediate Appellate Divisions (there are four), whose decisions, in turn, bind the much more numerous Supreme Court districts within each of their jurisdictions. But what of difference between parallel courts, between two Appellate Divisions? The general rule is that each stands on its own for binding purposes, committing only those below it in their hierarchy. This leads to the not very amusing situation where a resident's rights depend on the part of the state in which he lives. And, obviously, legal rights vary from state to state.

Out-of-state decisions have some persuasive value and usefulness even though the decisions of one state are not binding in another. Reasoning may be so compelling that it is accepted as
precedent through adoption. The weight of foreign (out-of-state or
alien) case authority usually turns on the reputation of the other
courts and their judges, and its special appeal to the sitting judge. Out-
of-state cases are customarily collected by lawyers to buttress points
on which their own state is silent. Citational nakedness seems something to avoid in any legal discourse.

A common feature of out-of-state case collation is the development of conflicting lines of authority. Fifteen states may have cases
passing on a point; nine may go one way, six another. The view of the
nine is known as the "majority" view, and that of the six as the
"minority" view. A state virgin on a point is free to pick and choose
between them. Sometimes a third position emerges.

State courts and lawyers generally tend to use federal precedents
freely, regardless of geographic location. Since there are so many of
them, a wide selection is available on almost every point of law.
Within the federal hierarchy, the trial court (District Court) is bound
by the decisions of its intermediate appellate court (Circuit Court of
Appeal), which in turn is bound by the highest court (United States
Supreme Court). There are often differences between the Circuit
Courts and the District Courts, and again accidents of geography
affect legal rights. The Supreme Court may intervene where there are
critical differences between the Circuit Courts of Appeal.

────── CONSTRUING STATUTES ──────

Simplified situations covered by clearly written statutes are the easiest
to research. For instance, it is simple to check the speed limit in any
given state, or the rate of income taxation, the number of days within
which to file a responsive pleading, or the degrees of manslaughter.
Penal statutes tend (or ought) to be clearest, because they are general rules proclaimed in advance whose disobedience can involve
serious penalty.

Statutes are legislation, but as a research body they include constitutions (federal and state), which are the basic sources of statute authority, and rules and regulations (delegated by legislative authority) of boards, commissions, bureaus, departments, and agencies. Foreign treaties also have statutory effect. Statutes include all legislative actions, whether they be denominated statute, code, resolution, ordinance, session law, or local law, and by whatever echelon of government, federal, state, or local.

Unlike cases, statutes are actual pronouncements ordering, forbidding, or setting standards of conduct, and are normally textual in form. Except for the more arcane subjects, their meanings tend to be readily absorbable, whether you like them or not.

As might be expected, statutes that are clear in their application to the facts presented are the least litigated ones. But even the clearest statute can be litigated in court to test constitutionality. When a statute is applied to the facts of the case and its meaning is found debatable, a court case looms to interpret the statute. Statutory issues have some special interpretative facets of their own in court: there are common maxims (ways) of statutory construction, some useless and some effective as technique.

Statutes should be read carefully. The initial way to construe a statute is to look to its most likely "plain meaning." This is fine for counseling if the meaning is plain. But the case is usually in court because the statutory meaning is not plain in the first place. It is safest in counseling statutory construction to consider things first to be as they appear to be. Many lawyers run into trouble with statutes because they are so busy with interpretative cases or with text commentary that they never read the precise statutory text thoroughly.

It is a mistake to assume that every statute must have a constructive meaning. Errors can and do creep into statutes through hastiness, lack of competency, political compromise, and simple oversight. Having seen enough legislative debacles, particularly in Albany, the New York State capital, I can stand witness that many drafting errors are made in devising statutes, that many legislators do not understand what they are voting on, and that omissions or ambiguities of meaning go unnoticed.

One sensible method for construing statutes that are unclear is to review a specific statute's legislative history for clues to its legislative intent. The policy and context of a statute are often keys to its importance. Where the roads run nowhere, the judge picks his own direction.

Rulings of such administrative bodies as the Interstate Commerce Commission, the Federal Communications Commission, and the Internal Revenue Service must be given careful attention. With heavy presumptions in court often effectively working in government favor, and client cost factors pointing the same way, it is important to consider not only what the courts will do, but also what administrative agency officials will do. In practical terms, decisions of governmental agencies, while technically appealable in court, tend in bulk to hold fast. Researching lawyers must therefore know administrative as well as case sources.

Many statutes are clear and not ambiguous as to authority or standards. However, they may deliberately leave implementation for administrative and then court interpretation. For instance, Section 10-b-5 of the Securities and Exchange Act of 1934 prohibits manipulative devices in the sale of securities. But when does given conduct become "manipulative"? What, for instance, is a "substantial" part of a corporation's assets; how does it differ from "substantially all"? In these instances, a hybrid area of statutory case law becomes necessary, and case precedents are used to flesh out a base-line statute.

CITATIONS

Citations are actually the names and addresses of cases and statutes, and a form of shorthand instruction. You have found the library. The walls are lined, floor to ceiling, with books. Lawbooks, particularly reports of cases, run on the large side. They are showy as a backdrop for pictures; so much so that many elective-office aspirants are photographed in their law libraries, sucking substance from a background oozing with recorded wisdom.

The books containing the reports of cases are separated alphabetically by state in a central library. In a smaller library, there will be just the one state. The federal books are divided numerically in three main echelons: District Court, Circuit Court of Appeals, and Supreme Court. The first two look the same from afar, but on close inspection the lettering on the spine tells them apart. The United States Supreme Court volumes are easier to spot; they are smaller in size and fatter in shape.

Go to the state reports shelves, take any book down at random, and look at it. Where are we? New York? "New York Reports–309" appears on the spine. "309" is the number of that volume in the series of the reports of the New York Court of Appeals. Usually the volume carrying only the name of the state relates to the state's highest court. Let us assume page 46 of that volume is the number of the page on which the case being researched begins. When this case is to be brought to attention, lawyers say it is to be "cited." For citation purposes, names are shortened or abbreviated to separate one or two of each side. The title is abbreviated by the official reporter. Thus, the 1976 case of *Elizabeth O'Connor* v. *Olive Papertsian* in the New York Court of Appeals, beginning on page 46 of volume 309 of the official reports may be cited as *O'Connor* v. *Papertsian*, 309 N.Y. 46 (1976). Similarly, the 1981 case of *Robert S. Shapiro* v. *The Prudential Insurance Company of America* in the Appellate Division, Second Department, is cited as *Shapiro* v. *Prudential Ins. Co. of America*, 81 A.D. 2d 661 (2nd Dept. 1981). "A.D." volumes contain reports of the New York Appellate Divisions, the state's intermediate appeals courts. Other states have counterparts.

A case on appeal to the Second Circuit Court of Appeals decided in 1978, and reported in the *Federal Reporter*, may be cited as *United States* v. *Kaplan*, 577 F.2d 923 (2 Cir. 1978). If a case appears in the United States Supreme Court, it may be reported in the *United States Reports* and cited officially as *Screws* v. *United States*, 325 U.S. 91 (1944). Again in each case, the number preceding the volume name is its number in the series, and that following is the beginning page of the case.

In sum, the citation shows a law researcher how to go right to the case. The system is simple in the hands of those accustomed to it. All states and jurisdictions have abbreviations that represent some easily identified contraction of their name and their various courts. There are variations in usages by private publishers. Always, the significant information is the jurisdiction, the volume number, and the page number.

In statutory material, which includes constitutions, statutes, treaties, regulations, and administrative releases, abbreviation and numerical consistency again are the keys to citation. For instance, Article I, Section 9 of the United States Constitution is cited as U.S. Const. art. I, §9; the Fourteenth Amendment as U.S. Const. amend. XIV. Citation of the New York constitution would be N.Y. Const. art II, §6 (1894); of New Mexico's N.M. Const. art. 4, §7.

Federal statutes usually are cited by code designations, which may be found in an index volume, or on the spine of the appropriate volume. The most common is the United States Code; for instance, Declaratory Judgment Act 28 U.S.C. §§2201-02 (1964). The United States Code Annotated may be cited as 21 U.S.C.A. §331 for a provision of the Food, Drug and Cosmetic Act. The word "annotated" means each statutory section is set with cross references and with interpretative cases, and, often, appropriate legislative and administrative histories and background factors are described. States like New York and California go by subject volume in their statutory codes. Thus, Cal. Agric, Code §351 (West 1954); N.Y. Banking Law §121 (McKinney 1954). West Publishing Company is the nation's leading private legal publisher. McKinney is a West property. The variations of statutory identification, beyond conventional citation, can make the search difficult. Sometimes there are no code citations; then individual session laws or acts must be located. Sometimes states simply publish their laws chronologically, not by subject.

Regulations and administrative rulings are also often abbreviation and codified; for instance, SEC Reg. A, 16 CFR, §16211 (1949). "SEC" stands for "Securities and Exchange Commission." "Reg" is an abbreviation of "regulation." CFR stands for Code of Federal Regulations. Internal Revenue Service rulings are in Cumulative Bulletins; for instance, Rev. Rul., 80-268 1980-2 Cum. Bull. 141.

Textbooks are cited by volume number (if more than one), author, title, section, paragraph or page number, and edition date. Thus, I. F. Pollock & F. Maitland, *The History of English Law* 518 (2d ed. 1898); B. Harnett, *Responsibilities of Insurance Agents and Brokers*, 76 (10th ed. 1983). The references are to pages 518 and 76 of the respective books. Interestingly, by tradition, British lawyers do not cite living authors. Law Review articles are also a useful source of information for serious lawyers. These are generally cited by volume number of the periodical, then page, and year, such as, 69 Harv. L. Rev. 88 (1955).

A booklet, A *Uniform System of Citation*, published by the Harvard Law Review Association with the participation of the legal periodicals of Columbia, Pennsylvania, and Yale universities, is the citation guide for Law Reviews and most scholarly works. Copies are available from Harvard and at most law school bookstores. Officially called the "Uniform Citator" or, gratingly to some academic ears, the "Harvard Citator," this valuable publication explains the citation of cases of all court levels, statutory material, books, pamphlets, letters, periodicals, newspapers, and commercial services. It gives forms of foreign citation, standardized abbreviations of common words, and various stylistic prescriptions.

Legal research is not a casual thing to lawyers; their livelihood and their clients' significant interests on many occasions depend on somebody's research. The lawyer working with cases and statutes can easily find the volumes in question. The library is the lawyer's workshop.

——GETTING INTO THE PROBLEM——

Let us assume X comes into a law office waving a written three-year employment agreement with a magazine publishing company which, by its terms, cannot be earlier terminated except for "cause." The contract provides that X will be company president, be assigned only duties commensurate with that position, and that he shall have perquisites customary to that office. A further provision is that in the event X breaches the contract, he cannot work for any other magazine publisher anywhere in the United States for the next ten years. X says that the owner of a majority of the stock of the publishing company, who is also its chairman of the Board of Directors, while not complaining of X's work, is harassing him publicly and undermining his authority by issuing direct orders to employees who supposedly should report to X. In addition, the chairman, over the past weekend, moved into X's sumptuous corner office, changed the locks, and posted his own name prominently on the door. When X arrived Monday morning, his secretary met him on the street in front of the building, told him what had happened, and reported that the chairman had directed he use a smaller room down the hall, adjoining the men's room.

What are X's legal rights? How does one begin?

The first step is to ponder the problem after reading the written employment agreement and carefully questioning the client. A full grasp on the facts, including all the contents of conceivably pertinent documents, not just the lines the client cherishes, is critical to research finding, particularly in distinguishing between cases on the subject. The lawyer analytically separates the issues.

1. What is "cause" for termination purposes?
2. What duties are commensurate with being company president?
   a. Must X have all these duties?
   b. Can others have some chief-executive-type duties so long as all X's own limited duties are the kind typically exercised by a president?
3. What perquisites are customary to being president?
4. Are the president's duties impinged on by the chairman's conduct in
   a. directing subordinates?
   b. scolding X publicly?
   c. switching the office?
5. Has there been a breach of the employment agreement by the company?
   a. Does the chairman's conduct amount to a breach?
   b. Is Board of Directors action necessary?
   c. What is the chairman's authority?
6. If X now leaves the company:
   a. Is he breaching the contract?
   b. What remedies does he have if there is a prior breach by the company?
   c. What is the legal effect of the ten-year noncompetition clause?
   d. If X works after termination, will his new earnings reduce the damages payable by the offending publisher?
7. What can X do?
   a. Wait and see?
   b. Leave the company?

    c. React aggressively in asserting his presidential powers?

    d. Send a written notice to the Board of Directors?

    e. Seek an injunction against the chairman?

    f. Something else?

In some general way such as this, an experienced lawyer will analyze the problem. Lawyers who plunge into their legal research with no written or mental outline will waste time. On the other hand, the initial outline is not gospel, and the lawyer must be alert for new approaches as he goes.

In his opening analysis the lawyer proceeds with certain tentative conclusions based on his general legal knowledge. No "cause" for the company terminating X appears. Presidential duties are pivotal but uncertain. The corporation's charter and bylaws must be consulted for the authorities of the chairman and the president. If the company is in material breach of the contract, X can leave; otherwise his departure is his own breach. The noncompetitive clause sounds too broad to be enforceable.

Most of the findings will be in terms of probabilities—the likelihood of a positive result against the magnitude of possible harm. The lawyer also must bear in mind that the facts are as his client gave them. What is the other side's story? And what will be the proof, with most if not all of the third-party witnesses remaining in the employ of the publishing company? The cost of lengthy litigation will be a factor the client must consider.

The principles of law that are applicable to the specific disputation must be clearly established. The subject matter is largely common law—not statutory—except as it may bear on corporate incidents. With the research course charted, the first books required are the "digests," which cover local and national levels, and which are organized and indexed by subject matter and topics. They furnish citations of cases in the area, prefaced by a one-sentence or one-paragraph indication of the case's contents. Topic headings to be examined in X's case will include "Duties of Corporate Officers," "Employment Contracts," and "Contracts Not to Compete."

There are other ways into the cases. They include recourse to treatises, textbooks, or encyclopedias prepared by responsible authorities, those that the researcher has tested by trial and found himself comfortable with. Text description by an established author is useful, since it organizes the area for the researcher, and gives him a framework of understanding in which to work, and itself cites many cases, often by state. An *Index to Legal Periodicals* gives Law Review citations, which are favorite sources because of the depth of current attention to a narrow subject in publications of their sort.

There are two particular research tools here to be emphasized. The *Shepard Citator* consists solely of numbers. It lists only numerical citations in abbreviated form by page and volume of case reports. With continued updating, including pocket parts, it gives current listings of cases cited in other cases. Once you have a case citation, you go to the *Shepard Citator* to locate every other time that case has been cited. Since cross-citation is customarily the result of commonality of issues, a collection of cases relating to an issue, if they exist, can be quickly built up. So common is this usage, that checking a case for later citation, reversal, or overruling is known as "Shepardizing."

For decades, the principal organized research method has been to employ the *American Digest System*, a digest of all state and federal cases. The West System is understood to digest the points of over 3 million decisions and adds to this at a rate exceeding 30,000 per year. There are 400 digest topics and over 80,000 subtopics.

The Digest features a decimal system under which a principal subject is given a number, and logical subdivisions are given subordinate numbers in the same decimal series. Its useful index is called "Descriptive Word Index." Each separate point has a drawing of a small key (as to a lock) printed to the left. Sometimes the system is called the "Key system." Possession of a key number enables a researcher to check any West-keyed publication in any jurisdiction to pick up the point. Moreover, in West-reported cases, the case headnotes employ the key numbers. Let me give you an example of how this works, both in the Digest and in the headnotes. Most reported cases have at least two systems of citation, the official and West. In the United States Supreme Court case of *Escobedo v. State of Illinois*, 378 U.S. 478, 84 S.Ct Rptr 1758 [e.g., the West publication] (1964), an issue was whether an accused could be compelled to incriminate himself. The West key number under Criminal Law, 393, is captioned "Compelling Accused To Incriminate Himself." 393(1) is subcaptioned "In general." Many cases are summarily described and cited under key number 393(1). In the official published reports of the case, 378 U.S. 478, there are no key numbers anywhere in view. But in the West reporter, 84 S.Ct Rptr, 1758, there are keys in both the headnotes and the text. One headnote in the *Escobedo* case reads "Criminal Law [Key] 393(1) . . . An accused may intelligently and knowingly waive his privilege against self incrimination and his right to counsel either at a pretrial stage or at the trial." This exact paragraph appears in the Digest under Criminal Law [key] number 393(1), which, incidentally, gives only the West citation for the case, not the official report.

This mechanical sifting of cases in a digest, scanning existing publications for case citations, and Shepardizing of wholly numerical citations quite obviously provide natural terrain for computerization. Apart from regionalized or specialized services, there now appear to be two computer systems used nationwide to help conduct legal research. One is Westlaw, a system of West Publishing Company; the other is Lexis, of Mead Data Central, Inc. They are both relatively expensive features, but their usefulness in breaking down big research projects in short order is compelling. Because of cost, most computerized research installations are found in large firms and central libraries. While there are a variety of important technical differences, both systems operate similarly. Each works on the principle of "storing" the contents of delineated volumes and documents. The user has a terminal, which resembles a typewriter, with a telephone-connected video screen and a printing unit. The terminal is used to formulate requests, in a language that is part code and part abbreviation. For instance, if you want all California cases in which a car strikes a bicycle, that request is fed in, and the answer appears quickly, on either a paper print-out or the television screen, setting out the caption, citation, and a very brief description of all summoned cases. Legal computer technology is continually expanding and improving. But, although computers telescope research, it is only human intelligence that can exercise the critical discriminations of case choice and analysis in terms of the facts on hand.

Points involving statutes, or the administrative rules and regulations flowing from them, are somewhat easier to pinpoint than cases generally. Basically, the way into statutes is through shelf placement, titles, tables of contents and indexes, whether by descriptive words, by phrases, or by subjects, and library card files. There are a number of different federal indexing publications by private publishers, including the ubiquitous West Publishing Company, with its United States Code Annotated, complete with key-number references to interpretative cases. Shepard offers federal statutory citator services.

In the various states there are local publishers who publish and annotate their state statutes. There are also periodic compilations and surveys of statutes of many kinds. A particular favorite is the *Law Digest* volume of the noted *Martindale Hubbell Law Directory*, published annually. This book digests very briefly the laws of all the states, with many current statutory citations.

——— THE MARCH OF EXPERIENCE ———

There it is, a description of finding the law, American style, cavalier enough to shake a law school dean down to his socks. But I stand by it as a communicative document.

A careful experienced lawyer will read his cases and statutory material and usually take notes for study or later memorandum construction. He will line up clearly in his mind the principal facts of his most relevant cases and who won and who lost. He will see his case in living terms. He will separate from the torrent of judicial language those statements that are essential to the holding, the minimum rule of the case necessary to sustain its holding on the facts. He will also study dissenting and concurring opinions, if any, for tangential insight. Sometimes today's dissent becomes tomorrow's majority with a change in the constituency of the court.

Where a statute or regulation is clear, or where the cases are close and consistent, the lawyer's decision follows more easily from them. But where the facts under review fall between the instances reported, the lawyer must synthesize his authorities. He must adopt a train of reasoning to support the conclusion he seeks. He does this by logical extension of existing case and statutory authorities, projecting reasons behind the rules, isolating principles, and finally weighing the practical factors that may appear—fairness, unjust enrichment, subversion of an apparent social good, conception of human nature—

in short, anything germane to making his position acceptable to an ultimate deciding authority. This pit of empiricism is bottomless.

Finding the law is similar for both lawyers and judges, but diverges at the moment of decision. The lawyer who is "counseling" must take into account the probabilities of the result going one way or another and express himself accordingly. The lawyer who is an "advocate" has the easiest intellectual part, for he has a given position to begin with and his task is only to gather means of supporting it. The judge, on the other hand, has the burden of decision, not for him the probabilities or the comfort of a necessary position to sustain. He does not engage in prediction about what the courts will do (unless he is worried about the appellate court above him); he is the court. He must concern himself with what he will do; his action becomes the law. Lest we feel sorry for the judge, let us recall that he faces no consequence for his error, short of bland appellate reversal. He does not have to face wrathful clients, or watch his economic fortunes fluctuate with his legal performance.

Careful inquiry, and further inquiry, into the facts appears in the work habits of all good seasoned lawyers. The methodical questioning in detail of everything of conceivable relevance, often maddening to clients, is designed to clarify to the maximum extent what really went on, because the assumption of what really went on forms the premise of the legal question put, and channels its answer. Many a lawyer to his sorrow has given a quick correct answer to a question, only later to learn the question was a different one. Clients rarely remember the questions; but they have long memories for wrong answers.

The experienced lawyer has background and is attuned to legal implication, and he learns where to look, then how to use his findings. This essential skill of lawyering varies greatly in lawyers, and, accordingly, in the law portions their clients receive. Its recognition forms further testament that the law is more art form than holy writ.

4

LEGAL
ETHICS

Historically, the statement of ethics for lawyers was known as the "Canons of Professional Ethics," although it is now called "The Model Rules of Professional Conduct." But use of the word "historically" may afford an overly grand perspective. Somehow, over the years, ethical prescriptions for lawyers in this country, once denominated "Canons," have assumed divine attributions rooted in Biblical antiquity. With divinity and morality in the wings, undue righteousness easily finds itself on center stage.

Without doubt, the Model Rules of Professional Conduct are not a morality play. Notwithstanding its critics, the Model has no plot, although it deals some in fiction. Its language tends to an elitism that has no true place in this country's tradition. From a common-law heritage reaching deep into Anglo-Saxon times, even before the Magna Carta of 1215, lawyering in England was done, albeit unevenly, by an elite fraternity. In that system, where traditionally the trial lawyers are barristers, who speak to clients only through solicitors, where their actual trial schooling comes through a series of ancient and restrictive voluntary associations for barristerial congregation called Inns of Court, a special class of distinguished gentlemen is understandable. The American claim of inheritance of this gentle legacy is, under the circumstances, somewhat illegitimate. In a brand-new country, settled principally by unlanded nongentry, the English lawyering institutions were never approached reverently. In the first century of the United States's corporate existence, legal training was a sometime thing, and in many places a person was a lawyer simply because he said so.

The original Canons of Professional Ethics were adopted by the American Bar Association in 1908. They were based on an 1887 Alabama Code of Ethics, which in turn borrowed heavily from a series of Philadelphia lectures by a local judge, George Sharswood, in 1854, the acknowledged starting point of the lawyering ethical regulatory saga. In 1969, the Canons were metamorphosed into the Model Code of Professional Responsibility. A prime mover then was another Philadelphia lawyer, Henry Drinker, who served for nine years as chairman of the ABA Ethics Commission. His book, *Legal Ethics*, published in 1953, remains the standard work in the field. It is particularly ironic that the term "Philadelphia lawyer" now bears the connotation of undue sharpness in practice, since between Sharswood and Drinker, Philadelphia can lay fair claim to being the legal ethics capital of the United States. In 1983, ABA changed the words; the "Code" became the "Rules" with little change in evident substance.

A six-year struggle over these present Model Rules was conducted within the halls of the American Bar Association with great emotionality. It culminated in a compromise to which all parties agreed, if only to end the pain. The 1983 Model Rules are plainly a lawyer's document, and are drawn by a committee of lawyers at that. Where the original canons were theocratic, and the 1969 Model Code was a mixture of the old-time religion and military regulations, the 1983 Model Rules, while still maintaining aspirational tones, lay emphasis on spelling out proper conduct so that lawyers will have specific guidance in their ethical applications. The reformative thrust to articulate greater public responsibilities of lawyers, which was a prime motive of the original drafters, crumbled before the basic thesis of the legal profession, private responsibility to clients.

ETHICS AND THE LEGAL MONOPOLY

The definition of legal ethics in that venerable standby of the profession, *Black's Law Directory* (5th Ed. 1979), reads:

> . . . usages and customs among members of the legal profession, involving their moral and professional duties towards one another, towards clients, and toward the courts, that branch of moral science which treats of the duties which a member of the legal profession has to the public, to the court, to his professional brethren, and to his client.

It is obvious that much legal "ethical" conduct has little to do with morality, even as that overburdened word is generally used. Rules that relate to limitations on advertising and solicitation of business, fee splitting, confidentiality of client communication, and singleness of interest in representing the client are essentially pragmatic, and not moralistic, in their content. Indeed, as we shall see, the requirement of maintaining confidentiality of communication may be downright immoral in ordinary individual terms, yet it is presumably justified in the social value of maintaining effective legal representation in the protection of rights.

Actually, the Model Rules, and the ABA itself for that matter, have no sovereign force. The states are the ones that, by statute or by rules of court, impose governing rules of conduct on lawyers. Traditionally, most of the states have accepted the ABA package pretty much *in toto*. While there has always been a certain amount of local self-expression, the ABA package has had the advantage of presenting to the states a careful assemblage from a "safe" source. Now the modern trend is for even greater local deviation on points of interest to trial lawyers particularly. There are also state rules which venture beyond the Model Rules with specific statutes on such misconduct as insider trading and hospital entry to negotiate retainers, settlements, and releases. There are specific statutory provisions in many states enforcing confidentiality of communication by virtue of a special relationship, such as lawyer-client, physician-patient, priest-penitent, and husband-wife.

In one form or another, the contents of ethical rules for lawyers drawn by lawyers become authoritative throughout the United States. Though developed by private lawyer groups, these rules have taken on the effect of law and their normative essences have been absorbed wholesale. Many policy decisions implicit in the Rules are judgments that sway society mightily. Many positions on subjects regulated as "ethics" in truth represent social value judgments and deal with the governance of society, yet they are largely self-imposed by the very profession sought to be regulated. These raise the question of the responsibilities of lawyers to the public, beyond their "hired gun" role for their clients, as do the questions of service to the disadvantaged and actions in the public interest. The charging of fees and the manner of distribution of their economic burden, the extent of the legal monopoly, the disciplining of lawyers, the ways people should have of learning their legal rights, all raise issues that go well beyond the confines of the legal profession. The keen and critical interest of the press in the protracted proceedings leading to the adoption of the 1983 Model Rules was, I believe, the first concerted focus of public attention on Rule adoption by the American Bar Association.

There is a growing social awareness of the need to improve the availability of legal services to all segments of the population. Largely through the impetus of concerned union and civil-rights groups and United States Supreme Court decisions giving primacy to rights of free speech, the ancient ethical rules guiding lawyers in advertising, soliciting business, and fee charging are being mauled. There has been no major reform of professional-conduct codes considered inimical to the interests of lawyers made in this century by the major Bar Associations that has not been prompted by pressure of civil-rights enactments of the United States Supreme Court in litigation pressed by special-interest groups.

The fundamental value judgment is that the legal profession operates a closed system. To repay that grant, the profession must work in the best interests of society. Licensing and discipline are correlative. There seems only positive value in reminding lawyers of their special role and obligations. Dean Norman Redlich, of New York University Law School, has trenchantly written:

> The legal profession is now engaged in a dialogue with the American people in which the lawyers are saying, "We want to retain our privileged position in the American system of law enforcement because it is in your best interests that we do so," and the American people are replying, "Unless we are convinced that the legal profession carries on its day-to-day practice in such a way as to provide compliance with the law, even among the rich and powerful, we will seriously consider restructuring the privileged sanctuary which *we* have created for *you*."
>
> As we lawyers work in the marketplace, and claim to have the ethics of the temple, we would delude ourselves if we failed to realize that the outcome of that dialogue is very much in doubt.

THE MODEL RULES OF PROFESSIONAL CONDUCT

The Model Rules are organized into eight general subjects. Within each subject there are separately enumerated "Rules." "Comments" accompany each Rule and are designed to illustrate the meanings and purposes of the Rule. They are guides to interpretation. While only the Rules are said to be authoritative, the Comments take on the coloration of Rules themselves through their interpretive devices. Finally, there are "Notes," which are research and source materials and not intended to affect the application or interpretation of the Rules and Comments.

The manner of professional discipline, enforcement, and penalty is not covered by the Model Rules. They are left for the enforcing agencies put in place by the states or federal jurisdictions, usually courts or local Bar Association committees.

The outline of the Model Rules, by official headings but without any text, is:

Client-Lawyer Relationship

Rule Number

1.1 Competence
1.2 Scope of representation
1.3 Diligence
1.4 Communication
1.5 Fees
1.6 Confidentiality of information
1.7 Conflict of interest: general rule
1.8 Conflict of interest: prohibited transactions
1.9 Conflict of interest: former client
1.10 Imputed disqualification: general rule
1.11 Successive government and private employment
1.12 Former judge or arbitrator
1.13 Organization as client
1.14 Client under a disability
1.15 Safekeeping property
1.16 Declining or terminating representation

Counselor

2.1 Advisor
2.2 Intermediary
2.3 Evaluation for use by third persons

Advocate

3.1 Meritorious claims and contentions
3.2 Expediting litigation

3.3   Candor toward the tribunal
3.4   Fairness to opposing party and counsel
3.5   Impartiality and decorum of the tribunal
3.6   Trial publicity
3.7   Lawyer as witness
3.8   Special responsibilities of a prosecutor
3.9   Advocate in nonadjudicative proceedings

Transactions with Persons Other Than Clients
4.1   Truthfulness in statements to others
4.2   Communication with person represented by counsel
4.3   Dealing with unrepresented person
4.4   Respect for rights of third persons

Law Firms and Associations
5.1   Responsibilities of a partner or supervisory lawyer
5.2   Responsibilities of a subordinate lawyer
5.3   Responsibilities regarding nonlawyer assistants
5.4   Professional independence of a lawyer
5.5   Unauthorized practice of law
5.6   Restrictions on Right to Practice

Public Service
6.1   *Pro Bono Publico* service
6.2   Accepting appointments
6.3   Membership in legal services organization
6.4   Law reform activities affecting client interests

Information about Legal Services
7.1   Communications concerning a lawyer's services
7.2   Advertising
7.3   Direct contact with prospective clients
7.4   Communication of fields of practice
7.5   Firm names and letterheads

Maintaining the Integrity of the Profession
8.1   Bar admission and disciplinary matters
8.2   Judicial and legal officials
8.3   Reporting professional misconduct
8.4   Misconduct
8.5   Jurisdiction

THE ADVERTISING AND SOLICITING BUGABOOS

Rules dealing with the availability of counsel have been among the most pregnant in terms of practical and social problems. In their sphere lies the whole public-policy clash of lawyers' advertising and stirring up litigation versus their promoting individual awareness of recourse to law and the courts. More than any others, they bring to the foreground the marked differences between the various segments of the Bar, and the inappositeness of using a single ethical-conduct standard to cover the outreach of all of them.

There is plainly high social interest in the accessibility of legal services and consequently in the means of communicating their availability. Yet, since lawyers as a whole are so strategically placed in society and government, and the public rarely pokes into professional mystique, self-regulation in the form of Bar Association rules, essentially protective of the lawyers' franchise, long rested easy, without any real contest. Over a period of time the established ethical rules took on aspects of faith and were unthinkingly renewed. Media advertising by lawyers was always prohibited.

Onto this serene scene of Bar Association equanimity, the United States Supreme Court (composed entirely of lawyers, it should be carefully observed) burst like an anarchist's bomb. The high court ruled, in the case of *Bates* v. *State Bar of Arizona*, 433 U.S. 350 (1977), that, notwithstanding the 1969 ABA Code of Professional Responsibility, which had been adopted in Arizona, a firm of Arizona lawyers doing business under the name "Legal Clinic of Bates & O'Steen" could advertise publicly. The law firm was upheld in running a newspaper advertisement captioned boldly "Do You Need A Lawyer? Legal Service at very reasonable fees." There followed a plausible sketch of the scales of justice, then a price list for certain normally uncomplicated legal proceedings. For instance, a change-of-name proceeding was quoted at $95 plus $20 in court filing fees. There was a $100 offering in the preparation of all court papers and instructions on how to do your own simple uncontested divorce. The advertisement finished with an invitation to inquire and listed the firm's name, address, and telephone number.

The bald assertions that advertising by lawyers is an automatic detraction from dignity was never supportable. Respectable businesses advertise, as do the Blue Cross and engineers. Under the 1969 Code, ABA sought to justify the ban on competitive advertising by saying, "History has demonstrated that public confidence in the legal system is best preserved by strict, self-imposed controls over, rather than by unlimited, advertising." Having said this, there was not a shred of authority offered; in fact, out of the 147 footnotes annotating old Canon Two, which contained the advertising ban, there seemed to be not one making any such historical demonstration.

Under the not so gentle hint of the United States Supreme Court, the American Bar Association has now broken its tradition of opposing public media advertising by lawyers. Under Rule 7.2, public media advertising is permitted if properly done. Yet, the choice of language of both Rules and Comments reflects the old distaste for the advertising process. While seemingly resigned to truthful public advertising which does not compare lawyers or exaggerate results, the Association remains overtly hostile to the enlisting of law business that it calls "solicitation." Rule 7.3 strikes at direct client contact by the lawyer himself or through intermediaries. However, this solicitation is only offensive where "a significant motive to do so is the lawyer's pecuniary gain." This limitation brings to my mind the story of the lawyer who fell from the canoe in the deepest part of the lake. His partner in the canoe called,

"Can you float alone?"

"Sure, but what kind of time is this to start talking about money?"

The relatively flat exclusion under Rule 7.3 of lawyers who earn fees from direct and indirect client contact is overly broad and not required by the undeniably poor effects which can result from unscrupulous lawyers drumming up legal business by questionable means. After all, the client who comes to a strange law office pursuant to a media advertisement is subject to solicitous activity once he sets his foot in the door. There are work among the disadvantaged, work in the public interest, and the effects of interpersonal communication to be considered in the generation of legal traffic. At the root, there is a policy nexus here between solicitation and paying for the case as discussed in Chapter Six below. The pecuniary gain of lawyers is significant in all private lawyering activity.

Economic competition, while odious to many lawyers, is desirable to the public. The client is concerned about cost, and some lawyers of equal competence and probity do charge less than others.

In the final analysis, the heterogeneity of the Bar diversifies the impact of advertising and soliciting, for in the upper legal registers advertising and solicitation restriction has had no real effect. The lucrative corporate and big-business legal trade is largely in the hands of large established firms. Yet, the infighting between larger firms for important clients can be fierce. The solicitation of big business is not done by media advertising; it is done, with more or less degrees of subtlety, through parties, political events, interlocking business arrangements, and contrived introductions and approaches.

Lawyers have always advertised within this business stratum and to other lawyers, accountants, bank officers, and insurance agents by professional lecturing and writing within the then governing rules. Many large firms carry partners whose basic functions are to market the services of their colleagues. This is known as "getting business." I find it amusing that the most devoutly ethical lawyers who balk at legal advertising and soliciting seem untroubled by deducting—for their own income tax purposes—such items as country club dues, on the grounds that these are expenses incurred in the production of income.

It is the single practitioner and the small firms dealing with the population at large who rely on the kinds of practice typically reached by competitive media advertising, including the telephone-book yellow pages, and on the solicitation of strangers. These practices cater to personal-injury (accident) cases, crimes, divorces, especially where little property is involved, small estates, debt collection, landlord-tenant affairs, and various governmental assistances.

The soliciting of cases and the "stirring up" or fomenting of litigation are companionate to advertising as an ethical problem. They are another facet of the same policy clash of professional restriction versus individual access to the courts. Actually, it was the solicitation of cases that led the Supreme Court to rule general advertising permissible.

In *NAACP v. Button*, 371 U.S. 415 (1963), the Supreme Court upheld activities by the National Association for the Advancement of Colored People in Virginia in promoting civil-rights litigation. A union was permitted, in *Brotherhood RR Trainmen v. Virginia State*

Bar, 377 U.S. 1 (1964), to recommend specific lawyers for personal-injury claims. (In England, tangentially, unions retain and pay for lawyers.) *United Mine Workers* v. *Illinois Bar Association*, 389 U.S. 217 (1967), upheld the filing of members' worker's compensation claims by a salaried union lawyer official. Under *United Transp. Union* v. *State Bar Michigan*, 401 U.S. 571 (1971), a union was permitted to recommend to its members personal-injury lawyers who agreed to work for a 25 percent contingent fee.

Obviously, solicitation and advertising overlap. A tow-truck operator, acting on behalf of a lawyer, who hands out the lawyer's business card at the scene of an auto accident is doing this double duty. Any communication that informs people, even a large group, of legal services can be both a solicitation and an advertisement and represent the same vice, if there be one.

The classic offensive solicitation involves a "runner," someone paid to go to a potential client and tout the lawyer. It may be at the scene of an accident or a crime, even in a hospital. There do seem to remain free commercial speech issues when it comes to striking down salaried "runners." This is, after all, another form of advertising, although more direct than media advertising. However, here there may be questions of undue influence and advantage taken, depending on the circumstances. But not all "solicitors" are "touts" or "runners." There are fine lines to be drawn between "stirring up" litigation and advising people of their existing legitimate rights to sue, even if people get paid in the process. The poor and the not so poor can, under a variety of circumstances, speak directly to lawyers they meet or with whom they are put in touch without realization of the panoply of terror promised by the Comments to Rule 7.3.

The Supreme Court decision in *Goldfarb* v. *Virginia State Bar*, 421 U.S. 773 (1975), seemed specially designed for Bar Association teeth gnashing. There the court held that a Virginia Bar Association minimum-fee schedule amounted to price-fixing and that the United States antitrust laws applied to lawyers' associations. In doing this the court said, out loud, where all could hear, that practicing law was a business.

The direction of the Supreme Court is plainly oriented to greater public rights and lesser legal exclusivity. When the chips are down, and they will be, we can anticipate a pruning of any professional-conduct restrictions that nibble away at the consumer's pocketbook and erode his rights to know his legal rights, to go to court, and to be protected.

CONFIDENTIALITY

Rule 1.6 deals with the most critical ethical problem a lawyer faces— that of preserving the confidences of a client. The privilege of confidential communication between attorney and client is so well known as to be part of the folklore of our society, and it goes to the heart of the profession. Basically, it means that an attorney may not divulge to anyone (subject to a few exceptions) anything he learns from or about a client in the course of a representation without the permission of the client.

Lawyers have people working with them, be they partners, employed lawyers, paralegals, secretaries, clerical help, or messengers. A lawyer is free to reveal a client's information within his law firm unless the client directs otherwise. This puts a burden on the lawyer to use reasonable care in selecting associates, particularly those with access to the files.

The difficulties of confidentiality have never been illuminated to me so dramatically as in a well-reported murder case in upstate New York; a subject carefully treated in Professor Monroe Freedman's controversial book *Ethics in an Adversary System* (1975). Defendant A was indicted for murdering man X. Two defense lawyers were appointed for him by the court. During preparatory discussions for the case involving X's murder, A told his lawyers he had killed two young women, Y and Z, and even where he had hidden their bodies. The lawyers went and saw both bodies, but reported nothing to the police. The woman Y had been a camping companion of the murdered man X, so it was natural that her father would come to A's lawyers seeking information about his daughter. But the lawyers refused to tell him anything. Later, but before A's trial, the bodies of Y and Z were independently discovered. At his trial, A made self-incriminating references to the murders of Y and Z. It was not until the day after that the lawyers revealed the full story of their knowledge of the Y and Z bodies.

Predictably, a storm of ethical controversy swirled around the events, and still persists. The two lawyers were praised for client fidelity in some quarters and excoriated for inhumanity in others. Most lawyers, particularly trial lawyers, I believe, agree with the decision of A's two lawyers, but many do not. There are some who do not criticize the conduct, although they personally would have done otherwise. In the end, A's two lawyers were not subjected to any professional disciplinary attention or adverse Bar Association opinion, although one of them was indicted for failing to report a dead body. But this was dismissed before the trial.

The justification for the privilege of confidentiality lies in the right to counsel fundamental to our legal system. If the client cannot tell his lawyer everything, and the lawyer cannot gather information for fear of compelled disclosure, the lawyer cannot develop his case fully. Individual morality is here put aside in favor of the pragmatic yet competing social value of the utility of the legal system.

Confidentiality is important to both civil and criminal causes, but more so in the criminal because of the imminent deprival of personal liberty. Constitutional right to counsel is more extensive under the criminal law for the same reason. No person can, under the federal Constitution, be forced to testify against or incriminate himself. If a disclosure to a lawyer were to be available to the prosecution, not only would the recourse to counsel be dampened, but also the accused would be incriminating himself by talking to his own lawyer.

Coming back to the case of the two dead women in upstate New York, a critical point is that the crime and the harm were already done. The obligation, if any, to disclose *intent* to commit a crime later on is most controversial. Under Rule 1.6, a lawyer may, "to the extent he believes necessary," disclose client information "to prevent the client from committing a criminal act that the lawyer believes is likely to result in imminent death or substantial bodily harm." Note carefully that the lawyer is not required to make this disclosure; it is a discretionary act. The narrowness of the lawyer's responsibility here illustrates plainly the ascendancy of the lawyer's commitment to his client's interest over any commitment to the public good.

The fallback on confidentiality can lead to some peculiar moral decisions by lawyers. In his *Crisis at the Bar* (1978), Jethro K. Lieberman writes, in connection with the celebrated Leo Frank murder trial, which was featured in book and motion-picture form:

> Just this situation arose following the Leo Frank trial in Atlanta in 1914. Frank was the wealthy Jewish manager of a pencil factory. An employee, Mary Phagan, was found dead; on shaky evidence, Frank was convicted of a sex murder and sentenced to death. There was a tremendous outcry from, among others, the Atlanta clergy and the Northern press; the governor of Georgia commuted Frank's sentence to life imprisonment. But xenophobia stirred up by a professional Jew-baiter, Tom Watson, led a mob to pull Frank from his cell and lynch him. Shortly after Frank's conviction had been affirmed on appeal, an Atlanta lawyer named Arthur Powell received a visit from a client who persuaded Powell that he had killed Mary Phagan and that Frank was completely innocent. Powell decided to keep this communication confidential. In an autobiography thirty years later, Powell, then a judge, noted that his conscience was relieved somewhat when Frank's sentence was commuted. (Was it eased still further when Frank was lynched?)

Only in 1982 did the true murderer come forward to relieve his own conscience.

—CANDOR TOWARD THE TRIBUNAL—

Rule 3.3 prevents a lawyer himself from knowingly using perjured testimony or false evidence, even though the communication of the information is within the professional relationship. He should try to persuade his client to be truthful. Assume, however, the client remains determined to lie and the lawyer is fearful of revealing the perjury under the confidentiality strictures. How does the lawyer handle the prohibition on his use of perjured testimony? It is one thing for the client to lie, another for the lawyer to swear to it. Still, the lawyer has a job to do. The comment to Rule 3.3 waffles through to an ultimate conclusion that even in a criminal case, the defense lawyer should not countenance his client's perjury. If he cannot convince his client to testify truthfully, the lawyer must withdraw if that would be helpful or permissible (pushing the problem on to the next lawyer), and if all else fails, he must make a disclosure to the court (pushing the problem on to the judge). What the judge should do is left open. In this undeniably knotty problem, the Comment acknowledges that various states have their own statutes regulating the conduct of lawyers, including those defending clients accused of committing crimes, based in part on local constitutional interpretations. In the face of these, ABA simply wrings its hands. Regrettably there is no firm stand on principle here, one way or the other.

My own experience has been that seasoned and well-regarded criminal lawyers, out of a belief in the superiority of basic constitutional rights, resolve the problem by examining the witness and then later summing up in their usual style. Most lawyers I know working on the civil side, without the constitutional imperatives of criminal cases, would withdraw from the case if they knew the client was giving perjured testimony or false evidence.

It must be emphasized that we have made perjured material our assumption. There is a great difference, however, between knowing something is perjured and suspecting that it is. Experienced lawyers rarely make the error of prejudging their clients in absence of a clear, informed admission or overwhelming circumstances. They do not usurp the function of the judge and jury, since they feel their client is entitled to a full trial run.

I have heard lawyers say, "It's my duty to do anything to win for my client." I have watched that theme pounded into the jury railing time and time again, and, of course, it is not so. It is not the standard of most lawyers; it is not even articulated aloud by the more astute of the unscrupulous who basically agree in silence. Lawyers are not to lie, deliberately mislead the court or the jury on the law, or fake evidence. The lawyer is required to be professional, courteous, dignified, and show other traits of good legal breeding, although there is enough deviation in practice to be downright discouraging. Obviously, the lawyer is not to tamper with witnesses, which introduces the thin wavy line between preparing a witness and coaching him. The way in which a prefatory inference is made or a question put may consciously or unconsciously affect a client's answer. If you infer to the client that it is in his interest to have had a controversial meeting at 7:00 P.M., and then ask the question of the time of the meeting, the client is likely to have a 7:00 P.M. recollection refreshed, even though he came into the interview room with an 8:00 P.M. recollection or, perhaps, none at all. In short, the demarcation between preparing and coaching will never in this world be satisfactorily delineated, particularly if lawyers question clients and witnesses in manners that are suggestive of the desired answer.

——HARASSING THE OTHER SIDE——

By the book, it is improper to harass the opposition by undue delay, by frivolous argumentation, or by abusive discovery devices. This is a proper ideal which founders in practice. In the profession, such practices lumped together may be known as "grinding down" the other side, by interposing endless demands, motions, and appeals in order to overburden the other side with cost, effort, and delay. Sometimes there is a deliberate calculation to delay to earn monetary interest, or simply to defer the payment of a loan the client cannot then repay conveniently. Litigation can be a way of buying time. These are undeniably tactics of many lawyers, particularly when backed by deep pocketbooks and when the opposing parties are undermanned or lacking in resources, which mostly means litigating money for fees and expenses. Yet grinding down to an offensive degree is rarely sufficiently identifiable for disciplinary action, although occasionally a court will fine or reprimand a lawyer for particularly abusive conduct. Delay is difficult to evaluate because of the differences in lawyer and court schedules, methods, style, pace, and temperament. Frivolity of legal argument is hard to pin down, since it is too easy for an experienced lawyer to fashion something from nothing.

A common practice to help collect a debt or to enforce a contract for the purchase of goods is to threaten to go to the district attorney. Actually, threats by a lawyer of pressing criminal charges to seek civil advantage are themselves unethical conduct. For this reason, most such threats are oral and, unless directed to the naïve, customarily useless.

A lawyer cannot ethically contact his opposing lawyer's client within the subject of representation without prior consent of that lawyer. This is an easy enough rule to observe between relative strangers, but where the parties and even their lawyers know and perhaps regularly deal with each other, it is a difficult stance to maintain.

———————SOCIAL IMPERATIVE———————

But let us abandon the ethical trees and seek the forest for an overview of the self-regulating charter of the legal profession. Professional Rules are simply the means to a larger end, which is the right conduct of our legal system for the benefit of society.

It is to be hoped that this recognition will ease the anguish of the knee-jerk righteous who see defilement in every innovation. As a social tool, the procedures of lawyering require constant review and revision to accord with the goals of society as they become spelled out in a democratic process. Social change is not necessarily heresy.

To be sure, some governing rules of conduct are moral in nature; they decry stealing, cheating, and fraud. Other rules are devoid of moral-value content in that they simply apply to the relationship between lawyers, such as following local rules of practice, being courteous, and, where it does not injure the client, acting to accommodate opposing lawyers in reasonable procedural applications. Other rules may actually run counter to governing morality. The nondisclosure of harmful information gained in confidential communications, cross-examination to destroy a truthful witness, diligent representation within the bounds of the law where the client may be legally right but is morally in the wrong—these tasks and others like them come to lawyers, and in their discharge lies the duty of lawyering, part of the foundation of the American system of legal justice.

Saints and sinners alike have personal rights to be protected in this country. The legal profession sets itself at the disposal of disputing members of society in the operation of a frankly adversarial system. It is the way our countrymen have chosen. The social weight of an effective legal system becomes the justification for conduct and associations sometimes required of lawyers that would be repugnant to their moral sense in their private capacities as citizens, parents, lovers, relatives, and friends.

CAN A DECENT PERSON BE A LAWYER

Lawyering and generally understood human ethics are often uncomfortably contradictory. Some commentators have gone so far as to question whether a decent person can be a lawyer at all.

If the client is a known thief or murderer, for instance, the lawyer nonetheless takes up his cudgels. Business-law advice to clients is constantly geared to shaving the rules, not how to abide by them more fully. Lawyers' effectiveness to their clients, whether rich or poor, is measured by how successfully they are able to pursue the clients' interests. How indeed, it may be asked, can a moral person stand upon an ethical platform poled in such a marsh? The lawyer's personal morality finds refuge behind his detachment.

Detachment means essentially that lawyers take their clients' cases, not their causes. The accused is presumed innocent until proven guilty. Right of counsel means entitlement to a lawyer, and the ability to confide in him freely without fear of exposure. Detachment is more than a lawyer's option; it is a necessity. If a lawyer clouds his judgment or conduct with inappropriate emotion or with conflicting personal attitudes, he fails to deliver to the client the objective test that is his due.

I read an article on the Op Ed page of the *New York Times* in which a successful criminal lawyer decried his self-brutalization, arising from his aggressive efforts on behalf of accused criminals. I wonder sometimes if all of us in the law do not do a variety of this to ourselves, without the extreme of shielding violent criminals, even in the peaceful context of commercial routine or ordinary civil cases.

The law profession turns on taking maximum advantage of a situation, putting the other side to its proof, finding the loophole, engineering the potential escape from the seemingly inescapable obligation, and on the thirst to win, to get the edge, to profit. Lawyers are professional manipulators who understand well the differences between morality and enforceability, and who gauge the extent to which enforceability is effective or can be ignored.

Some lawyers may seek to justify their roles by saying they act circumspectly within the system, that there are lines they never cross. But that does not relieve the fundamental moral onus of lawyering. It only says that some will not go as far as others; it ignores that all lawyers must go part of the way.

If a lawyer can switch client allegiance at will, and by training can cut into any transaction he approaches without compunction, is he not more susceptible to corruption than lay people? Was the lawyer debasement so vividly portrayed in the disgraceful Watergate affair, an aberration where a number of lawyers simply lost their heads, or was it something deeper? Were they predisposed to immoral conduct by their essential professional conditioning, with its mobile morality? Is moral lassitude built into lawyering?

I believe it need not be. There is a place for the private person in that special moral universe of lawyering, for the person who, consistent with the obligations of his calling, adheres to decency. In this world we all occupy multiple relationships, yet must remain true to ourselves. We must remember there are many free choices constantly open to lawyers in the honorable performance of their chosen work and in society beyond.

5

THE
ECONOMICS
OF LAWYERING

Many lawyers who support themselves in private practice vigorously assert that their vocational activity is a "profession" not a "business." But, most assuredly, if they neglect the financial end of their profession, they will be out of business.

It is clear that the bulk of practicing lawyers do relatively well financially in varying degrees throughout the country. For example, partners in firms of forty or more lawyers nationwide, now have estimated median incomes of $110,000; $60,000 in firms with two to six lawyers. Starting law firm salaries average $26,000, although big-city firms typically go up to almost twice that. Nonsupervisory attorneys employed by corporations enjoyed a median salary of about $40,000, rising to about $47,000 in major cities. Obviously, higher and lower earnings go into any "median" computation. Top city and high level corporate lawyers are very substantial earners.

It is estimated that in 1982 the gross national product of the legal profession approximated $30 billion, up from $10.8 billion in 1972. This takes in the earnings of lawyers and those who work for them, apart from the rather extensive infrastructure that supports lawyering, such as landlords, suppliers of all manner of paper and equipment, and countless servicers. In all, it seemed a thriving legal decade.

About 65 percent of all people working as lawyers are in private practice, with about 35 percent of those in solo practice and the balance in law firms. The remaining one-quarter or so work for governments and as house counsel for business companies and nonprofit institutions. Approximately 8,000 lawyers teach full or part time in law schools.

Traditionally, law firms have been partnerships, and remain overwhelmingly so. Most have ten or fewer partners. Some have incorporated to gain tax deductions for pension fund contributions and other tax benefits. Incorporated law firms may be identified by suffixed initials, such as "P.C." (for Professional Corporation) or "P.A." (for Professional Association) following the firm name. There are even law partnerships where individual partners are themselves separately incorporated as professional corporations.

LEGAL FEES

Payments to lawyers for their services are "fees." Hiring a lawyer is "retaining" him. Generically, a "retainer" is a fee arrangement, payable either in a lump sum or periodically, covering services to be rendered over a period of time. Fee charging is a skill all its own, not found in any law school curriculum, and not learned from books.

A unit of legal work may be generally referred to as a "case," although, strictly speaking, "case" relates to a lawsuit or "claim," actual or pending. The generic word covering the full scope of legal piecework is a "matter."

Fee-charging methods relate to the type of matter, the size of the firm, the nature of its practice, and sometimes the client at hand. They may be described as:

1. Percentage of Recovery (Contingent Fee)
2. Units of Time Spent (Time Charge)
3. Retainer by Calendar Period
4. Fee Fixed by Court
5. Standardized Charge for the Kind of Matter
6. What the Traffic Will Bear
7. Loss Leaders
8. On the House

1. *Percentage of Recovery (Contingent Fee).* Easily the most controversial method of lawyer billing is the percentage-of-recovery method, known as the "contingent fee." This fee is a percentage, agreed upon in advance, of any proceeds actually collected. Claims for injury to person or property in accidents caused by the negligence of another are wrongfully synonymous with contingent-fee practice, for there are other legal fields that also customarily employ the method.

In personal- or property-injury cases, the payment is almost invariably in the fee mode for the lawyer for the plaintiff, the one bringing the suit. The defendant is customarily represented by a lawyer retained and paid for on a per diem time basis by an insurance company covering him for legal liability. Because of a perceived potential for abuse in the personal-injury field, a number of states impose limits on plaintiff contingent fees in negligence cases and prescribe a scale according to recovery. The scales may start at 50 percent of the first one or two thousand dollars of proceeds recovered and scale down to 25 percent, one-fourth, of the balance, or perhaps a flat one-third.

Contingent-fee charging applies to many contract and debt-recovery claims, real estate condemnation and real estate tax assessment reduction proceedings, insurance-policy recovery, workers' compensation claims, and others. Charging percentages vary by area and type of work.

Controversial as the contingency-fee practice may be, the greater bulk of American lawyering is done with other means of charging. All office legal work—such as drawing of contracts, wills, trusts, real estate documents, securities registrations, and more, and the whole gamut of business and personal consultation, negotiation, and advice—is beyond the scope of contingent-fee work, as is criminal work, and much general and commercial litigation.

2. *Time Charge*. In corporate-serving law offices, particularly the larger ones, fees are generally calculated on the "time charge" basis.

Chargeable time is expressed on an hourly basis, and computed in multiples or fractions of an hour. Time charges are recorded by lawyers under diverse systems, from casually entered time slips to carefully computerized data cards. But all systems depend on an opening manual entry, in a diary or on a slip of paper, noted either by the lawyer himself or, more remotely, by a watchful secretary. Time units are kept customarily in denominations of six, ten, fifteen, or more minutes. A sample time entry might be *"Folger Art Works Corporation*: research into question of Security Act 1933—exemption letter—4.5 hours," or *"Levine Will*: preparing first draft of Mrs. L's Will—3.75 hours."

Telephone calls are always a problem. Common practice is to charge the minimum time unit of the office's system for every call unless the call is plainly longer. Letters tend to be recorded at thirty minutes each as a standard. Most firms charge portal to portal when a lawyer leaves the office. Out-of-town travel is generally carried as seven hours per day unless particular overtime takes place, such as extended negotiations into the night. If a lawyer works on another matter while on a plane or a train, that is often separately charged in addition to the prime matter taking the lawyer out of the office.

After giving effect to holidays, weekends, and one-month vacations, a seven-hour workday for twenty-two days per month for eleven months is a minimum annual-time-charge anticipation for employed lawyers (called "associates"). This approximates 1,700 chargeable hours per year; 1,500 hours approximates the annual norm for full working partners. Obviously, we are dealing here with averages, and an assumption that compensable business is always on hand.

Young employed lawyers, even junior partners, tend to put in more time than older ones, for all the reasons one might assume. Many firms expect young employed lawyers to work between 2,000 and 2,500 chargeable hours per year, which is very burdensome. I have seen lawyers, sometimes partners and not so young, log over 3,000 chargeable hours in a year, sometimes for several years.

Not all legal work has the same recordability. Lawyers who specialize in litigation, with trials, court appearances, and endless pleadings and legal memoranda, tend to charge the most time. For one thing, their whole process is necessarily time consuming, with much waiting around in court, legal research, and a great deal of digging up and analyzing of facts to reconstruct the happening of a disputed situation. It is also easier to keep track of litigation time than commercial time, because very often the litigation is the only chargeable matter the lawyer works on that day or that week. He figures when he came to work and when he left, with maybe time off for lunch, and the result is his time charge. On the other hand, a commercial lawyer may attend to more than ten different clients in one day, with a potpourri of telephone calls and correspondence constantly breaking his attention continuity. His difficulties of recollection and recordation invariably reduce his chargeable time entry. Litigation time is more law-intensive, and commercial time more client-intensive.

At first blush, a litigation may seem well confined. Brown contracted to deliver crude oil in a grade expressed in an exchange of telegrams in the abbreviated telegraphic terms solemnized by industry usage to Wright at a terminal in New York City, at a price to be agreed upon by a formula, ranging between $300,000 and $550,000.

Brown in fact delivered oil, but now the parties cannot agree on whether the oil was the right grade or its price under the formula. Brown sues for his money. The only real issues presented are the definition of the grade to be delivered and the price determination. Compare this litigation with closing a ten-million-dollar loan Brown intends to take from an insurance company, pledging all his company's assets, including his inventory, with a simultaneous use of the loan proceeds to purchase new machinery under a separate purchase contract to be negotiated. The insurance company whose loan will enable the purchase of the new machinery will also receive a mortgage on the newly purchased assets. This large commercial transaction may well take less lawyering time and carry a smaller legal fee than the *Brown v. Wright* litigation involving significantly lesser sums and business importance.

Consider the *Brown v. Wright* litigation. The lawyer in charge of the account will first confer with a Brown principal, and then other employees. The case is described, sharp questions are put by the lawyer, initial legal reaction is forthcoming, and usually some program of establishing the facts, including further questioning of possible witnesses and studying relevant documents, is put in place. When the lawyer is satisfied, he serves a summons and complaint on Wright. Some preservice discussions are usually held, with an eye to settling a case by way of compromise before the expensive war of lawyers begins in earnest. While settlement is not unusual at this early stage, the fact that the parties have been to lawyers means probably that some lawyering will have to take place before any settlement is hopeful. A certain amount of client muscle-flexing and indignation inevitably vents at this juncture. The Wright side answers the complaint, moves to make it more particular, which Brown's lawyer opposes; bickering ensues, motion papers are traded, and finally order is restored. Later, Brown and Wright conduct "discovery" proceedings; they question each other and witnesses under oath, for a stenographically transcribed record. Eventually, the case is noted for trial, a jury is selected, a trial takes place, briefs and reply briefs are filed, a decision is rendered, someone wins and someone loses, and one or two appeals, with all their own paperwork, ensue. In a nutshell, there is the litigative prospect. At every stage there are papers being drafted, and there is research, both into the points of law that will be urged on the court, and into the legal effects of various contingencies. More than in any other branch of law practice, in litigation lawyers write long memoranda to each other and talk among themselves. While a certain amount of conferring goes on with Brown officials, it is rarely continuous unless the litigation is critical to the client or there is a house counsel who keeps in touch. Legal time piles up in three principal areas: the internal research, memoranda, and conferring; discovery procedures; and court appearances and papers. Five to six actual trial hours a day is a goodly sum; figures that are reached only with determined judges. But for each trial day there are days spent waiting to be reached, adjournments while the judge considers legal applications, and, inevitably, logistical delays when any one of the many characters who fit into a lawsuit is late or absent. Once in court, litigation is an unhurried process, where patient questioning of a witness and careful laying of the case foundations are the hallmarks of success. Cases take a lot of time, while the law firm meter ticks on inexorably. Appeals have their own delays. It would not be unusual for that whole litigation to consume between 1,500 and 2,000 hours.

Commercial matters may be extensive, but on average a completed commercial transaction takes a lot less time than a full-blown lawsuit. The Brown $10 million insurance company loan, for instance, might be generously handled in from 750 to 900 hours. Because of their nature, commercial transactions take place very conspicuously in the presence of clients. Negotiating, which is continuous in a commercial transaction until the papers are actually signed, requires heavy client presence for business decisions as to terms. Moreover, unlike litigation, which is extraordinary to many clients, commercial transactions are part of the daily conduct of the client's business. Clients know more and do more here, and are informed in the business-law implications that bear on their own parochial activities. Business clients are in a better position to monitor their lawyer's activities. Often the client carries out part of the commercial transaction himself. He is more aware and less tolerant of multiplying the number of lawyers on the job, whereas litigation is more of a blind item to him. Business time pressures accelerate the rate of legal execution of transactions, often on overtime. The work may be short but powerful; there is less occasion for legal research, multiple office memoranda, and court-engendered delays. There is no deliberately obstructive adversary; typically, the other side shares an interest in expediting the matter.

While there are exceptions for sophisticated or unusual transactions, office work on the whole features client advice and consultation grounded in existing knowledge, or quickly gathered replenishment, and the drafting of familiar written instruments. The more common contracts, leases, mortgages, wills, trusts, and securities tend to follow set forms. Indeed, the first drafting step is usually to start from a previous form, either from a form book or the office precedent files. The client reviews commercial papers, which he sees in advance, much more critically than all litigation papers beyond his own sworn affidavits.

Senior lawyers tend to be employed in greater proportions in commercial advising and planning, since many clients are, often erroneously, reluctant to accept younger lawyers in their business presence. It is the more experienced lawyers who are usually assigned to significant negotiations and client relations.

A prime problem in estimating a litigation time charge fee is the inability to forecast how far the case will go. What will be involved in grasping the full facts, including the business setting? Will it go to the highest appellate court available, or will it end earlier? Moreover, the depth of the work varies with the intensity of the effort of the other side, what he puts you through, and this is beyond your client's control. If the case is to go "all the way" on a time charge basis, the client is totally in his lawyer's hands, both for the fee and for legal representation. The high cost of litigation, even without taking into account the risk of adverse outcome, hangs heavy on both sides and contributes to the settlement of the great majority of cases before they reach final judgment in court. Here is one of the prime collisions between having rights and paying to enforce or protect them.

It is small wonder that many business clients, able to afford a fair fee on any basis, prefer the contingent-fee method in commercial matters. They do not want to wonder whether time recorded is well spent, and, more important, they are uncomfortable with the thought of the money charges being open-ended. Their theory is that the lawyer working only on a percentage will not do unnecessary procedures and will try harder. In this way they satisfy themselves as to their case potential, reasoning that if the lawyer is taking a chance with his fee there must be something there. They want to relate the legal expense to an affirmative result.

Personal-injury litigation, which is complicated only on occasion, as in the determination of defective products or the assessment of medical malpractice consequences, is in the main a more contained pursuit than commercial litigation. The cases tend to be more factually narrowed, and consistently find Mr. Pragmatism himself, in the form of an insurance company, controlling the defense. His close relative, Mr. Realist, represents the plaintiff, and by virtue of his contingent fee and client naïveté usually controls the plaintiff side. Since vocational litigators control both sides of these cases, they tend to run on more predictable and, oddly enough, businesslike grounds than commercial litigation. The righteous indignation of clients less often clouds these cases.

Time charge rates are high all over, but nowhere higher than in the large busy law firms. In 1982, time charge rates for senior partners in medium- to large-sized firms, roughly those with more than fifty lawyers, fell between $165 and $250 per hour; some now go to $350 per hour. Certain specialists, such as tax lawyers or specially regarded lawyers with unique professional standing, may command higher rates than their fellows of equivalent seniority. The youngest partners start at about $100 per hour, and the scale is typically constructed by seniority ladder between the most junior and the most senior. Associates (employed lawyers) are scaled at approximately $65 per hour for beginners to about $100, with upwards exception for long service. Smaller firms and those not in metropolitan locations tend to lag behind by 10 to 20 percent in time charge rates, although there are always exceptions. Time charges are, of course, items of gross income and later translate into profit only after allowance for expenses and reserves.

It is a rare legal partnership of any size that allocates profit equally to all partners. This is because of disparities in business production, ability, work capability, age, professional standing, communal reputation, and length of firm service. New firms may start on an equal-sharing basis, but time normally takes its experiential toll. The common method is to establish a minimum sustenance draw, often scaled somewhat by rank within the firm, based on a minimum net income estimation. This is a basic "salary" the partner can anticipate with regularity. Beyond that, the profit-percentage differentials set in. There is customarily a "float" of a few percentage points held in reserve in some form for unusual performance by partners not anticipated at the beginning of the year when the profit-sharing formula was established.

In the event the unthinkable occurs, and the firm fails to cover its minimum draw, or even loses money, each partner is charged with his share of loss according to his capital account. The partners may be forced to skip their draw for the lean period. Some firms may borrow money in this circumstance to meet their minimum draw schedules and rely on later fee production for repayment.

Capital investment in a law firm is a surprise to many, but it should not be so. A good deal of money can be tied up in leasehold improvements, furniture, fixtures, library, and the sophisticated equipment used in maintaining a modern law practice. In the firm's early development period, before the fees come washing in, the need for funding is essential, and is normally supplied by bank borrowings or individual capital contributions. In addition, unreimbursed disbursements advanced to clients can amount to sizable outstanding sums, especially under careless management.

The ideal of a time-charging law firm is to record, bill, and collect a scale charge for every minute of legal energy devoted to a client. However, the facts of legal life are that while time charges are to be entered on the firm records, not all time spent can be recompensed. This is for a great variety of reasons, many internal to the law firm, and some rooted in simple concepts of fairness to the client.

Large problems result from inaccurate entry, which in turn comes from clerical duplication or file misassignment, overly casual time estimates, the faulty recollections that go with late entry, and cheating. The last is morally indefensible but often understandable because of the pressure some large firms put on their people to log time.

Closely related to inaccurately recorded time is the properly recorded time unnecessarily spent, which cannot or should not be billed. This is often the result of lax supervision. There may be need to discard poor work, particularly of younger associates, and to discount work that took too long to produce, even taking juniority into account. Another major offense is using too many lawyers on a job and duplicating their efforts.

The determination that too much legal time is being used on a matter can be edgy to the extreme. Often the conclusion is the result of compromising a difference of opinion between equally able lawyers as to what needs to be done under the circumstances. There can be small differences between imaginative work and hopeless forays, often measured in hindsight.

The problem of the doubling up of lawyers grows with the size of the utilizing firms. Quite apparently, the bigger firms have more lawyers around, and more temptation to inefficient utilization. Moreover, while smaller entities possess no greater innate morality, if they are busy, their immediate work priorities are more likely to forestall careless use of their customarily tighter lawyering force. The personnel deployment of too many large firms generates significant cost hazard. Doubled (or tripled or more) lawyering time comes about frequently when too many lawyers of the same firm sit through meetings or court sessions or when competitive research teams are used. Too many lawyers may be assigned to a case. They may confer with each other too much. They may seek out things to justify their presence, a faculty seemingly built into overlawyering. Large firms maintain a work force to handle big jobs and crisis situations which suddenly arise, and this causes periods when too many lawyers are employed only marginally. Larger law firms today also tend to over-hire to ensure their pool of sufficiently talented "comers."

The multiplication rate of lawyer usage is greatest where client contact with the work is most remote and where relative work values are not easily assessable. This normally singles out the litigation sections of large firms. The other side of the coin (in this case, literally) is that clients come to large firms because of their ability to do complicated jobs well on short notice. They want careful attention and exhaustive legal research and are willing to pay for it. The clients give the firms they respect the benefit of the doubt, and, indeed, recognize and tolerate their lawyer's excesses so long as the billing cloth fits the suit.

Size does have its virtues: it enables a healthy exchange of ideas, and it ensures continuity of work. Sheer size is not, however, to be equated with quality, or, after a certain point, even with real productive capacity. The common wisdom notwithstanding, there may be substantial differences in fees charged by law firms of similar size and quality. This turns largely on the precise time charge rates, the strict monitoring of time activity, deployment of personnel, and flexibility in departing from mechanical billing of all clocked time. Administrative efficiency in keeping down the overhead tends to have a beneficial effect on fee construction. This, too, can work a significant variable in net income.

Everyone, it seems, is willing to charge the other person's client full rates, but has reasons for entitling his own clients to concessions. As a result, many firms articulate an inflexible time charging rule, the computer print-out of hours multiplied by charge rate equals billing. Actually, however, firms often do not adhere strictly to time charges. Large clients may get volume discounts. Sometimes promising young clients are favored, as good existing clients in temporary distress may also be. The most common time deviations are for regular clients who lose an expensive case or negotiate a potential acquisition that falls through (the so-called burnt deal).

Theoretically, a time charge rate is derived by adding to the estimated expense of doing business the aggregate partners' planned profit and spreading that sum over the total number of hours of lawyers' work anticipated. The process is essentially an estimate, kept within bounds by comparative pricing and past experience. One newspaper reported that some large firms arrive at hourly rates for their associates' by doubling a given lawyer's salary and dividing by 1,000. Other firms estimate that the services of each lawyer should bring in between $100,000 and $150,000 annually.

Where more than the anticipated base time is charged, law firms can do very well, for their principal expenses are their rents and salaries, and these have elastic productive capabilities without real cost expansion. Rent stays the same no matter how many hours the offices are used, with only small service and utility cost increments. Associates do not get paid overtime, and clerical-staff overtime cost is passed on to the client. On the other hand, if the meter has run insufficiently, the overhead expenses remain, and proprietary income levels will be lower than expected.

Theoretically, time charge firms get paid for time regardless of result. The formula for their success is in labor intensity, particularly among their associates. Take a young associate hired at the sum of $40,000 per year right out of a top law school. The firm may charge $70 per hour for his time. If he logs 2,500 hours per year, the firm grosses $175,000 on his time, as opposed to an originally anticipated $119,000 (1,700 average hours × $70, used in making up the rate base). While the expense-to-income ratio may be 50 percent for the firm as a whole, his particular ratio is lower, since, as a young charger, he inevitably does much of his work in the evening, without added pay, in the same rent-paid premises in which he works during the day; with a secretary who is paid overtime on charges passed through to the client as disbursements. In short, if there are enough lawyers putting in enough billable time, the enterprise thrives. There are those who unkindly suggest that these law firms thrive on the exploitation of labor. Of course, it is exactly that. The ratio of associates to partners has a marked effect on net profits.

By now you may be grateful you are not paying for this book by the hour, but there are some summary observations that are useful. Larger firms tend to be more fixed, but not necessarily exclusively, to the time and rate method, since their overhead costs are constantly high and it is considered unwise for them to speculate on nonpayment for whatever reasons, including contingent fees. These firms are often among the largest and strongest, and try to take only business that will bear their tariffs. If a client is a new one or otherwise unknown to the billing partner, he likely will be asked, delicately, to be sure, yet firmly, to make a down payment against time and disbursements. This, incidentally, is not a bad rule for all practicing lawyers.

Smaller firms and individual practitioners tend to be more flexible than the large ones in discounting or adding premiums to time. For one thing, they have to be. The corporations and wealthy families that sit still for the massive time-based bills typically prefer the larger bigger-name firms. Smaller firms may risk greater contingency based on results in attractive cases. For instance, a tough piece of litigation may be charged out at half time, with an understanding that a specified result will be rewarded by a billing of four times the time spent. Some of these lawyers may, when pressed, quote very generous flat fees, with some catastrophe escape clause for unexpected massive time spent. Customarily, smaller firms measure more carefully their client's circumstances, and the outcome of the work, in adding or subtracting from a strict time measure of billing. These firms tend to consult more with clients in advance of billing.

3. *Retainer by Calendar Period.* When I first came to private practice in 1949, those firms fortunate enough to have sizable clients would, more often than now, bill "retainers" for fixed calendar periods. The client might pay $1,000 each calendar month, or $3,000 each calendar quarter, or perhaps $12,000 per year payable in monthly or quarterly installments. There is implicit in this type of arrangement a gamble by both lawyer and client as to how much work will in fact be done. The lawyer who works excessively during the retainer period is the loser, but if the work is light he is the gainer and the client the loser.

An appropriate level of payment for the client's business will become apparent over the years. In the event of gross discrepancy, after a reasonable period, lawyers and clients of good will mutually agree on an adjustment, either retroactively or in the future retainer.

There was a time when lawyers preferred this arrangement because it assured a flow of income with which to meet constant overhead expenses. The clients liked the arrangement because it controlled the fee exposure by preventing sudden surprises. The stress on measured time has tended to reduce the incidence of this billing form.

The obvious key to this system is the ability to forecast a reasonable work level. For this reason only "regular," "ordinary," or "general" business representation and counseling are appropriate. Extraordinary transactions, not in the recurring course of business (mergers, acquisitions, securities offerings) and litigation, would be excluded for mutual agreement when the occasion arose.

4. *Fee Fixed by Court.* There are a number of lawyers' fees that are set by a judge of a court as part of a legal proceeding. These are usually a mixed bag and have no fully unifying principle.

Courts may determine and award fees to lawyers for creating, safeguarding, or enlarging funds of an entity under court protection. Typical cases might involve the forcing of an executor to put back money in a decedent's estate, or, in stockholder actions in which dissident shareholders establish management misconduct, forcing a restitution of corporate assets. Class actions for civil rights or environment protection may also fit into this category. Matrimonial, bankruptcy, estate, and antitrust matters and the legal affairs of infants and incompetents usually involve court-awarded fees for successful plaintiff lawyers.

Many stockholders' suits, although not all, are frankly pursued by opportunistic lawyers who see a promising situation and proceed to find small shareholders or class members to be the nominal plaintiffs. The practice often features lawyers filing covering suits, known as "strike" suits, willy-nilly, claiming "you should have done" whenever corporate giants stumble or go down, on one knee, both knees, or flat on their back. The race to the courthouse is reminiscent of the "sooners" in the land-claim rushes of the American West, for the first lawyers accredited by the court may become the lead counsel. Legal fees go to a winning plaintiff lawyer, or combination of lawyers. Fees vary from court to court, but generally take into account time spent, results, time risk taken, and reputation and experience of the lawyer. Losing plaintiff lawyers usually get nothing but a huge set of useless files containing, tangibly, a big bundle of time slips and a write-off memo to the bookkeeper for time and disbursements.

5. *Standardized Charge.* There are transactions that have more or less standardized fees fixed by common practice. Usually, fees are based on a percentage of the dollar amounts involved in the representation. These are percentage fees—not contingent fees. The lawyer is not at risk for his fee, and frequently the fee is known going into the transaction.

In many areas lawyers charge 1 percent of the contract price for the purchase or sale of vacant land. This sort of percentage charging is also standard in sales of single-family homes. Adjustments are made for unusually large or small prices.

Many criminal-trial defense representations by counsel in private practice are charged on a fixed-fee basis, paid down immediately. Prices vary greatly, depending on the lawyer's reputation, the court, the place, the charge, and the defendant's apparent economic circumstances, including those of his family, friends, and business associates. If there are installments, they are invariably to be completed before the actual trial starts.

Smaller-scope economic items tend to carry fixed prices. These include simple or uncontested matrimonial arrangements, leases, landlord-tenant disputes, adoptions, and the like. The charging guidelines are usually what is customary in the area, what the traffic will bear, and, increasingly, what the competition charges. The emergence in recent years of permissible legal advertising and legal "clinics," which may be storefront operations, is significant in this regard. Their fees are established and advertised.

Clients who use lawyers as a part of a regular processing activity of their own business particularly like to fix their legal costs. Fixed unit charges are not uncommon, for instance, if lawyers perform repetitive work for a real estate client and experience suggests a fair rate. Lawyers who represent residential or shopping-center developers, for instance, might charge owners $500 per lease, or $750 per closing, but they get all the legal business of the project, and work with tight forms.

6. *What the Traffic Will Bear.* This is a grand old legal tradition which many clients insist is the basis of all legal charging. Snide criticism aside, there are circumstances in which the charges do not relate to time or quality of work or, even, results. Well-known trial lawyers in all branches, criminal, antitrust, matrimonial, corporate-takeover, and others, command great premiums for their service, even for the fact of their availability. Often, clients will pay handsomely, even if mistakenly, on the notion that the best charge the most, or its corollary, he must be good to charge so much.

Lawyers like to tell of the old country lawyer of German or Scottish extraction who was a master of billing. He would sit the client down, stare deep into his eyes, draw out a clean pad of paper, a sharp pencil, and proceed to write: "April 4th—one hour of meeting $35, one letter $15. April 9th, two hours of drawing papers $70." This continued, the lawyer always watching the client from the corner of his eye. After a while the client grew restless, squirming, then impatient, and the old man, still gauging him with sidelong glances, accelerated his pace accordingly. Finally, the client had stood enough. But the old boy anticipated the explosion and declared, "And that is that." With a flourish he drew a line for a total and quickly added the column. "The bill is $4,236.75." It may never have happened—I never saw it—but I can tell you of at least a dozen lawyers who swear that one of their seniors has been known to do some variety of the routine.

The "traffic will bear" charging principle effectively applies to a great variety of charges to small businessmen and individuals. The clients are not sophisticates; sometimes the charges are excessive, sometimes too low. For the lawyer, if he wants the piece of business badly enough, or needs it, this may be his method.

7. *Loss Leaders.* Inevitably, there are "loss leaders," like wills, which, under competitive conditions, cannot be paid by time charges. The lawyer who deals with wills can hope to be rewarded by receiving representation of the estate when the client dies.

People in special relationships receive special treatment. Time devoted to the personal affairs of officers or directors of important business clients may be discounted, or may be buried in the time charges of the sheltering corporation. This seeming largesse may extend to peripheral instances, perhaps the wife of a chauffeur of the president of a major corporate client.

Obviously, there are other deviations. One of the most interesting is the ubiquitous "low ball," the classic effort to attract a prized account from another firm by flashing a capability of good work at low cost, a practice that appears more often than users in the most respectable places will admit. The theory is that later on, once the client is firmly aboard, his fee for future work will rise to their proper level. This practice, however nobly enshrouded, is sometimes referred to as "buying" the business. Professionals, you see, are not inclined to use words like "stealing" in any strict nontechnical senses.

8. *On the House.* We all know of the businesses that did not start out to be nonprofit organizations but wound up that way. This can apply to law firms, too.

In the past, lawyers generally were loath to sue clients for fees, and defaulted payments were written off as part of the professional life. There was the rampant feeling that suing a client was just not a thing to do; courts traditionally did not relish lawyers suing clients. In current practice, this reluctance has abated, although a lawyer suing a client is creating an extra burden for himself. The fear of a malpractice counterclaim can often be a deterrent to suing for a relatively small sum.

While sentiment and business may go poorly together, some of the more warm-blooded law firms have old clients who can no longer afford current bills. These people are often afforded courtesies.

A constant source of nonpaid legal work is in the parade of

relatives, friends, charities, political associates, minor inquiries, and client favors that marches through all law offices. This is inescapable, and its drain is minimized only by careful discipline. Larger firms tend to have fixed monitoring rules. But lawyers do vary in their empathy for the human condition and their own reverence for legal tender, notwithstanding Abraham Lincoln's supposed declaration that time is a lawyer's only stock in trade.

DISBURSEMENTS

Except in contingent-fee billing, where disbursements "come off the top," lawyers will bill for disbursements—or "out of pocket" expenses—in addition to their legal fees. Disbursements are essentially advances, sums laid out by the lawyer for the client's account.

The practice of billing for disbursements, whatever the nature of the matter, reaches its full flower in time charging. This entails passing on to the client expenses laid out for travel, photocopying, special postage, long-distance telephone, messenger service, overtime paralegal and clerical charges, overtime meals for all personnel including lawyers, Lexis, Westlaw, or other automated research retrieval services, and word-processing-facility cost allocations. No firm that I know charges overtime for lawyers.

Since clients habitually regard disbursements with suspicion, and usually consider them as legal costs and undifferentiated from fees, well-managed firms monitor overtime charges and are quite careful about what they pass on to the client. There is a wide discretionary element in charging disbursements, particularly where "hard" costs (those paid directly out of pocket, such as filing fees and traveling expenses) are concerned, as opposed to "soft" costs, which are allocated items of regular overhead, such as in-house photocopying, word processing, and employed messengers. Although the time charge rate is theoretically calculated to cover the firm's fixed and working costs and to yield a profit to its partners, the separate billing of disbursements has its irksome elements. Because of this, as a matter of practice, some firms absorb more disbursements, and charge a higher time rate. There are, too, those hungry firms that include some expenses (for instance, word processing) in their overhead base for fixing time rates, and then go ahead under cover of standard billing practice to bill word processing separately as a chargeable disbursement.

─────── MAKING PARTNER ───────

Admission as a partner in a prestigious law firm is the career goal of its young associates. This has two roots, one financial, the other psychological. Financially, an assured proprietary interest in a big profitable law firm affords good income and all the prospects for its continuance. The psychological factor, on the other hand, is less quantifiable. For the successful associate, partnership comes as a rite of passage. As much as anything, the attainment is a mark of personal triumph and a validation of Herculean effort that can take seven to twelve years. For those who do not tolerate competition well, big-firm partnership is a poor goal.

Yet turning employees into owners (the economic translation of raising associates to partner) is not always so simple. Meaningful partnership carries financial increases over associate status, with a share in the profits of the firm. Where the firm itself is under economic pressure, and the existing partners feel they are not making enough money, there are reasons for refusing to open up new proprietary shares, quite apart from the high regard that may be held for the poised associates. The number of pressing associates at any one time is similarly relevant. "Superstars," as outstanding prospects are known, retain a priority, which often enables them to climb aboard in the most trying times. Unfortunately, many an associate, amply deserving partnership, who has served his time, fails in his quest simply because his name comes up at the wrong time in the firm's economic history.

More than a few law firms in recruiting interviews will state that partnership status is determined on the solitary merit of the lawyer himself and is unrelated to the firm's business condition. There should be a "truth-in-hiring" statute protecting innocent applicants from such professional predators. Any firm that distorts the significance in partnership competition of the firm's financial prospects, the associate's business production, his social, business, and governmental contacts, his religion, his color and ethnicity, and perhaps the phases of the moon is perpetrating nothing short of fraud. In major law firms less than 5 percent of the associates make partner.

Recruiting associates is a significant job, which requires organization and dedication. Firms that work at it do best at it. Unfortunately, ruthlessly competitive firms sing siren songs of partnership prospects, of associate democracy, of little night work or overtime, of easy fraternization with partners, making promises that in their real world they cannot deliver on. The law student who swallows whole a tale of blue skies and balmy nights may later find that he is blue, not the skies, and that it is not the night that is balmy. In weighing law firms, applicants must be coldly analytical. A law firm is essentially an economic enterprise. It may be a benevolent employer, but employee status has inevitable limitations in a demanding profession. Night and overtime work and pressure come with the franchise.

GETTING BUSINESS AND HOLDING ON TO IT

Getting legal business depends on four factors: lawyering presence, exposure, goingness, and luck. "Lawyering presence" is, by my definition, a combination of the appearance to the client of legal talent, determination, and the inspiration of confidence. No one personality holds the key to success. The whole gamut of personal style may apply, but that inevitable blend of elements must appear. The ability to enlist confidence is probably the major introductory factor, although in the end the client, once fooled, may be lost with the dawn of reality. Many good business producers work in tandem with technical lawyers to nail down the client catch.

"Exposure" means displaying your lawyering presence to potential clients. This exposure may come to a client's attention directly, or to someone who will inform a client. Direct exposure is gained in endless ways; a principal one is in the ordinary conduct of legal practice, where others see you in action and become sufficiently impressed to want to use you or to refer to you. Reputation is a form of exposure, both within the profession and to the public at large. Specialists are more particularly apt to get clients from reputation. Writing and lecturing to lay and legal audiences help. The classic route to exposure is through activity in organizations, whether they be political, professional, civic, fraternal, veteran, sporting, social, or charitable. Outright media advertising, the latest method of exposure, promises a potential quite beyond anything now being done.

Modern law firms of stature are beginning to use public-relations experts in the pursuit of more clients. Such services produce handsome printed and pictorial presentations, letters, and legal-news reports for clients and potential clients, publicize the important or interesting cases in which the firm is participating, and see that particular lawyers' names appear in gossip, social, and human-interest stories and columns.

Political lawyers may hope for references from courts, as guardians or referees, but for the majority these are slim pickings. Politics can enhance fees, largely because more people are met, and more people become aware of personal ability and reputation. As a career, however, politics can be a trap for a lawyer, since its legitimate economic rewards are generally meager compared with those of private practice. Overattention to politics and neglect of private-practice opportunity have ruined many a lawyer. There is, too, a widespread client feeling that political lawyers may not be really as professional in lawyering as they could be, although this is not universally true. Many clients are uncomfortably aware of a controversial political side and they prefer their business to be neutral.

"Goingness" relates to exposure. Being in practice, working daily, seriously, openly, exposes the lawyer to legal business. Building a legal practice is largely a cumulative affair. One client, one friend, recommends another. One piece of business leads to another. Lawyers who have always been with established law firms are often puzzled by the way sole practitioners succeed. Yet able and tenacious lawyers who are willing to make sacrifices to cultivate clients are likely to succeed if they stay with it. Building a practice takes time and staying power.

The established firm is the epitome of "goingness." Here is an established practice and clientele in place. From generation to generation, there is a tendency for business to adhere. Clients do not lightly transfer their legal trust. Once a lawyer becomes acquainted with the client and his affairs at a law firm, he has an opportunity to capture that client's total trust. In fact, if the lawyer leaves the firm, the client often goes with him. This kind of early client rustling has laid the foundation for more than one prestigious law firm.

"Luck" as a factor requires little explanation, except perhaps for the observation that the persistent tend to be luckier than the rest. Every lawyer has friends and clients, but few clients go on to great economic heights taking their early lawyers with them. Some business firms fail. Some clients acquire others by merger; others merge themselves out of existence. Many clients who start small with a young lawyer may feel they have outgrown the lawyer who nurtured them. They may lean toward a prestigious law firm more in keeping with the new image they have of themselves. Happily, there are enough clients of all varieties to go around.

The fortuities of personal fortune, rich family and friends, and social and business connection are all lucky incidents. So is being in the right place at the right time.

Fresh business is the economic lifeblood of any law practice, but it is also as important to keep clients in the office as it is to march them through the front door in the first place. Holding on to a client is a matter of continued service, mutual loyalty, reinforced confidence, good results, and, again, luck. A competent lawyer must stay in constant contact, and not take his established clients for granted. Competent client handlers leave unturned no opportunity to speak with their clients or to write to them; they stay in touch. The lottery of available clients, thriving or going on short rations, living or dying, individual or corporate, is always in progress. The client handlers never forget that. Tickets in this same lottery are held by new sons-in-law, golf-club friends, sharpshooters, sure-thing artists, and a whole host of miscellaneous parties in some way in touch with the client, including, sad to say, a number of other very good lawyers.

In most law firms, fees produced by partners simply go into the firm's "pot" as part of the partner's anticipated performance. In the longer run, those who produce more fees will be rewarded by an increased percentage of the firm's income. Unusually high fee production in a particular year may be applauded with a special year-end "bonus" over and above normal percentage shares. Firms differ in encouraging associates to bring in business. Large firms tend, as a rule, to discourage anything but major fees, since they want the associates concentrating on firm business and not the small matters typically available to young associates. Some firms encourage associates to take on business of their own, within reason, to learn close up the practical problems of client handling. Where associates are entitled to their own clients, they usually share from 20 percent to 40 percent of the fee, depending on firm practice.

Unlike government and corporation lawyers, those engaged in private practice must, in spending their time, always weigh just what their clients will pay for, and which client to spend time for, and when. While the average client is irritated to find that a lawyer has other clients, whose work, either by importance or by accident of scheduling, takes priority to his own, he also tends to think less of the lawyer who does not have other significant clients. And, of course, the client will be more inclined to accept a hefty bill from a busy and successful lawyer.

————————THE BOTTOM LINE————————

Lawyering is the way lawyers make their living. To disregard this plain observation is to miss an important point about what lawyers do. Whereas there may be a public preference to revere ideals of Law, the cold fact remains that those who implement the law, indeed, who are the law in material respects, hold it in the most personal of economic interests.

Lawyers' income is paid to them by clients, and costs to fee-paying clients have ascended to dizzying heights. Many rights are forgone now because the cost of procuring or securing them has become prohibitive. Between the very rich who can pay their own way and the very poor who can qualify for social assistance lie the massive middle classes, who feel the legal-cost pinch most personally.

In its upper reaches, the law profession is big business in every way. The profits of many a firm, well into the millions, compare most favorably with successful corporations whose securities are listed on stock exchanges and trade well. The economic momentum of relatively big law firms has been astonishing during the last two decades. With income and expense accompanying each other to the stratosphere far past expectations, it is unsurprising that lawyers are now running into client resistance. There is currently considerable concern that private lawyers are pricing themselves out of business.

The trends of more affluent corporate clients using in-house lawyers, of house counsel spreading their company's legal work to forestall one-firm complacency, and of clients generally shopping around for better price and service are subtly changing the economic ways of many firms. Litigation strategies are being rethought to bring down the cost of going to court. Automation systems, time monitoring, and the other devices of modern business management have moved into law offices to stay.

There is a growing awareness in good-sized law firms in metropolitan areas of a need to emphasize so-called boutique services: complicated litigation, bankruptcy, trademark and copyright, taxation, and other areas that, by dint of deep law office resources needed or the special knowledge and ability entailed, few corporations could handle adequately for themselves in house. There are even major law firms now taking in matrimonial and white-collar-crime specialists, where once those practitioners were scarcely considered gentlemanly enough to grace their corridors.

Lawyers are generally poorly prepared for their economic challenges. Their own training, which steeps them in precedent, wariness of change, and minimization of risks, is at odds with the entrepreneurial mentality. The most successful survivors of the legal economic revolution now going on will be those who can enthusiastically adapt to the new circumstances and the new business methodologies available.

6

PAYING
FOR THE CASE

A pivotal principle of our legal system is that each party to a lawsuit pays his own legal bills, win or lose. This generally is not the subject of any constitution or statute, has never been the subject of extensive or meaningful public debate, and passes into our social ways essentially because it has been that way for a long time.

When a case is lost in court, the loser may be directed to pay "costs," but typically this refers to relatively few dollars in filing and service charges, and not to legal fees.

A defendant who is unjustly sued and fights off his persecutor is, in fact, a loser, for despite having won his case (unless he is insured for his defense) he is out of pocket the fee he pays his own lawyer. Similarly, plaintiffs with just causes who become obliged to sue for their legal due remain shortchanged to the extent they have to pay a lawyer to collect what is theirs. For these reasons, plaintiffs and defendants often elect to settle cases themselves and save on the legal fees. The burden of having to pay legal fees in order to vindicate one's rights is a built-in unfairness of our legal system, although in modern practice exceptions have sprouted, both by statute, by common law, and in the state of Alaska.

This situation is worst in cases where the plaintiff's lawyer is working on a contingent-fee basis. In effect, the person doing the unjust suing pays no legal fee at all if he loses, and effectively never stands in any risk of paying one from his own pocket.

——CONTINGENT-FEE PRACTICES——

Under the pure contingency fee the lawyer's total fee is a percentage of the money he recovers. If he collects nothing for the client, he collects nothing for himself. Essentially, the lawyer finances the case.

A significant number of lawyers in this country depend on contingent fees from personal-injury negligence cases. While many may maintain daily practices of more diversity, the windfall of that good personal-injury case can be considerable. A general practitioner attracting a negligence case may settle or try it on his own and reap the full legal harvest, or forward (refer) it for an agreed share of the ultimate fee to one of the sizable corps of lawyers who specialize in negligence work. Referral fees range from 20 percent to 50 percent of the final fee. The more successful negligence lawyers, as might be anticipated, pay out the lower percentages to forwarders.

Forwarding fees are, strictly speaking, unethical under the existing Code of Professional Responsibility for lawyers. Although numerous lawyers neither pay nor accept them, the practice of forwarding fees, particularly in contingent-fee cases, is actually institutionalized throughout the country. In defense of forwarding, lawyers often cite the rule that permits sharing of fees according to relative work. The forwarding lawyer may do some actual work in the case (interviewing clients and witnesses, and assembling data) and is theoretically paid for his time and services. The work, however, is largely fictional and typically includes only the interview during which he landed the case.

The difficulty in a generalist trying a negligence case is that negligence trial work is time consuming and calls for a certain amount of professional expertise—particularly in accident investigation and with medical issues. Moreover, lawyers who work in negligence cases are "street smart" in dealing with insurers and co-parties. The leading negligence lawyers for the plaintiff or the defendant (they tend to separate into those two categories) work in the negligence specialty almost exclusively. Many of the country's most skilled trial lawyers are, in fact, negligence specialists.

Part of the negligence mystique is in the standing of the plaintiff's lawyer. There are lawyers whose name on a litigation file is worth thousands of dollars in settlement value, since insurance companies respect and defer to their abilities. This is a tough field, not designed for the fainthearted or the bashful. If an insurer defending a negligence case believes the plaintiff's lawyer is particularly strong, it will not want to risk easily a court scene before a jury. The insurer knows he will not be able to "steal" the case. Inversely, the insurers will concede much less to a lawyer they perceive as weak.

Contingent-fee charging is not limited to personal-injury work. A good part of the nation's claim-collection work is done via the contingent-fee route: the lawyer gets paid only a percentage of the contract or debt monies collected. This is also the case in much commercial litigation. Claims under fire, theft, marine, life, and accident and sickness insurance are also commonly subject to pure contingency payment for legal services. Reasonable debt-collection fees range between 15 and 33⅓ percent of the actual collection; in insurance-policy matters the range is between 25 and 33⅓ percent of the collection, depending on the values and the difficulties. Fees for services in procuring real estate tax reduction are almost always contingent, varying from 25 to 50 percent of the tax savings.

An intermediate type of contingent fee may involve such instances as the condemnation of real estate by government authority for public use under the principle of eminent domain. The owner whose property is condemned (taken by government) for a highway right of way, or for any other public use, is entitled to fair compensation under due process of law. Even some private corporations, such as utilities and railroads, have limited rights of eminent domain under different states' laws. If the lawyer's fee is 5 percent of the eventual award for the taking, the fee is not wholly contingent, since the owner will surely realize some value; only the size of the fee is contingent. Predictably, some fee is assured. However, the contingency may be, instead, 15 percent of any excess collected over the assessed value of the property; or perhaps 33⅓ percent of any excess collected over the amount offered by the government preliminary to the taking. In these instances, the lawyer can wind up with nothing if the recovery fails to attain stipulated sums; so that type of fee is purely contingent.

———CONFLICTS OF INTEREST——— BY CONTINGENT FEE

The contingency lawyer is a partner in the case. To the extent of his share, he is a co-owner of the case. Although the lawyer and the client may seem to have a total coincidence of interest in a successful outcome, this is not always so. A particularly destructive conflict of the economic interests of the lawyer and the client is built into the contingency arrangement over and above the customary economic adversity of the lawyer and client stations.

Contingent-fee law practices hinge on a large portion of settled cases. If all cases went to full term, that is, trial and appeals, the lawyers could not maintain themselves; the time and expense involved would be too high and the relative volume of high-fee/low-risk cases that could be attracted too low. Litigation is a long-drawn-out process, oozing delay and expense at every pore. Contingent-fee practice feeds on volume; the chanciness of the enterprise is hedged by one case against another. Enough good cases balance the bad ones, enough quick easy fees balance the long hard ones. The costs of carrying too many contingent-fee cases through lengthy litigation have destroyed many a negligence practice.

The lawyer's judgment in settling a case may be based on his own assessment of the trial probabilities and the time delay in damage collection occasioned by continued litigation. However, suppose he needs the money represented by his fee right away? Suppose he feels it is not worth his while to continue the case, since the largest fee he can hope for is already on the bargaining table? Suppose he feels he has no more time for the case? Suppose the client needs the money and the lawyer does not? Suppose the client would welcome a risk-free smaller sum in settlement, but the lawyer wants to gamble for higher stakes? After all, he, and not the client, has borne the time burden and expense of preparing the case.

Since the contingent-fee lawyer is a partner of the client, he no longer has exclusive loyalty to the client's interests, and has an investment of his own to protect. In dealing with him, the client has no lawyer.

——IS CONTINGENT-FEE PRACTICE—— DESIRABLE?

Lawyers who support contingent-fee charging argue that only through it can people of limited means (by no means restricted to the poverty level) have available to them high-quality legal services. They urge that if lawyers cannot recover exclusively from their clients, but instead must rely on a court award or, worse, the opposing side, the independence of the Bar, both for itself and for the clients, will be jeopardized. They also urge that lawyers and clients should have their freedom of contract.

Opponents of the process claim that contingent fees result in excessive litigation of no merit. They fear that since payment comes only with winning, contingent-fee lawyers will do unscrupulous things to avoid emerging empty-handed. They fear transgression of the indisputably fine lines between preparing and coaching a witness, and worry about fabrications of evidence, the partisanship of experts, improper examination, furious resort to jury sympathy, bigotry, unscrupulous medical collaboration, and groundless legal argument. They remind us that even if a case seems to lack merit, it may not be immune to unscrupulous contingent-fee undertaking, since a play to jury sympathy even in a case with low legal merit might just hit a jackpot. In the hands of a skillful lawyer, almost any case has some chance, if only of being settled for its nuisance value. Opponents also assert that insurance liability premiums increase unfairly for coverages in the areas where personal-injury contingent work flourishes— notably, automobile accidents; professional malpractice; accidents on staircases, in hallways, on the sidewalks, under broken lights, with glass doors, in the parks and the schools, on loose rugs; and the panoply of household and everyday personal danger. Finally, it seems to critics of this system that injustice is done to a client who pays a high fee for little work, either by charging too much in the first place, or by cutting the legal process short by early settlement without trial.

Inevitably, someone points to England, which is legendary for legal excellence and does not permit contingent fees. But an astounding irreverence, doubtless of a piece with crumbling empire, is uttered by those who counter that the British litigating system does not compare with the American in quality for precisely the reason of contingent-fee unavailability. Those who argue that the British legal-aid system is superior in its consideration for plaintiffs of modest means are met by those who argue that the very highest-quality lawyers can and do represent the lowest-stationed claimants in force only under the American contingent-fee system.

It may even be that the gamble caters to American instincts. Although the undeniable speculative aspects of contingent fees affront a classic professionalism, they appear to have originated with a society who liked it that way. To a people whose trial lawyers seemed sacrosanct, like the British, contingent-fee charging may be sullying. But in American culture, perceptions held of early trial lawyers were that they were business operatives, and not always savory ones at that. No bars of gentility or professional indignity here. The British tradition is to cut down on litigation; the American way is to promote access to the courts. In any event, the practice of contingency charging is so rooted in American theory and practice that it is plainly here to stay for our lifetimes, those of our children, and beyond. Modifications are likely to be addressed only to particular abuses.

Is this so wrong? If one puts aside the self-fulfilling prophecy of professionalism, contingent-fee theory fundamentally centers upon the desirability of encouraging litigation. The day in court is a fundamental American expectancy, nurtured over a national lifetime. Litigation, if it is to be had, must be paid for in some way. All systems of maintaining litigation obviously rest on somebody paying the bill. "Legal aid" may be free to the recipient, but somehow the lawyer is paid, the typist is paid, the paper is purchased—all from public sources, or the coffers of a nonprofit organization supported by public or private grants, or the contributions of lawyers whose availability is afforded from income gained elsewhere. Under contingent-fee charging, the very fund that is the litigative objective does seem a likely source for fee underwriting. After all, the client does not pay unless he collects; the lawyer is encouraged to take on meritorious claims lest he waste his time. If the lawyer estimates the case correctly, and handles himself competently, and has that little bit of luck that never hurt any case, he earns a fee that carries a premium for the economic risk he runs.

A remarkable factor in contingent-fee personal-injury work is the uniformity of its charge (which is about one-third of the recovery) all over the country, and its imposition regardless of the size of the recovery. While there have been inroads into the percentage for very high verdicts, often called "jumbos," the one-third measure remains the rule rather than the exception. It is a warm tribute to the persistency of legal custom, unless met head on by an organized opposing constituency. The *American Lawyer* compared a book written by a well-known negligence lawyer and one written by another almost thirty years earlier. The article commented on the vast monetary increases in negligence recoveries that juries seem willing to award, and concluded that if one were to review the earlier book and compare it with the more recent one, it would be "much like looking at the prices in the 1903 Sears, Roebuck catalogue." Newspaper reports indicate that million-dollar recoveries for personal injury are increasing, particularly in New York, California, Texas, Illinois, and Florida. The first million-dollar personal-injury jury verdict in history is said to have been handed down in 1962. Now, there seems to be one a week in the United States. Indeed, there is a million-dollar corps of personal-injury lawyers, who have formed their own Inner Circle of Advocates.

Apparently, inflation has a lot to do with increasing awards. Among the intriguing activities of the personal-injury field is the work of a Cleveland company that publishes statistics on four kinds of injury: neck strain, knee injury, vertebrate fractures, and male wrongful deaths. These are the principal injuries flowing from auto accidents. The average verdict for a knee injury in one year was cited as $27,905, up $1,000 from the previous year. It would appear that knee futures are hopeful. Among the wry witticisms of personal-injury lore is this dialogue. Question: "How do you value the loss of a leg?" Answer: "Yours or mine?"

Some states restrict contingent-fee charging by statute. In Maine, contingent fees are illegal, and in Massachusetts they are limited. Some administrative agencies, such as the Social Security Administration and the Veteran's Administration, bar contingent-fee representation before them. I suspect in these latter instances the government believes that their claimants really do not require representation at all, and should not be subject to charges they can ill afford.

The economic impact of contingent-fee legal work forms a vast public cost, the true extent of which is immeasurable. If unworthy cases were cleared from the court calendars, civil trial court congestion could be drastically curtailed, particularly in the major metropolitan population concentrations. Available facilities and personnel would be freed to service criminal-justice systems, and ease the social burdens and costs that flow from inadequate discharge of criminal justice. With the decreased personal-injury litigation would come a great reduction in wasted medical services and equipment used only to prop up the litigation. Much of this medical drain is financed by the public through Medicaid, Medicare, and social-assistance payments.

—SAFEGUARDS IN CONTINGENT-FEE—
LAWYERING

In my view, contingent-fee lawyering is justified because the alternatives for those who cannot afford legal representation are even more doubtful. This decision comes hard to me, since the system as it now works simply affords too much abuse. My own years on the bench have cultivated a distaste for the immorality now rampant in the negligence field. I do not refer to fake claims in the sense that the "accident" was contrived or did not happen at all. There is doubtless enough of that, as there is crookedness everywhere. The real vices are in exaggeration of injuries and in distortion of the facts. In contingent-fee availability, the courts sponsor immoral enterprise of a staggering proportion. It is a standing joke (on whom?) in the New York Supreme Court that a claim in a personal-injury complaint for only $50,000 means that no one was really injured at all.

But, on balance, I would continue contingent-fee lawyering, with some distinct limitations. The question is really whether the most underlying policy is appropriate: should litigation be encouraged or discouraged? To me, that day in court is American to its core. The contingent-fee model caters to that recognition, as the most feasible way for some private claimants to get that day in some kinds of cases.

Castigation of contingent fee practice can be overdone. Character weaknesses and financial drives are hardly unique to lawyers working on percentage contingencies. Lawyers working on public salary may be searching for advancement; they may yearn for job security, or their political ambitions may polarize attitudes. To lose a new client, or to fail to keep an old one, because of unsuccessful litigation is spur enough to most time-charging lawyers to seek successful action by whatever means their personages permit. Is it not easier for a time charger to sponsor meritless legal work if the lawyer is to be paid in any event? Who will argue that all noncontingent fees are fully earned, or done for necessary or proper work?

The only real alternative to contingent fees, something resembling the British system of making more widespread public legal aid available to private claimants, seems even more dubious. The public expense would be large, though I know of no way of comparing it to that of the existing contingent-fee cost structure. There is, I suppose, an apples and oranges comparison here in terms of increased payroll and facility costs as well as only problematic effects on court flow and medical abuses.

The cream of the American bar, and, I believe, even the British bar, is largely in private practice, not in legal-aid offices, and I very much doubt that this state of affairs will change in this country given the incentives underlying our society and our economy. I would also find a huge government presence (in essence, a preemption of a sizable portion of the civil side of the legal profession) atop the huge present public criminal-defense presence to be a dangerous encroachment on the independence of the private bar. Tarred though the profession may be, it is still one of the most formidable institutions in the preservation of our liberties.

For business people and their lawyers, the contingent fee is a form of business payment. The parties deal at arm's length. The client can pay a fixed fee, but he prefers the contingency because he likes to keep his lawyers "hungry." He suspects any other charge basis. The lawyer and his client are parties to a business transaction in which the client is a sophisticate. Additionally, the business case deals in known, often fixed amounts, and arises from circumstances independent of any lawsuit. In personal-injury work, it is often the case that is the only business.

The ordinary citizen with his sometime accident claim is normally an unsophisticated client wholly in his lawyer's hands. Knowing neither the lawyer's capability, nor the flexibility of his charge, nor what is actually involved, he signs a retainer agreement, and he floats on the current. He may be more or less injured, and he is dazzled by the monetary prospects held out to him. He is a "one-shot" client without the protective milieu of a relationship involving later need of client good will by the lawyer. It is here that court regulation of contingent fees has been greatest, and more is indicated. Where this regulatory activity exists, it is significantly directed to personal-injury litigation. There is, typically, a court-prescribed scale of permissible charges, usually 33⅓ percent of the recovery, with a higher percentage allowable if the total recovery falls below two or three thousand dollars. The retainer agreement must be officially filed so the circumstances of acquiring the case may be investigated; for instance, whether there was bribing of a tow-truck operator to recommend clients, or splitting of fees with a layman. Sometimes there is unethical overt solicitation by lawyers themselves of victims of serious multiperson accidents, such as train, bus, or airplane crashes, with many identifiable victims. Here the spectacle of the lawyers bidding against each other is, if nothing else, hygienic for the price levels. Many a fee in cases like these has been dropped from 33⅓ to 20 percent, or to X percent over Y amount of recovery, by lawyers who have appeared in the family kitchen, living room, or, much worse, a hospital room to bargain against known competition. Safeguards are needed against taking advantage of the injured, the distraught, and the unsophisticated.

A principal reform required is the scaling down of percentages where the amount of recovery is so high as to render the agreed percentage unconscionable as a fee. There should be no finder's fee on human misery. There should also be some limiting correlation between the amount of time and expertise spent in settling or trying a case and the size of the fee. The classic lawyer's defense of an excessive fee for one case is that his cases balance out; he wins some, he loses some; his winners pay for his losers. This is not good enough. It is justice to the individual client that is the concern, not the economic balance of the lawyer's practice. The good cases should not pay for the bad. The lawyer must be bound to stand by the exercise of his judgment in taking each case on its individual merits. Lawyer laxity in taking on meritless cases should not be encouraged; lawyers should not be permitted to roll the legal dice in the courthouse, financed by the taxpayers, and play the odds of the system.

But the individual claimant is not the only person with an interest in contingent-fee charging. All members of the public have an interest in its practice, since it fills the courts at great expense and distorts the priorities of criminal justice. Probably more than two-thirds of the civil court's volume in this country, at least in state courts, is made up of contingent-fee litigation. The proportion is likely similar in federal courts after taking out the enforcement cases in which the government is the plaintiff. Various studies suggest that as much as 25 percent of the legal income in this country comes from contingent-fee work. When you consider that the high-earning lawyers of the corporate and commercial fields do little or none of it, you can easily visualize its prevalence in the rank and file of our country's lawyers as a whole. This relates to the high cost of justice generally, the willingness to pay for its support facility, and the recognition that, although the best things in life may be free, our court system is neither.

———"NO-FAULT" AUTOMOBILE——— LIABILITY

Contingent-fee patterns have contributed in an important way to at least one significant social change. "No-fault" automobile liability proceeded directly from excessive legal expense and its relation to the insurance-premium dollar. A United States Department of Transportation study concluded that over half of every automobile liability insurance-premium dollar went for legal expense, for both the lawyers' share of benefits paid to claimants and the insurer's own legal expense in defending against the claim.

Moreover, the huge aggregation of auto-accident cases in all urban court systems was viewed cynically as a monstrous morass in which the worthy and the unworthy were lumped indistinguishably together, and their distinction lost to the pressures of an adversarial court system. In the maw, many a just cause is lost, not pursued at all, or bought off for a pittance. So unappetizing is the whole process that many people will not pursue an honest auto-accident claim.

Some background observation is necessary to understand the automobile no-fault controversy, since, in fairness, its philosophic base extends beyond any evils of contingent-fee lawyering. If Jones negligently causes his Ford to collide with Smith's moving Chevrolet, hitting the Chevrolet's rear end and causing injury to Smith's neck and back, Jones may be liable for both the personal injury to Smith and the damage to his Chevrolet. In most states, Smith's recovery is limited if he was himself guilty of fault, to a degree that varies from state to state.

All of this stems from the ancient common-law rule that liability for negligent conduct depends on fault, both the plaintiff's and the defendant's. But rules of fault in vehicular accidents stem from rural medieval England, whose lawyers could never have fathomed the population and technological status of our time. Today, on a narrow strip of paving, bordered by people walking, sitting, or conducting their lives, masses of metal rush by at great speed. The automobile is inherently a dangerous instrument, but by social consensus we tolerate this open danger. It is a necessary evil of modern society.

The fault or faultlessness of any party as a basic premise in automobile liability is questionable, for social fault is factored in from the outset, in the very consensus that permits free operation of the dangerous things under dangerous circumstances. Fault of one side or the other in an accident is too often an immeasurable thing, where the law result is clouded by personal sympathies and the availability of anonymous insurance funds.

Auto liability insurance, like all insurance covering a person against legal liability to another for personal injury, is known sometimes as "third-party insurance"; the three parties are the insurer, the person insured, and the person who is injured. This differs from "first-party insurance," for instance, fire insurance, where the insurer pays its insured because of fire damage to his own property. There is no injured third party. Actually, automobile collision insurance (as opposed to liability for personal injury caused) is first-party coverage, since the insurer pays its insured directly, under his own insurance policy, for physical damage to his own car.

The thrust of no-fault automobile liability is twofold: it is to provide for payment to victims of damages of specified kinds without regard to fault, and, in the case of a car owner, to have his own insurer make the payment. It provides for first-party coverage for personal injury, making payment to the victim prompt and automatic, it is to be hoped, on behalf of the insured.

The institution of a no-fault system is, however, more than an insurance arrangement. It is akin to workers' compensation insurance programs, which eliminate fault as a factor of personal-injury liability in work-related accidents. Where auto accidents fall within the restriction of the no-fault law, there is no right to sue any third party for negligence. This is a plain abrogation of traditional rights to hold someone liable at law for negligent injury. Proponents of no-fault— largely governmental and labor groups—justify it in terms of sure benefits paid by the victim's own (first-party) insurer without litigation. Inflated claims based on inconsequential injury become reduced by fixing the scale of first-party insurance payments available. There are built-in penalties against the malicious and the reckless actors, and provisions to protect those victims who have no access to auto insurance of their own and therefore no first-party insurer to fall back on.

Because of strong state policies to protect motor-vehicle victims, some form of auto liability insurance coverage is compulsory or urgently indicated for drivers throughout the country. An insured defendant means one good for the money if he is held liable, words and music for the ear tuned to the irresistible beat of the contingent fee. The cycle is self-generating, since wealthier people, aware of their liability risks, carry far more insurance coverage than any statutory minimum. The temptation factors in automobile-accident litigation under present contingent-fee circumstances are inevitably and unacceptably high.

While under a no-fault scheme there will be individuals who will recover less money for their injuries than they would if they were able to sue freely in court, the main point is elsewhere. Most of the more serious injuries can be set aside for regular "fault" litigation meeting statutory threshold standards. But in the miasma of lesser injury, where legal fever rages, no-fault automobile liability means more injured people collect more money, and on a higher plane of decency.

Understandably, trial lawyers are not ones to stand idly about when any of their oxen are being so vigorously gored. Since they include, as a group, many of the most adroit arguers in the country, their reaction might have been expected to be forceful, and it has been, and it is. The trial lawyers' associations and lobbying groups fought for years in the states that now have or at one point considered no-fault systems. In some areas, their efforts succeeded in trimming down the programs that exist. But their involvement in the ongoing battle has turned from the offensive line to rear-guard action.

There is something dismaying in the spectacle of these lawyers battling shoulder to shoulder to protect their economic interests, particularly when they cloak their words in pious phrases alluding to the constitutional rights of their clients and social injustice. In fact, there is rarely, if ever, a vigorous struggle by an organized trial bar or any other bar for broader horizons of justice or human rights. The improvement of the law and the protection of the rights of those downtrodden by poverty, race, religious, or economic constraints are seemingly alien elements to concerted bar action. It seems that for these lawyers the pressing matters of principle are mostly those of principal.

Amusingly enough, a number of the most successful negligence lawyers are closet supporters of no-fault. They cannot admit this in public, because they depend heavily on referrals from lesser legal lights whose social benevolence is as yet insufficiently buttressed by economic affluence. However, most of these agreeable topnotchers are not born-again legal reformers; it is just that they are now fairly distant from those small auto cases they once had to take in order to get the bigger cases from referring lawyers.

Personal-injury litigation is by no means limited to auto accidents, although they are the most frequently litigated instances. Airplane accidents, medical malpractice, and faulty manufactured products figure prominently in high dollar recoveries. Less remunerative, but in great volume, are falls due to unlighted staircases, cracked sidewalks, loose carpeting, running into glass doors, and more.

——— SHOULD THE LOSER PAY ——— THE WINNER'S FEE?

Still another party stalks the contingent-fee trail: the innocent defendant in a commercial case who has been cleared of wrongdoing and who leaves the courthouse with both a sigh of relief and a bill for legal services he never wanted and cannot afford. Take the uninsured party who did no wrong, yet is sued, in any number of civil instances, (debt, sales contract, breach of trust, employment contract, and more), by a party whose lawyer will not be paid unless the defendant is found liable for a sum of money. The plaintiff has zero risk of exposure to legal fees except from a new cash fund the lawyer brings to him. Aside from investing time, and being responsible for modest legal disbursements, such as court costs, if they are ever called for payment, the plaintiff will never pay his lawyer if he loses. But what about his adversary, the defendant? He cannot be a winner under any circumstance, unless he is backed by an insurance company who carries the defense cost as part of the policy coverage. Whether the uninsured defendant wins or losses, he must pay his own lawyer. The suing party, the plaintiff with a winning and just cause, can also fall victim to the principle of each party paying his own bill. Theoretically, the winner recovers the sum or gets the result to which he is entitled, but his recovery is inescapably diluted by the cost of his own legal fee. Essentially, he is taxed in his recovery, and has no chance to be made whole.

This is the theme of a larger problem: the principle that under our legal system, except in Alaska—and unlike the practice of other countries, including England—the parties almost always bear their own legal fees. Exceptions do exist, although they are few. These allow a plaintiff to recover his fees in common-law causes of action, such as aggravated fraudulent behavior, and in statutory actions, such as antitrust, consumers, civil-rights, or, in some states, insurance-policy claims that specify reimbursement, often in combination with punitive damages. The federal government is now experimenting with an Equal Access to Justice Act, which reimburses limited-fee costs. The language of an instrument involved in a lawsuit, such as a lease, mortgage, or explicit contractual provision, may also specifically authorize legal-fee recoupment.

Unfortunately, I can cite many commercial cases from my own experience where clever lawyers, working on contingent fees, by incessant legal attack wound up with substantial recoveries to their clients and fees to themselves on meritless cases, paid just to be rid of them, the risks they create, and the hemorrhages in legal cost and inconvenience they cause. These made me ashamed to be a lawyer.

Lawyering can be an economic license to steal; this is not limited to the contingent-fee area, although the fact is clearest there. Any competent lawyer can just about select a victim at random, and if any colorable relationship can be established, can take that victim for a few dollars, if only for nuisance value.

Brave words of millions for defense but not a cent for tribute spout in parties' mouths early in suits, but resolution typically fades into despair when the realization sets in that it costs $10,000 to avoid paying $5,000. There are only a few of those who admirably stand on principle and refuse to compromise for any sum in a patently spurious claim.

I have long believed that a winning party is entitled to some fee reimbursement by a losing party who causes the trouble. While there should be allowances made for close bona fide cases and for great economic disparities, some recognition of fee restoration seems fair. Where the plaintiff is attacking with a contingent-fee lawyer, it is even necessary. Contingent-fee selling of representation in low-merit cases might be significantly abated if the plaintiff himself understood that he could be personally at risk for legal fees of his chosen target.

A winning plaintiff dragged through a spurious litigation by an obstructive defendant deserves to have his fees reimbursed, too, although more caution is indicated for a plaintiff who by definition initiates the case. There are countless ways for unscrupulous defendants to prolong lawsuits and delay their day of retribution. An emerging method in several states for handling such defendants is to assess some form of punitive damage for provoking lawsuits as forms of economic duress.

FIXING THE LOSER'S LEGAL COSTS

If the loser is to pay, how would the payment be implemented? This aspect offers its own difficulties. The matter is probably best left to the trial judge's discretion; he should determine first whether the loser should pay, and, second, what would be the fair amount of reimbursement. This solution is not limited to contingent-fee cases, although I believe the contingent-fee basis of the plaintiff could be an important element in deciding whether to charge successful defense legal-fee expenses to the plaintiff. There are bases, I believe, for articulating fair standards: necessity of the actions taken, the parties' relative ability to pay, the colorability of the respective claims, and the surrounding circumstances of the questioned litigation. The principle of reimbursing the winner holds the same philosophic base for both plaintiffs and defendants, but the injustices of ruthless contingent-fee strikes are particularly compelling.

The approach to allow courts to assess legal fees against the loser is usually met with three objections: it discourages recourse to the courts by the less affluent, it prejudices the independence of the bar, it gives judges too much power and discretion.

I believe the first objection should be met by the competence of the judge to take into account the ability to pay and the relative merits of the case. Recourse to the courts does not necessarily imply license to tread with impunity on the rights of others. The second point, concerning the independence of the bar, has substance, but there are many instances where the courts themselves award legal fees. Moreover, the courts have not encountered recent howling objections to their imposing scales of contingent fees. The courts are unquestionably accepted as regulators of the bar. The third point, that it grants too much judicial power, I deem absurd. If judges are to have the power to decide cases, to rule on admissible evidence, to sentence people to jail, and to do all the other fundamental things judges do, why in the world is the fixing of a legal fee so holy? Is it that the lawyer's fee is more important than the client's substantive rights, which indubitably fall within the judicial realm?

Perhaps the judicial discretion to charge the plaintiff for the legal fees of the innocent defendant might even extend in a contingent-fee case to the plaintiff's lawyer personally to the extent of his interest. While this is a radical step, with obvious potential for punitive abuse, it would take place on grounds where lawyer abuse is already rife. After all, the contingent-fee lawyer is a partner with his client in the case, and in many cases the real moving principal. If a plaintiff is "sold" by a lawyer on a case on the basis he has nothing to lose—and this is indeed being done in various fields of contingent-fee enterprise—the "seller" could fairly sustain some consequences of actions. Since the courts in all states have the power to discipline lawyers, even to disbar them, it has always seemed reasonable to me that simple economic sanction according to the damage inflicted is a justifiable principle for regulatory guidance.

An alternate and intermediate method of introducing fairness in legal-fee sharing in civil suits enjoys some very limited statutory and regulatory use in the country now. This is a procedure where at some time before the trial, under proper safeguards, each party declares to the judge a sum for which he is willing to settle. If the ultimate trial result proves as favorable or better to the party suggesting it than his settlement offer, he collects from the other side the fair value of his legal services. This compromise gamble is favored by a number of commentators, but I feel it is less fundamental than the more direct approach of laying the legal fee on the judicial table. Maybe the gamesmanship implicit in the compromise-gamble approach bothers me.

Little has been said to this point about criminal-case defense-fee charges, other than to indicate that contingent-fee practice is not used there, and that the great bulk of defense work is done through publicly financed legal-aid or public-defender agencies. However, there are many individuals who retain private counsel. Criminal cases that go "all the way"—trials, jury verdicts, appeals, and with much intermediate procedural wrangling as to the protection of civil rights—cost significant money. I have known defendants who have forfeited their rights and bargained for a plea of guilty to a lesser charge simply to save the devastating expense of a full criminal trial. It has always struck me as grossly unfair that where government directs its elaborate criminal mechanism against an individual in a criminal accusation, and fails to prove its case, the innocent party should not receive some allowance for his defense legal fee. People of lesser means are constitutionally protected in their defense through publicly provided criminal-defense funds. Unjustly convicted persons serving jail sentences are often compensated by special legislation if the injustice to them is uncovered. By the same token, it seems reasonable that innocent victims of governmental attack are entitled at least to escape any heavy legal-cost burden unjustifiably put on them.

——LEGAL ADVENTURES WITHOUT—— PRIVATE FEE RESPONSIBILITY

The sad fact of the matter is that anyone who is sued by a party with no burden of legal expense is in extra trouble. This is a further facet of attacking bad-faith litigation by exposing the moving party to liability for his adversary's legal expenses.

The average person who has to pay a lawyer from his own

pocket is intimidated by the governments, the utilities, the railroads, and the major companies who can litigate ceaselessly without any real regard to legal cost. Indeed, the utility companies are particular offenders where they can pass their legal costs directly to the consumers in their rate bases and even arbitrage a small profit.

In government practice, where oppressive suits can go on for years, through changing administrations, the legal fee is not the only irritant. There is a limitation in government's susceptibility to compromise, a reluctance to take the responsibility for giving up a weak suit or to settle it when circumstances and probability would commend that course of action to any reasonable private party exposed to all its true costs.

Many clients need not concern themselves with their lawyer's economics or lawsuit economics, since they do not pay the legal costs of their actions. These users of legal services range from government officials who can fall back on government lawyers, to major corporate and institutional personnel who use lawyers on the corporate payroll, to the poor who may benefit from government-financed legal-assistance programs in many forms, including poverty-law programs, legal-aid societies, and public defenders for those accused of crime. In practical effect, those people charged with causing accidents and represented by lawyers furnished by their insurance company under the terms of their liability insurance policies are similarly cost unconscious. But these latter "clients" are largely indifferent to outcome altogether, since the insurer bears the burden of loss and is in reality the lawyer's client.

Just as government and large corporations are able to grind down litigants with lesser financial resources, by attenuating the legal process so that mounting costs and hindrances eclipse their adversary's zeal in proceeding, so can publicly or institutionally financed legal services do the same. With small exception, a party with an adequately supported lawyer for whom he has no personal financial responsibility holds an edge over the party who must retain a standard-charging private-practicing lawyer. The disadvantage may extend to effective loss of rights by inability to stand the financial gaff.

A tyranny of the underprivileged may be a novel and disturbing recognition, particularly in a subsidized setting designed to promote the public good. Nonetheless, it is present where there is excessive pursuit by publicly supported lawyers who wear down, for instance, smaller landlords seeking to enforce their rights as to their tenants, or vendors seeking legitimate collection. I do not refer here to legal action in legitimate pursuit of genuinely believed rights; this is the very intent of supplying legal assistance. But where the legal-assistance agency takes advantage of the legal system in much the same way as a major corporation would, with repeated legal motions, examinations, delays, and constant court appearances and blocking tactics to thwart rights by legalized chicanery, the moral equivalence of abuse is clear. It is only an added embarrassment that the taxpayers pay directly for these immoral expeditions financed from poverty-aid funds.

It may be argued, as it has been, that the poor should have all the rights of the rich, including the ability to get their way through pragmatic abuse of the legal system. This line of argument is doubly disturbing for it accepts normatively the moral abuse of legal process by anyone, rich or poor. The goal should be to encourage responsibility by all, not to widen abusive practice to the point where there is no abuse because there are no standards. The complication here lies in distinguishing vigorous and thorough legal action from grinding for the sake of grinding.

In criminal cases, many believe as I do that extra leeway should be afforded to those protecting personal liberty. Unfortunately, the seeds of this belief may grow disappointing fruit in the fields of the public defender and legal-aid societies. Here again, payroll lawyers with clients at least innocent of financial responsibility may turn to the worst evasive tactics of which the outer fringes of the private bar are capable. The question repeats itself: to what kind of defense is a publicly supported defendant, or then for that matter any defendant, entitled?

A fundamental point germinates. Is there a tempering influence on maneuver where the client is willing or able to pay for only so much of it? Stated another way, does dispensing with personal financial obligation to a lawyer encourage high legal adventure? Have we not seen this potential in contingent-fee lawyering in which the attacking client is free of the net risk of legal cost?

7

HAVING YOUR "DAY IN COURT"

To have your "day in court" is the most American of resorts. The phrase implies that if you are charged with a crime or with a breach of contract or anything else, you will have an opportunity, sometime, to go before a judge and maybe a jury, to tell your side of the story. More than that, the people to whom you are telling your story will listen to you. You will be heard. And, in the best of worlds, you will be believed and have your own way.

Justice (to you) follows your day in court. Or does it?

That day in court is not always what it is cracked up to be. Even putting aside the time, expense, and emotional strain accompanying lawsuits, we can parse lexically "your day in court" and demonstrate its fragility in every word. To begin with, "your" day is also your opponent's day. One of you is going to lose. In your day in court, you may not be believed, you may be unsympathetic, or you may just not be yourself. You may even have a poor case and lose because of it. But to come to court with the fervor of the righteous and to lose because you are not believed is the adding of injury to insult.

"Day" can be many days; court proceedings take time to unfold. Much of its time is spent on wooden benches, struggling to hear, or perhaps simply waiting when nothing at all is played out before your eyes. Trial participants also tend to log considerable courtroom-corridor time. It is the rare trial of any substance that runs its full course in one day.

Even the "in" can be a joker, because most civil cases that come into the hands of contending lawyers, even into the courtroom itself, become compromised (settled) by agreement, to save expense, but mostly to hedge the risk of an adverse outcome of the cherished day in court, or perhaps in despair of the time in which it will take to be reached or to finish. Since compromise is by definition a mutual giving, as well as a getting, many people feel frustrated at settling without going to trial on their actual day in court. In retrospect, they often entertain a regret at missing, even a curiosity about, that lost official outcome. Lawyers are familiar with clients who willingly settle their cases and who later hold it against the lawyer that he foiled that day in court. Long after the anxiety of the day has melted away, when the cocoon of distance has wrapped around, the client may think back wistfully to that chance he lost to be in court that day, his day, and to have it all his way right from the judge's mouth.

By far the incisive word is "court." It is the place for the day, it is society's ultimate forum for directed decision which sends the litigants out into the streets or into the jailhouses, sad, glad, or confused. For all the prologue, the courtroom remains the pivotal place of the legal system. The happenings of each case not only affect the particular parties, but also have more distant effects by way of precedent. Even the empty courtrooms, standing available, send emanations. The availability of this ultimate forum of decision underlies voluntary compliance with law, and foreshadows a legal consequence that enables counseling and drawing documentation in some comfort of confidence.

But the day in court may never come for economic reasons. On the whole, commercial cases for less than $50,000 are marginal in terms of risk and the expense to bring them in metropolitan areas. This forces parties either to abandon smaller claims or to settle them unwillingly. Current initiatives to substitute arbitration or mediation for lawsuits in cases of modest monetary proportions are results of drives to cut costs as well as to save time. California has been notable for its Pilot Project in Economical Litigation.

Court nomenclature is uneven throughout the United States, although the underlying pattern offers three courts in a hierarchical order: a basic trial court, an intermediate appellate court, and a higher appellate court. There are two general systems: the federal and the aggregate of all the separate states.

———————— THE FEDERAL COURTS ————————

The federal scheme offers, for instance, the District Court (its basic trial court), known usually by the vicinity of its location (such as the Northern District of California); the Circuit Courts of Appeal (numerical regions from one to eleven and the District of Columbia), and, above all, the United States Supreme Court, a solitary court of nine justices, sitting in Washington, D.C. There are also a number of specialized federal courts, such as Bankruptcy, Tax, Customs, which function essentially as trial courts, appealable to one of the Circuit Courts of Appeal.

While an individual federal District Court judge now and then receives publicity for a newsworthy decision, the judges of the federal Circuit Courts of Appeal are surprisingly anonymous to the public. Their coverage is important because these federal regional appellate courts are second only to the United States Supreme Court in prestige and judicial significance. The increasing dominance of the federal court system, because of its jurisdiction over such publicly attentive affairs as constitutional rights, civil rights, international relations, taxation, securities, labor injunctions, environmental challenges, monopolistic trade practices, and the ever-widening panoply of federal administrative agencies, has taken its toll of state judicial notability.

Of the federal Circuit Courts of Appeal, the Second, including New York, the Ninth, including California, and the Circuit Court of Appeals for the District of Columbia stand in highest renown. The District of Columbia court may be eclipsing the others because, by virtue of its location, it oversees much federal regulatory mechanism, and it hears appeals from the federal District Court of the District of Columbia, which itself is the forum for presidential activity, such as Watergate, and other federal questions.

Generally speaking, only cases involving rights under federal legislation and the Constitution go to the federal courts, as do regular private cases with a diversity of state citizenship of the participants.

STATE COURTS

The state courts are similarly divided into trial courts, intermediate appellate courts, and a high court. As in the federal system, most all cases from the trial court can be automatically appealed to the intermediate appellate court, and then, under certain conditions, to the highest court. Each state is unto itself; each has its own system, and disposes of its own cases, but may be responsible to federal courts if federal issues are raised. Subjects in state courts that involve federal constitutional questions can go on appeal from the highest state court directly to the United States Supreme Court.

The various state, district, and territorial courts readily identify themselves and their area by name. Little doubt exists as to the geographic clutch of, for instance, the Supreme Court of Kansas or that of Maine. Even within a state, the further breakdowns are mostly self-identifying by city, county, borough, town, or village. Sometimes numerical district designations are used, making things harder.

Every state has a basic trial court of general jurisdiction, but of varying title, whether it be Supreme, Superior, District or otherwise. It means that every kind of case can be brought in that court, excepting only those specifically excluded by state statute or a state constitution. Each state also has an assortment of "limited" courts. Some are for specialized purposes, such as family affairs (Domestic Relations or Family Court) or decedents (Surrogate's or Orphan's Court). There may be courts for claims against the government, such as a Court of Claims. There are also lower courts in the state system for lesser crimes, for civil cases involving no more than a limited sum of money, and for only some kinds of civil actions, such as tenant's eviction. These lower courts in the state systems are habitually known as "courts of limited jurisdiction" or "inferior courts."

TRIALS

Trial courts are where the action is, where the people are. The facts from which the decisions flow are determined from the raw data of witnesses and conflicting contentions in the trial courtroom. Trial judges preside over a busy scene. Witnesses appear, are sworn, and testify before the judge, the jury, the parties, the courtroom staff, and any spectators who may wander in.

Courtroom spectators are sparse in ordinary trials; occasionally, there are some supportive friends or relatives. There may be lawyers or parties from adjoining courtrooms in recess who are killing time, participants waiting for the next case, not to mention courthouse buffs, investigators, insurance claims adjusters taking settlement temperature, even classes of schoolchildren or civic groups being given the courthouse public-relations tour. In those sections of the trial courts that busily process many proceedings—for instance, criminal court rooms or those for traffic nonjury cases, or uncontested matrimonial cases—there are large crowds, clients with their lawyers and witnesses, waiting their turn. Depending on the discipline imposed by the trial judge, those scenes may be restless, even noisy.

Normally, newspaper or press representatives appear only when cases are matters of public interest, either for the issues or for the celebrated personalities involved. The day in court, so critical to those having it, is typically focused on them alone. Their drama passes in obscurity, without the world watching, as some aggrieved parties expansively anticipate.

Court reporters (stenographers) at trials, working by hand or, most usually, with a stenotype machine, transcribe everything said to create the "record" of the so-called courts of record. Some courts use tape recorders, either alone or to back up reporting personnel. The skills of competent court reporters are extraordinary, since they take down for hours on end not only the questions and arguments of the lawyers, the witnesses' statements and answers, and the judge's comments, but all the give and take between lawyers and judges. With people talking at the same time, it is remarkable how court reporters are able to follow and separate their sayings. During many a wearisome trial I've wondered how they manage to maintain such sustained concentration. Nevertheless, it must be said that some reporters are more accurate than others: some never make mistakes, others I could not trust with a grocery order. Given the vagaries of the Civil Service, weeding out is hard to do. While theoretically there are procedures available to correct records, these are rarely employed; recollections of precisely what was said, including gaps, tend to fade quickly. Even if recognized, the defect may not seem important enough at the time. One may also be reluctant to make an issue, in a jury trial, because there an implicit lay presumption is that the reporter is correct. The best that emerges is the lingering suspicion that the witness changed his testimony.

Reporters vary in skills, and speakers vary in their recordability. The mumblers, the low-voiced, and those with speech difficulty are not as recordable as the resonant speakers with the pear-shaped tones. For all that, what is taken down and later typed out is the record. For purposes of reviewing the record, particularly on appeal, the written record is what the reporters make it to be. Quite obviously, that record is devoid of facial expression, tones, inflections, and the other nonlanguage manifestations that bear on the meaning of speech. The supposed objective record, then, offers elements of personal frailty, a fact that is also part and parcel of the linkage of justice.

Trials may be conducted by a judge and a jury, or by a judge alone. In this country, jury trial is a matter of right in criminal cases carrying penalties of more than six months' imprisonment and in most civil trials, particularly in the state courts. Not all civil trials carry jury entitlement; for instance, cases traditionally denominated "equity," such as labor injunctions, tenant evictions, and child-custody proceedings. However, the reason a good many nonjury trials take place is that both the parties waive their rights to a jury trial.

That people voluntarily do give up their rights to jury trial, and allow the judge to assume the jury function, is surprising to some. Reasons for the waiver vary. They normally center around the presentation of issues too complicated or personal for the parties to wish to entrust them to a lay jury, or avoidance of popular wrath where there is contested conduct of social contempt. Sometimes the waiver is meant to curtail time and expense, since jury trials tend to become more drawn-out than nonjury trials. There may be no substantial dispute as to the facts, and a realization that the disposition of the case turns only on interpretation of law, not on what actually happened. Jury waivers are not often chosen in criminal or accident cases, but are commonplace in commercial ones.

Actually, there is a facet of trial judging itself that partakes of an appellate nature, and that is motion practice, where issues are presented, usually before the trial, solely on paper, without evidence being taken. These motions are essentially applications to regulate the stream of preliminaries as they course into trial. Here, we see rulings relating to timeliness, to propriety, and particularity to pleadings and to permissible depositions. There is, however, one particular motion that can actually decide a case. It is called a "demurrer" at common law. In modern practice, it presents some variety of summary judgment or motion to dismiss, in which the moving party says, in effect, "Even assuming everything my opponent says is so, I should still win the case on the law." The decision on such a motion by a trial judge puts him very much in an appellatelike stance, since he decides the law on granted facts. These motion rulings are also subject to regular appeal.

The essential point for laymen is that there are two different kinds of courts in which to have their day, trial and appellate. In determining the outcome of cases, they are both important. At first impression, the lay view is that the appellate courts are more important because they are higher. This is true in the sense of final disposition of a particular cause, because an intermediate appellate court can affirm, modify, or reverse a decision below, and a higher appellate court can do the same to it. Appellate courts rank higher in their establishment of general principles of law for other courts to follow. However, the great bulk of litigated cases never go on to appeal, which is costly and time-consuming, with uncertain prospects, and for all practical purposes the trial court is the only court for most litigants.

Raising an "issue of fact" in a trial is an elegant way of asking "What happened?" The chief purpose of a trial is to make the official determination of what happened. Factual determination is in the jury's province unless the trial proceeds with a judge alone, without a jury, in which case the judge has sole responsibility for all aspects of the case. The trial judge presides over the trial, ensures orderly and proper presentation, and rules on issues of evidence and permissible questioning. The trial judge advises the jury, after both the testimony and the arguments are completed, of its responsibilities and of the rules of law applicable to the case. This advice comes in the form of the judge's "charge" to the jury. The judge, classically, tells the jury in his charge, and maybe in an introductory statement at the beginning, that it alone determines the facts, that it must accept the law as he gives it, and that the jury reaches its verdict by applying that law to the facts it finds.

Trial juries (once called petty juries) are to be distinguished from grand juries, which do not sit on trials of cases. Grand juries are investigative in nature and are used to determine whether there is good reason to put a citizen to criminal trial; their indictment is a way to continue criminal proceedings.

In a typical jury trial, the proceedings start with jury selection, at which a judge may or may not preside, according to local rules and customs. In federal courts the judges usually conduct the jury voir dire (the seeking of qualifying information), for bias or interest, allowing the lawyers to supplement their questions. In state courts the lawyers more often than not wholly conduct the voir dire, going to the judge only for rulings if the lawyers cannot agree on their procedure. Trial lawyers prefer to question jurors themselves rather than have judges do it. For the judge, it is a case of getting a neutral jury and expediting the proceeding. For the lawyers, it is an opportunity to mold and sway a favorable jury in advance.

A panel of prospective jurors is normally selected by lot. If the judge is to question, he takes over. Where the lawyers question the prospective jurors, the plaintiff starts first. Each party is empowered to challenge and disqualify any number of jurors for good cause, usually statutory, stemming from relationship or demonstrable prejudice. Parties are also entitled to a certain allotted number of additional challenges, which are called "peremptory," since no reason need exist for them. Peremptory challenges, limited in number, are the key to jury gamesmanship. The lawyers by their questions test whether a prospective juror will be susceptible to his client, or at the least be fair. Lawyers' theories of what is good and bad in potential jurors are endless. When controlled by the participating lawyers, the jury-selecting process is not so much an exercise to get an impartial jury as it is to get, to the maximum extent, a partial jury, one calculated to be as favorable as possible. Jury selection is seen by many lawyers as an opportunity to size up the jurors and their reactions, and to salt them with attitudes and impressions in the questioning process itself. It is a way of prearguing a case, of implanting points, of arousing sympathy. The lawyer searches for the telltale signs of empathy or hostility to him as a person, as well as to his client's situation.

An interesting, and controversial, modern development is the use in some cases of research or market-survey firms to test communities for attitudes important to the case at hand, and to use the results as jury-selection and strategic guides.

After a full jury is selected, usually twelve, although it can be as low as six by local statute, with one or two alternates in case a prime juror becomes disabled during the trial, the jury is sworn. The judge gives a short welcome, usually with some preliminary advice as to conduct: do not jump to quick conclusions, listen all the way, sit back, be comfortable, I will be advising you more later. The judge may remind the jury that it will have to judge the facts, and that he will give them the law.

Then the lawyers approach the jury, first the plaintiff ("prosecution" in criminal cases), then the defendant, to indicate what they hope to prove. These opening statements are usually shorter than the later closing statements (summation). The plaintiff, who has the burden of proof, brings his witnesses to the witness stand first. Each witness is sworn. If he objects to an oath, he is permitted to testify by affirming he will tell the truth. He is subject to direct examination by the lawyer calling him, then cross-examination by the other side. When the plaintiff is finished with the personal testimony of his witnesses and the submission of his exhibits, such as photographs, guns, tools, and documents, the defendant's turn comes, and he repeats the process. Questioning of witnesses may be punctuated with objections as to form or content by either lawyer.

Witnesses are frequently not permitted as spectators until they have finished testifying. This is so they will not be influenced in their own testimony by any other testimony they might hear. Expert witnesses, on the other hand, engineers, doctors, scientists, may be allowed to hear testimony, since part of their very role may be to evaluate some part of the testimony, particularly that of other experts.

After the defendant rests, the lawyers again approach the jury, this time to sum up. Each lawyer comments on the evidence, adds his reasoning and exhortations, pleads a bit, and sits down. In civil cases the defendant takes his turn before the plaintiff. The summation is in reverse in criminal cases, although in many places the prosecution may have a rebuttal opportunity.

Typically, the suing parties sit up front with their lawyers, immediately before the judge. The judge charges the jury right before their eyes and ears. The jury is to one side in a low enclosure called the "jury box," and the spectators sit to the rear of the courtroom behind a railing dividing them from the operating space of the trial participants. In his charge, the judge tells the jury that it has an important job to do, that it should weigh the evidence carefully and decide the case as it sees it, without fear or favor or regard for personal popularity. He might go on to add that personal credibility is hard to determine, but that the tests used in everyday life to determine the credibility of what is being told to you may be relied upon. He cautions the jury to consider the manner of each witness testifying, any limiting capacities such as impaired senses, the opportunity the witness had to observe the things he said he saw, any interest the witness might have in influencing the outcome of a case, and the plausibility of the witness's testimony taken in light of all the other facts and circumstances of the case. Judges vary in the completeness of this prefatory charge material according to their own senses of diligence or proportion, sometimes tiredness, and sometimes lack of patience, perhaps lack of time.

When, in giving his charge, the judge reviews the facts, as many do, in different degrees of detail, this is known as "marshaling the evidence." Great care must be taken to be objective here, for jurors are greatly swayed by the presiding judge. It becomes clear as a trial unfolds that there are really three sides present: the plaintiff, the defendant, and the court, which is made up of both the judge and the jury. While the court is not partisan in the sense the parties are, its members are trial participants, people in their own rights, conscious of their own roles, anxious not to be considered wanting in their performance. An alliance, if you will, tends to link the judge and the jury, for they alone in the courtroom share the burden of studied neutrality during the trial and, afterwards, of articulated decision for one party and against the other.

After reviewing the facts, the judge informs the jury of the applicable law. As earlier indicated, he tells them they alone judge the facts, but they must accept his instructions on the law even if they disagree with him.

Let us follow the essence of the charge in an automobile-accident case, a variety of the most common charges in the state civil trial courts. "Each person has a duty to operate his car as a reasonable person might, exercising the due care under the circumstances of an ordinary person. All traffic laws must be obeyed, including those relating to rates of speed and making left turns. The speed limit in the accident locale is thirty-five miles per hour. Drivers can properly make left turns into side streets, off the main highway, if they first stop, signal with a left-turn flashing light, and then proceed with caution into the intersection, being satisfied no other car is so close as to make a collision probable. On the other hand, all drivers of cars on the road have a duty to see what there is to be seen, and to act reasonably to avoid accidents. No party may drive recklessly or collide with another car at will, and all parties have an obligation to do all reasonable within their power to drive safely." (Note: For the sake of simplicity and brevity, I am here addressing only the question of liability and omitting the approach to damages.)

Charges of judges are on the whole very cumbersome messages; excessive attention is given to the possibility of being reversed on appeal and too little paid to the need to communicate a meaningful message to the lay jurors. Since so few cases are actually appealed, this practice is regrettable. Jurors with inadequate instruction, faced with the requirement of decision, are left to decide by their own devices.

The judge concludes his charge by telling the foreman of the jury that the members of the jury must agree on a verdict by a specified consensus. At one time all jury verdicts had to be unanimous; now it is common to permit a consensus to be less. Sometimes only a criminal verdict need be unanimous. According to local rule, verdicts may suffice if nine or ten jurors out of twelve, or five of six, for instance, agree on the verdict.

The jury is then led to a separate room and starts its deliberations. Normally, no one is allowed in the jury room but the jurors, not even the alternate jurors. Their deliberations are in closed sessions.

Jury deliberations and verdict reaching are quite unique. Here, a group of people chosen from the population at random, none of whom are lawyers, hold in sway the fate of the parties to a lawsuit. They may be totally disparate in education, economic level, life experience, and in the endless ways people can differ. Jury construction is based on the assumption that all eligible jurors are equal, and that jury decision is accordingly an act of the "peers" of the parties competent to judge their actions. This is a valid enough assumption in cases of straight-forward human misconduct, such as robbery, rape, automobile accident, or causing falls on poorly lighted stairways. But it is less so as affairs become more technically complex. Cases that turn on expert medical, scientific, or engineering perceptions go to juries all the time, as do those involving high finance and intricate transactions, often well beyond the comprehension of most of the jurors charged with their resolution.

How do juries reach their verdicts? There have been studies of the subject with concealed microphones and questionnaires, as well as countless stories told by jurors after their jury has been discharged.

After the verdict, jurors can in most places talk about the case, although not reveal how any individual juror voted or acted, an injunction often honored in its breach.

The foreman of the jury, usually the first juror picked, presides in the fashion of a chairman of a meeting. He may express his own opinion first, but more often throws open the discussion. A common procedure is to take an immediate straw vote to see where the jury stands. Questions are asked of each other, personal verdicts are announced. Votes are taken periodically. Juries generally take their tasks quite seriously. The substance of the case is discussed in detail, and personal opinions of both the merits and the parties flow quickly. An opening quiet dignity gives way to informality and finally to irritation and frustration as the proceedings wear on and agreement is not reached. Much persuasion takes place in the jury room, as individuals reason with those who disagree with them.

Juries tend to have a leader, a standout, more respected or persuasive, around whom a consensus coalesces. Lawyers look for this person in jury selection and when he is thought to be spotted follow his reaction throughout the trial. Some comments are really addressed to him, because he may do a lot of explaining of points to other jurors not so quick or analytical. Education in the case is part of the jury-selection process. Where there are two leaders who disagree, it can take a long time for a verdict to break through. Very often a majority of a jury comes to a rough consensus relatively soon, but the requirement of unanimous or supermajority consent requires bringing dissenters around. The dissenting people, sometimes called "hold-outs," come under increasing pressure from their colleagues as deliberations wear on and tempers thin. In jury selection, a lawyer may look for seemingly "safe" votes, hoping in that way to place on the jury some sympathetic jurors who will be sufficiently persuaded by his argumentation to hold firm against an adverse decision. Usually, however, isolated individual resistance crumbles in the end and a group decision, known as the jury's "verdict," is reached. Often the whole jury is dissatisfied with the precise verdict, but because it is a compromise termination of the seemingly interminable its toleration becomes necessary. A common informal, but improper, compromise, in a case where money damages are at issue, is for each juror to submit a sealed number to the foreman, who then adds up all the numbers and divides by the number of jurors for a compromise figure.

If jurors have questions to ask of the judge, they are usually put in writing by the foreman and taken by an attendant to the judge, who notifies the lawyers. In conference, on the court record, the language of response is agreed upon. Sometimes the jury request is merely to be supplied with a document or a thing that was in evidence. Where a question cannot be answered simply in an agreed note, or where the jury expresses the desire to hear some parts of the testimony or the judge's charge read back, the jury is brought again to the open courtroom, where session is restored and the judge may comment further or the reporter read aloud for the jury any requested portions of the record. The jury is then returned to its deliberating room.

A jury that cannot reach a verdict because enough affirmative votes cannot be mustered is "deadlocked," or, if the deadlock persists to the end, a "hung jury."

Judges do not really accept announcements from the foreman that the jury cannot agree. The jury is usually sent back for further deliberation a number of times after reporting a deadlock. Sometimes the judge gives it a supplementary charge, known in judicial quarters as a "dynamite" charge, which is a stern reminder of the obligation to agree if possible, normally centering around the thought that a lot of time, effort, and expense has gone into the trial, and that there is no assurance that another jury on another and later day would, in doing its duty, be any better constituted to reach a verdict.

Quite naturally, the insistence on reaching a verdict puts pressure on members dissenting from any majority consensus; the fewer the holdouts, the greater the focal pressure. While pressure to agree is not calculated to reach justice in any pure sense, within the dimensions of the real world a certain amount of head knocking is helpful in deriving concert among twelve people on anything. Still, it is unsettling to observe in hallowed halls.

Trial judges are less reluctant to accept deadlock or mistrial in civil cases than in criminal ones. After all, the disputation is private and usually boils down to money, and may be tried again. Criminal matters, however, involve a whole skein of complication, starting with the possible need to return a defendant to jail, and including the difficulties of retrial because of the high burden of proof required of the prosecution and various constitutional issues of double jeopardy in the proper handling of criminal defendants.

Jury trials are normally ended by "verdicts." In a civil trial, the jury foreman announces the result: "for the plaintiff in the amount of X dollars," if he is to prevail, or "for the defendant," if he is to be the winner. The judge may, on request of the losing lawyer, direct the court clerk to ask each individual juror, on the record, whether he subscribed to the verdict. This process is called "polling the jury," and is designed to check up on the jury count. The judge thanks the jury, excuses it, and the jury is led from the room, either to be set at liberty or to be returned to the jury pool for further assignment. In the courtroom, the judge gives the lawyers a chance to make motions addressed to the verdict. Everyone then leaves the courtroom, except the court clerk, who is busily entering his report of the proceedings in the court records.

Where the trial has proceeded without a jury, judges usually reserve decision in civil cases and hand down a written decision some weeks or months later. If the decision is delayed excessively, that itself works injustice. The old saw remains that "justice delayed is justice denied." Some courts require decisions from the bench because of the nature and volume of their cases. This is true in lesser criminal cases and traffic offenses. In Family Court (domestic-relations) cases, an unlucky urban judge might find himself snapping off as many as sixty or seventy rulings a day, amidst the highly charged emotionality and meanness that unhappily characterize much familial disputation.

In a criminal proceeding, the jury merely reports "guilty" or "not guilty." If "not guilty," the case ends there. If "guilty," the matter of punishment remains. Sentencing practice varies by jurisdiction. In some, the trial continues for the convicting jury to fix the punishment. In other places, the judges impose the sentence.

In criminal cases, the sentence is normally deferred pending the acquisition of posttrial sentencing information for the judge or a separate trial on the issue of punishment, according to local practice. If the judge is to sentence, he will want investigatory reports and recommendations, as well as information as to prior convictions, in determining factors of clemency or severity. Where the question of criminal sentencing is left to the jury, a new hearing ensues on the punishment issue. If for some reason a new jury is used, the action amounts to a whole new trial, except for the issue of guilt, which is assumed. Where the same jury is employed, the evidence set forth at the trial need not be repeated, although much of it often is gone over again to refresh recollections, to set perspective, and to serve as a line on which to hang the colorations of good faith, evil intent, intelligence factors, accident, coincidence, and plausibility that go into the mitigation or maximization of punishment.

Trial judges have the authority, subject to appeal, to set aside jury verdicts as being contrary to the weight of evidence, which means a new trial in civil cases. In civil cases, judges may even enter a verdict contrary to the jury's, or, more usually, take the case away from the jury, commonly after the plaintiff's case is over, and dismiss it, thereby deciding that the plaintiff has no case at all.

APPEALS

In a trial, the case for the judge and jury begins on a blank page. Except for the preliminary pleadings, which the judge and lawyers alone have seen, and for the questions preceding jury selection, the judge and jury have no perception of how the facts will fall in the development of the proof. The appellate courts, on the other hand, deal retrospectively. Appellate judges work from written transcripts of the trial testimony, with all the recorded oral conduct by the trial judge, the jury, and the lawyers.

Only manufactured products come before appellate courts. The flavor of personal variability is lost; credibility, intuitions about witnesses based on watching them, impact of sympathy, and misconduct of lawyers and judges by facial gestures and voice inflection go unperceived. In short, the human flavor that helps size up situations is lost to the appellate judge. The written record is truly cold. To compensate for that generally appreciated factor, appellate judges are not supposed to determine facts afresh. The legal verbiage is that they do not, in normal circumstances, determine facts *de novo* (from the beginning). They do not make new, or fresh, findings of fact apart from the trial evidence. Appellate judges may, however, set aside findings of fact and return the case for a new trial, or even make new and different findings of fact based on the evidence in the record, if the court believes the finding or verdict to be against the weight of the evidence. The formulation of this legal concept takes many verbal symbols, but reduces to the simple notion that the appellate judges may reverse a trial verdict if they find it to be simply unbelievable on the face of what the witnesses have been recorded as saying and of the documents that were marked in evidence.

Sober safeguards are necessary to forestall arbitrary or unreasonable trial findings of fact, as well as erroneous applications of law. The function of the appellate courts is to check the trial court for error; they are barriers against fallibility below. Unfortunately, there is a tendency in too many appellate judges to divine, as an original matter, what really went on in the facts shaping the case, notwithstanding the trial record.

Appellate courts are not lively; the personal action of the parties is missing. Trial courts, on the other hand, are the epitome of personality in action. Appellate courts in session simply monitor and sometimes participate in dignified formal argument of lawyers. A party having his day in trial court has an intensely personal experience. His name is mentioned endlessly, his conduct is analyzed in detail, and he is a constant focus of attention as he sits prominently in the center of the arena. On the other hand, his day in appellate court is peculiarly bloodless. Often, the party does not even appear, for on appeal no evidence is taken, no witnesses are questioned, and the popular oratorical devices designed to sway lay jurors are suppressed.

The appellate courts are places for lawyers. The parties who were "plaintiff" and "defendant" become "appellant" and "appellee," or "petitioner" and "respondent," depending on who won below and who now seeks the appeal. Personalities are dehydrated in the proceedings. Legal arguments suffuse the appellate papers filed by the lawyers, such as summaries of grounds for appeal, the transcript of the proceedings below, and new briefs discussing the facts and the law.

Appellate courtrooms have a general similarity. They are usually formal, wood-paneled rooms. From three to nine judges sit side by side on the inevitable raised console. While on the "bench," the appellate judge, like his trial colleague, sits in a large, comfortably padded, high-backed leather chair. Proceedings are more dignified and much quieter than at a trial. For one thing, the courtrooms are rarely occupied by spectators. The hubbub of the trial courtroom is conspicuously missing. Unless it is a specially newsworthy case, the only people in the audience are lawyers waiting for their cases to be heard and a sprinkling of clients. Sometimes other lawyers come in to hear an interesting legal issue aired or to watch a particular lawyer in action, one noted for forensic style or simply for a big reputation.

Appellate argumentation is often low in tone, quite inaudible at the rear. Appellate courtrooms are more distinguished for their design trappings than for their acoustics. Lawyers customarily present their arguments in dignified style, setting a factual background before attempting their legal analysis. This is the professional occasion to which a good deal of their law school training has been addressed. Law school moot courts are usually appellate courts. The rough and tumble of a trial in all its logistical elements is not readily simulated in law school.

Appellate judges usually question lawyers arguing before them. Indeed, some judges delight in breaking into a carefully arranged argument, throwing the lawyer off stride. Oral argument is more often than not required to be completed within an allotted period of time. If before the arguments the judges have already read the papers the lawyers have submitted on appeal, the court is known as a "hot bench." Sometimes a thermometer of extreme sensitivity is needed to make this observation. Judicial questions may betray an unawareness of the papers that were supposedly absorbed in advance.

Nonetheless, the hot bench cooks up the best of the appellate process. Judges who are well prepared in advance may take the opportunity to question lawyers about points insufficiently covered, or manifestly deficient, in their appellate papers. Good oral argument is helpful in appellate practice, for although the bench may be hot, the record is always cold. Unfortunately, time and calendar pressure preclude many appellate courts from review of the record prior to argument. This is almost invariably true of intermediate appellate courts, which typically work with impossibly large case loads. Hot benches are most often found in the higher state courts, and a good number of the federal Circuit Courts of Appeal.

Most appeals are submitted on papers alone, without oral argumentation. There really is no day in the appellate court in the trial sense. The appellate activity is simply an extension, perhaps a correction or affirmance, of the day had earlier. Indeed, it may lead to a new day if the trial court is reversed.

Appellate decisions are almost never issued from the bench, since they are group decisions. Upon review of the records on appeal and completion of oral arguments, if they take place, appellate judges meet in conference to discuss a number of cases. Their chief judge, by whatever title called, acts as chairman. When a decision is reached as to how the court will go, one judge is assigned to write up the case. In practice, appellate judging relies heavily on legal clerks and law assistants; and depending on the habits of their judge, the assistants' duties vary, from full-opinion drafting to specifically directed research. The draft prepared by the responsible judge is usually circulated to the others, at which time dissenting or concurring opinions may mushroom and be circulated. Fellow judges may induce others to change their minds, but, as time wears on, judges become committed and attitudes harden. The instances reported in the press and in literature about the drama of backstage judicial turmoil in deciding well-known cases are exceptional. Actually, in lower appellate courts with huge case loads, opinions, particularly those in routine matters, are drafted entirely by clerks and law assistants and become the court's opinion with little or no change. The parties may be receiving much shorter shrift than the imposing courthouse façade suggests.

A determination of a trial court is deemed final after time for appeal has expired without timely appeal being taken. Depending on local rules, determinations of appeal become final after the appellate court has acted or its decision can no longer be appealed. "Opinions" of courts are really memoranda of reasoning. The actual result is set forth as a shortened entry of judgment on the court's records and filed with a record-keeping functionary, who recites the names of the parties and the result of the litigation in specific and concise terms.

———ESSENTIAL UNCERTAINTIES——— OF PROOF

By all measures, the main stuff of a trial is in the resolution of factual issues, because the trial forms the official version of what went on. For case purposes, it *is* what went on. Did he do it? Did he say it? Did he sign it? Did he hear it? Did he know it? Did he mean it? The case is decided not necessarily by what went on, but by what the judge and jury believe went on.

A cradling yarn of trial lawyers recalls the law professor bidding solemn farewell to his favorite pupil, who is graduating and leaving to practice law downstate. "If ever you are in trouble and need advice on complex issues, call on me without fail." The years passed. Then suddenly the young lawyer landed the biggest case of his career, representing a defendant in a lurid murder trial. Because of the complexities of the legal issues, he needed considerable analytical assistance, and thought back to his old professor's offer. He promptly dispatched a long letter describing the facts and legal issues of the case as he saw them. No reply came from the professor. He sent another letter, and still no reply came. The trial started, and, sensing the depth of his trouble, he sent a night letter to the professor, detailing the testimony of the case, but more silence followed. When the prosecuting lawyer finally rested his case, our young hero was distraught, and telegraphed to his mentor long and pleadingly, explaining what the prosecution witnesses had said, and begging for advice. After two days of presenting his side in trial testimony, he despaired, only to have his associate put in front of him a telegram from the elusive professor: "Not to worry. Am arriving on the one o'clock plane with three witnesses."

In approaching litigation, a party must take into account that where one person's word is stacked against that of another, the result is fragile. Legal opponents, with their lawyers, can be counted upon to deny or to shade. It is never enough to know in your heart you are right; you must prove it. The number of cases that turn on one person's word against another is legion.

Sometimes, however, the contest of word is lodged in a familiar fact pattern, which by human experience leads to presumptions. An automobile case may serve as an illustration. Assume an automobile accident in which you are the driver of a car going south on a main road. The defendant is driving his car northerly on that same road. He makes a left turn at an intersection unregulated by any traffic-control device, and there is a collision of your two cars, injuring you both. Both of you were alone in your autos, and no witnesses to the accident came forward. The police, alerted by radio, arrived on the accident scene. Moments later, often behind an assortment of tow-truck operators and photographers, who also own radios, the usual gathering of helpful and curious people attracted to accident scenes in inhabited areas arrives, sometimes even before the police. It is amazing how many business cards are flourished on these occasions. This case is known in the legal negligence fraternity as a "left turn," not to be confused with a "rear ender" (stationary car hit from behind), "knockdown" (struck pedestrian), or a "fender bender" (minor damage to a car). All these cases are common in court. They are so common that insurance companies, who typically bear the burden of both sides in automobile-accident cases, have their own rules for settling them. For instance, our left turn case would be considered for adjustment on a "one-third / two-thirds" probability, meaning that two-thirds of the fault belongs to the car making the left turn.

Cases turn upon the burden of proof. In a civil case, to win you must prove your case by a fair preponderance of the credible evidence. In a criminal case, the prosecution has the burden of proof to establish beyond a reasonable doubt that the accused is guilty. In both cases, the defendants win if there is a tie.

The trial has been prefaced by months or years of costly paperwork, and lies on the far side of an economic hurdle. You come into the courtroom with your story in mind, with your documents, your witnesses, and your sturdy lawyer, only to find your opponent does the same. It is a mistake to underestimate the capacity of lawyers to spin skeins of argument and to make inferences from the events leading up to the litigated controversy. When the opposition is represented by a skilled lawyer, no cause or defense, no matter how certain it appears to its proponent, is quite secure, particularly where a jury is concerned. No case has a 100% probability of victory.

Factors of prejudice affect trial outcome, although they appear in no lawbooks. Consider the New York builder in a Texas court being sued by a local subcontractor, the mortgagee evicting a widow, the slum landlord, the rich insurance company, the big corporation, the black, the Jew, the foreigner, all in the wrong place at the wrong time, but trying there for their day in court. "Venue," place of location of a trial, can be fateful.

In addition to the variables of the place, the jury, the judge, the parties, and the lawyers, the witnesses present their own problems. Some are available, others are not, at specific times, and show uncertain willingness to mix into a process that promises them little good. Witnesses bear different degrees of relationship, if any, to the parties. The closer the relationship, the more likely their appearance and their steadfastness. But even the close ones can be troublesome. The assurances of loyalty, the positiveness of recollection, the willingness to stick out the neck weaken in trial performance, or even in its contemplation. On the witness stand, alone, at the mercy of the lawyers, many witnesses become confused, upset, forgetful, unconcerned, doubtful. They worry, fear, and weaken.

Superimposed on all this is just plain luck, good or bad— fortuity, as luck is formally known in the law. A crowded calendar may motivate a judge to move ahead too quickly and impatiently. A holiday looms and the jury is anxious to break away. A lawyer has a diverting problem. Illness afflicts an important participant. A crime wave is on and the community is unusually upset. Many things affect the course of a particular trial, apart from its merits and even the normally anticipated range of variability.

Where his civil case is weak on legal principle, the plaintiff's driving legal effort may be "to get the case to the jury." This means to avoid having the judge dismiss the case on the law at the conclusion of the plaintiff's presentation. While not unique to them, weak personal-injury actions are prime instances. The hope is that the idiosyncratic aspects of jury practice will somehow work gain for someone seen as the underdog, oppressed, or highly sympathetic, but with a poor formal case. The jury verdict is the acid test of the proof.

———CHOICE OF TRIAL LAWYER———

Many people think all lawyers are equal. This is not true in any field of law, let alone trial practice. The manner of presentation of a case has a material bearing on its outcome. Thus, another variable for your day in court: how good is your lawyer? how willing is he? Technical legal ability is a subordinate factor in trial conduct, where preparation, persuasiveness, quickness, sense of timing, believability, and the ability to judge which points to press and which to soft-pedal are prime factors. In a case with nineteen possible points of argument, a typical client will insist on all nineteen. Lawyers, however, know cases must be reduced to manageable proportions, that too much argumentative weight sinks a case, and that some points are boomerangs.

Please note that "preparation" is the first attribute cited in this litany. The placement of the word is not accidental; more than by anything else, trials are won by careful preparatory work. This means that beyond analysis of the legal problems, there are painstaking investigation and study of the facts, pretrial depositions, marshaling of witnesses, grasping of the business details or the techniques involved, strategic planning, and, not insignificantly, arrival at court clear of mind and eye and ready to concentrate wholly on the case at hand. The drunken, flamboyant *bon vivant*, up until the wee hours with beautiful women, but vivaciously awake for the trial on a Thermos of black coffee, dashing off the tearful phrase and the masterly trick, so dearly fathered by fiction writers, is just that, fiction. Most trial lawyers are serious, hard-working people. Some are predisposed to dramatic dress or approach, but trial lawyers are largely professionals, many family-oriented, who know well the cold legal dawn is a hostile environment for frivolity and tricks.

Trials are best handled by adequately paid lawyers who concentrate on trial work. Skimping on preparation and attention is often a result of inadequate compensation. Unfortunately, many lawyers will take the fees that are available and tailor their efforts to their reward. Litigation is an expensive business, with uncertainty in the time it will take. If the lawyer's estimate of cost is too high, the client may leave; if it is too low, the lawyer may be stuck with an unprofitable workout.

Financial considerations are, accordingly, critical to whether the day in court is even available at all, and then as to its quality.

Trials take time and concentration. Lawyers who are able to give maximum effort can do better than those forever diverting their attention by running to the telephone in the corridor during intermissions, attending to other clients, other matters, other priorities. Lawyers who specialize in trial work are better able to schedule court appearance in more or less orderly sequence; other trial courts are prone to grant adjournment by accepting in excuse reasonable prior courtroom engagement. Contract closings and board meetings do not sway deadline-pushing trial calendar judges. The advocate harried by events external to the trial before him handicaps his client.

Many clients, however tough they may be in business negotiation, are in awe of the judicial process; they see it as a discipline out of their hands. They are right in this, for nowhere else in the law is a client so firmly in his lawyer's hands as when he is on trial.

THE COMPETENCY OF TRIAL LAWYERS

Along with the many fine trial lawyers of this land there are many incompetent ones. In a provocative 1973 lecture at Fordham University Law School, in New York City, Chief Justice of the United States Warren E. Burger launched the extraordinary assertion, repeated before the American Bar Association in Dallas in 1979, that "from one-third to one-half of the lawyers who appear in the serious cases are not really qualified to render fully adequate representation." Other judges have hastened into print with even more dismal estimates. While there is no way of documenting any figures here, all commentators agree that the trial lawyer incompetency quota is excessive.

The root causes of trial lawyer incompetency are lack of preparation and lack of know-how. Many intelligent lawyers, capable of good work, are simply inadequately prepared in the facts of their case or the legal principles affecting it. This poor preparation may stem from bad habits, disinterest, or laziness, or because the lawyer is untrained or incapable, intellectually or emotionally, of better effort.

The problem may be overcommitment, too many cases or clients to service properly, or inadequate compensation. But under any of these circumstances, poor preparation affronts the client and the court. Cases should not be undertaken unless there is a resolve to devote adequate resources to them. Case acceptance for low or marginal fees does not preclude the necessity to exert effective efforts. If the time planning for a case blows up in a lawyer's face, it remains still his obligation to honor the commitment he made in taking the case. A lawyer who gives his client less than full measure is both cheating him out of any fee paid and harming him by prejudicing his rights.

A prime lawyering fault is the failure to develop in the minds of the judge or the jury a clear narrative of what happened. This task is particularly essential to the plaintiff, who normally has the burden of proof. Many lawyers lose sight of the fact that they have intimate prior association with the case, its issues and its people, whereas the judge and jury see them only in fleeting courtroom sequence. Superior lawyers are careful to impress their story.

Another recurring fault is the misunderstanding of the letter or the spirit of the rules of evidence. Evidentiary rules are necessary to filter out unwarranted and prejudiced conclusions, and to screen rumor, hearsay, and insufficient bases to testify, including inexpert experts. Rules of evidence help separate the supportable versions of fact from the mass of irrelevancy, misinformation, and rhetoric surrounding every human controversy.

The most famous and butchered rule of evidence is that precluding "hearsay" testimony. "Hearsay" is where a witness repeats as fact something someone else told him happened. For instance, where a time of arrival is a critical point, an illustrative example might be:

Question: Do you know what time Crohn came to his lawyer's office that night?
Answer: Yes, he came in at 9:15 P.M.
Question: Would you tell the jury how you happen to know that?
Answer: His secretary told me.

Question: Objection; hearsay.
Judge: Sustained.

The testimony is obvious hearsay on the issue of when Crohn came in, since it is really the secretary's version of the facts being offered. But suppose the secretary later testified herself that Crohn arrived at 5:00 P.M. Then it would be proper to recall the first witness to ask him what the secretary had said to him about time of arrival. Now, the purpose of the question is to throw doubt on her credibility.

However, hearsay evidence may be used to establish a collateral point, for instance, an ability to enunciate clearly.

Question: What, if anything, happened after that?
Answer: Cummings said to me, "I heard on TV that the
           Dow Jones ticker was running thirty minutes late
           at the closing."

The answer may not be used to establish that the ticker was late, but it may be used to prove Cummings could speak coherently at that time. So it may be legitimate to raise a hearsay statement for some purposes and not for others. Many lawyers do not understand this subtlety; they simply do not grasp the nuances of the hearsay rule, with its infinite exceptions and modifications.

Rules of evidence commonly extend to when opinion testimony, as compared with fact recitation, may be elicited. They extend to the identification, authentication, and proper use of pictures, bloody shirts, weapons, neck braces, official documents, letters, and other physical things (called "real" or "demonstrative" evidence). These rules bear on the question of "foundation," which means the establishment that the witness could have seen what he said he saw, or that the expert had the qualification to render a professional opinion.

Perhaps the best-known objections are the classic "irrelevant" (nothing to do with the case), "incompetent" (cannot effectively prove anything), and "immaterial" (unimportant). Courts overrule these objections more often than not, except where the questioner is totally exceeding the bounds of reason.

Another notable line of objection is that of "leading the witness." Strictly speaking, leading has no particular form, except that its effect is to suggest an answer to the witness. Examples:

Question: Did you not meet the real estate broker at Powell's restaurant on Wednesday night?
Question: That is your partner's signature right there, isn't it?
Question: Were you in Mr. Folger's room at 11:30 A.M. talking to Mr. Korn when Mr. Lesnick walked in?

Leading questions are permissible only on cross-examination; although on direct examination, the court, or the parties by nonobjection, sometimes permit bringing testimony beyond undisputed material towards a crux. "Are you Tom Levin, the plaintiff in this case; do you live at 34 Cox Street, Albany, Georgia; and do you work for the Peachtree Sales Company?" Some lawyers cannot, particularly under stress, phrase questions that are not leading. Because of their universality, the practical judicial tendency is to tolerate leading questions unless they touch on disputed matters of substance.

A staggering number of objections are wasteful knee-jerk reactions to matters factually uncontested. Absurdly, many lawyers object to questions solely because they fear the answers will harm their case.

Actually, the permissibility of questioning and the admissibility of evidence are as much involved with the individual dynamics of each trial as they are with the rule books. Able judges lean to broad admissibility of evidence in the interest of hearing a maximum presentation. If they are to err, they prefer to do so in the interest of full disclosure.

Trial judges rule quickly on most evidence questions from the seat of their robes. These rulings customarily involve quick perceptions of the relativity of the prejudice to the probative value of an offering. Where counsel persists, judges should have no hesitation in reconsidering their rulings, based on a reading back of portions of the transcript or legal citation by counsel.

If there are incompetent lawyers on both sides, the trial situation becomes intolerable, and a good trial judge must take matters in his own hands. A judge may feel obliged to allow more than usual leeway to a bumbling lawyer if the other side is not overly prejudiced by the allowance. Sometimes the judge must intervene and ask clarifying questions. It is bad practice for judges to question excessively, since they are not advocates or inquisitors. Of course, if the judge himself does not really understand the rules of evidence, and this is an uncomfortably common state of affairs, law school is out for fair in that trial.

Incompetency also surfaces in oral and written argument. The failure to organize thoughts in advance and then to present them cogently when opening or closing to the jury is common. Some lawyers have fatal tendencies to "wing it." A basic error is to neglect forceful presentation of one's own affirmative points in favor of chasing the adversary's like a greyhound after the electric rabbit. Strangely, more lawyers than supposed do not enunciate clearly, or speak poorly or haltingly. As many times as I have admired a legal presentation, I have watched stumbling lawyers and wondered whatever made them think they should be lawyers in the first place.

CERTIFYING TRIAL LAWYER SPECIALISTS

Increasing publicly expressed doubts of trial lawyering competency have led to a controversy as to whether trial lawyers should be required to receive separate certification as specialists to be eligible to try cases. This would be a form of sublicensing of trial lawyers.

Chief Justice Burger's 1973 Fordham address was a watershed occasion because of his candid thoughts circulated to the public. In remedying trial lawyer mediocrity, he would require increased law school educational interest in trial technique and add to it a system of certification of trial advocates as a licensed subspecialty of the law.

But in arguing for a separately licensed trial corps, the Chief Justice is considering only some of the trees in the forest. Incompetency in lawyering runs far beyond trial conduct; it permeates the profession. The real need is to upgrade the professional qualification of lawyers in all areas of practice; the courts are only the tip of the iceberg. It is in the law office that most people meet the law, become advised, are handed papers, and carry themselves forward, accepting all consequences, in the belief of competent legal ministration. Unfortunately, more lawyering harm is worked in law offices than in courtrooms, although the former may lead to the latter. Litigated cases involving written documents, business and commercial activities, and noncompliance with statutory or administrative requirements stem significantly from poor legal transactional execution. In medicine, the word "iatrogenesis" means doctor-induced illness; its legal counterpart is lawyer-induced lawsuits.

The emphasis should be on proper legal education for all lawyers before practice commences, and on continuing professional postgraduate education throughout the course of practice. Most lawyers effectively bring formal education to a grinding halt on leaving law school, and later learn only from what is put directly in front of them in the course of their practices. The most pressing need is for periodic professional recertification of all lawyers and their maintenance of mandatory continuing-education standards.

Criminal cases are serious by any definition, both to society and to the accused. No one can disagree with the desirability of competent counsel for both sides. The prosecution is always government. The great majority of defendants are represented by governmentally funded public defenders or governmentally subsidized legal-aid agencies of different kinds. There are excellent trial advocates in both public prosecution and defense efforts, but the ranks are thin. The undeniable deficiencies in general competency level here do not trace to anything curable by sublicensing trial lawyers, because the basic problems emanate from the lack of will to depoliticize public-prosecuting offices and an unwillingness to provide sufficient funding to support superior legal efforts, particularly for the defense. Both public facets of criminal law, prosecution and defense, would attract a ready flow of qualified applicants if public salary structures were appropriate and professionalism, not politics, controlled the office workings.

To the extent that trial lawyer incompetency results from greedy assumption of too many cases, laziness, indifference, personal economic considerations, and lack of energy or zeal, all the sublicensing in the world will be unavailing. Sublicensing is not divinely inspired; it would go largely to education and experience prerequisites, not to the personal traits that result in incompetent advocacy by those with proper paper credentials and the ability to do better.

It is the obligation of judges to preside over trials fairly, but with firm hands. Judges have the power to hold lawyers in contempt if they persist in obnoxious professional conduct, and by virtue of their power to impose standards of conduct. The power is insufficiently exercised, however, for a variety of reasons. Most important, there is an exceedingly fine line between permissible and impermissible conduct in a heated trial. Remedial options are limited, since interference with a lawyer's leeway may result in depriving his client of full representation, or prejudice his client in front of a jury. Trial judges know that appellate courts tend to be critical of exercise of contempt and other coercive powers, and they are reluctant to get out on that limb. The cold appellate record, divorced of the flavor of the moment, unable to convey gestures, voice tones, and expressions, makes it particularly easy for the appellate court to look in retrospect more kindly on trial transgression. Also, the longer the trial goes on, the less anxious a judge is to declare contempt or compromise a lawyer. The time investment in a proceeding that may have to be tried again becomes a consideration. Even another is the fact that contempt citations make judges unpopular with lawyers, and many judges are eager for the general approval of the bar, eager to hold a good common reputation as a judge, through pleasing those whose views create the reputation. Lawyer regard may be necessary at a later time, such as for judicial reappointment or promotion, upon Bar Association recommendation. There is also the fraternity of lawyers linking the judge and the trial advocates. They do associate with each other a great deal in the course of their working days.

Judicial monitoring of trial conduct is not restricted to disruptive or obstructive tactics; it can also go strictly to incompetency, although here the ice is even thinner. There are great dangers in judicial trial intervention until the whole race is run, and then it may be too late. Playing possum and using country-boy tactics are common to trials, as is lying low with even worse factual skeletons than have become apparent. While gross incompetence, such as total unfamiliarity with the case, is intolerable, under existing authorities the judges have largely only moral force to compel removal of an incompetent lawyer from a case. Disciplinary action for legal incompetency is rare. Sometimes an essentially extortive judicial threat to the errant lawyer that he will be reported to professional authority facilitates his willingness to resign from a case "voluntarily." The more valuable judicial role in upgrading lawyers' performance must be an instructive one.

It surely must be obvious, in all events, that judicial monitoring of lawyers is inescapably bound up with the ability and personality of the judges themselves. The judge who lacks judicial temperament or legal ability can scarcely be expected to have a refreshing professional effect on lawyers appearing before him. Judges who themselves lack legal ability are poor choices to educate trial lawyers.

The Chief Justice's 1973 commentary on sublicensing of trial lawyers proceeded from his admiring references to British barristerial supersuperiority and ethical elevation, and to the ostensible selection of English trial judges entirely from the ranks of the lawyers having the highest trial advocate qualifications. Presumably, these British judicial selections are made on the merits, without political, social, or economic intermediacy. Given the closed nature of the British social structure, and the barrister system, the fundamental nature of all these assumptions is most doubtful. In simple language, and certainly not the Queen's English, they smack of elitism. Moreover, given these observations, how can one conceptually seek the certification of trial lawyers without first having true merit selection of judges? I have not the smallest doubt that the need to work for better selection of judges remains an infinitely higher priority of the American legal system.

In this country, unlike England, the guiding tradition is to encourage access to the courts. In these times, when a critical lack of the justice system is insufficient delivery of legal service to the middle and lower economic groupings at reasonable cost, any system that seeks to limit the number of lawyers who can try cases in court has to be socially wrong. There are growing indications that existing barriers to the exercise of the lawyer's franchise are even now too exclusive. Witness the rulings of the Supreme Court in the last several decades limiting states' rights to prevent bar admission on various political and moral grounds. And surely it is clear that restricting the trial lawyer class will work to increase the cost of their lawyering and to no demonstrable public purpose.

Government seems quite obtrusive enough in the affairs of its citizens without stimulating further means. A pride of the American system of justice is the right to counsel of one's own choice. The lawyering class is itself a restricted one, not only by its qualifying requirements, but also by the social and economic processes inherent in acquiring substantial education and using it to productive end. Many of our citizens, when they face their need for lawyering, of any kind, prefer to have a lawyer who is empathetic with their situation; the feeling of instinctive confidence that one person has in another is not to be disregarded. Personal loyalty, innate ability, courage, special knowledge, and conscience can outweigh technical competence in trial adventure. There comes a point when a person has a right to be wrong, to help make the legal bed in which he may find himself.

——————YOU NEVER KNOW——————
WHAT A JURY WILL DO

Juries represent the major imponderable. The common legal lore is that you never know what a jury will do. Is that so surprising? The jurors see and hear the cases with radically different legal sensory apparatus than do the lawyers and the judges. For one thing, they sit confined silently in a tight little area, often cramped by long periods of inactivity. Theirs is not the comfort of the judge. Jurors do not stand and move around like the lawyers or the witnesses. In most places they are not permitted to take notes. Their experience in legal matters is assured from the process of their selection to be almost nil. Lawyers and their spouses and employees are generally disqualified from jury service, as are those in many law-oriented positions such as insurance-company or law-enforcement background.

In many places, successful people, those who best understand business transactions and economic expectations, are also successful in evading jury service. Juries picked from the population at random and those found eligible to serve tend to be law-abiding people without litigious records. In their qualifying process, they are selected precisely because they are not notably mixed up with the sort of thing that forms the basis for the litigation. They are picked for their amateur standing.

At no time during the trial do jurors normally see the pleadings joining the issues of the case, nor can they review any past records not before them. All they know of the case is what they hear in open court, which is theoretically good, but often poor in practice. In the course of a lengthy trial, the threads of the case come together confusingly slowly, sometimes not timely enough, to form a pattern. Many objections to questions and answers are made by lawyers; some are granted, some are denied. The jury is then told to disregard matter put firmly into its consciousness. Much of what lawyers and judges do is to protect a record on appeal, without real consideration of comprehensibility to the live jury in front of them. All this disrupts continuity and understanding.

There are such things as depositions or examinations before trial, where parties or witnesses are questioned under oath by lawyers. These depositions, parts of a wider practice known as "pretrial discovery," are recorded in typed form, and may be read to the jury for hours in place, and with the force of live testimony. Their purpose is to help discover information so that trial preparation is facilitated and surprise averted. The judge and the opposing lawyer have transcripts to follow the reading, but the jury has nothing to help it with the droning assault on their ears, which may take hours or days. The record may be protected, but those who would give a verdict shortly are not.

Trials of lawsuits are essentially dull, unlike the theatrical versions that are edited for sustained lively matter. Lengthier trials ooze forward, replete with droning voices, marking of exhibits, mumbling, recesses, and often petty disputation. Their dramatic content is low, in the main. It is to be wholly expected that summaries of the case by the judge but mostly by the lawyers, who do it more expressively, often twisting the occurrences and adding innuendo to innuendo, move juries in ways that evidentiary presentations fail to do.

In fact, the jury's view of the case may be so incomplete or twisted by the way the case is presented to it that it reaches out for any prop to ease its decisional dilemma. It may award the defendant something because he seems like a nice person, or acquit an accused because the district attorney was thought to be a sneering bully. Years ago, a lawyer friend of mine questioned his next-door neighbor, an elderly lady, who had just returned from jury duty. He asked her about her experiences, and was startled by the lady's explanation of one case. "Oh, that one! We gave him nothing. We figured since he had such a crook for a lawyer he couldn't be much good himself."

In addition to disappointment, losing litigants are often surprised that the outcome is so different from their expectations of justice. Much of this stems from an incomplete understanding of the process. Rules of law are not immutable inscriptions on stone, nor are criminal sentences or money judgments, and a sure knowledge of having been wronged does not translate assuredly into litigative success. The proof that is accepted is controlling. Being disbelieved or being seen as unsympathetic or in inappropriate perspective are difficult potions for most to swallow, but those bitter medicines are in full stock in all courthouses. Lay people just do not see their day in court, their trial, as the chancy enterprise it almost always is, beset by uncertainties engendered by the personal characteristics and the fortuities of all of the many participants and processes in it.

8

TO BE
A CLIENT

Lawyer-client relations actually proceed on two levels. On one level, the lawyer is the representative of the client; he acts for him and speaks for him. The lawyer owes loyalty to his client, holds his confidences, and, by the book, does what is necessary to further his cause, ease his distress, or counsel his action. This is the level of cooperation, of coidentity of interest.

The other level is something else; it holds germs of adversity between lawyer and client, the most usual of which is economic. While the professional relationship entitles a client to fiduciary and ethical protections, the client is also a customer of a person who makes his living practicing law.

The lawyer in private practice survives by keeping the patronage of clients. He runs the risks of hurting himself economically by dispensing advice that could lead to less legal work, such as "Drop the case," or advice that could culminate in the end of the legal relationship, such as "Your merger into your competitor is legally feasible." Conversely, "Sue the man" or "The merger will cause insuperable problems" help to fund the private legal economy. A lawyer's practice may also compel different priorities between clients at different times, so that his sense of timing may be at odds with the client's in settling cases or in moving forward forcefully. In the ideal professional world, no financial considerations impinge; but there is no ideal world.

Nor need lawyer-client adversity be simply economic. It may also arise where the client's activities cut against the lawyer's moral grain or in some way compromise his independent professional position.

To assume that every lawyer in every instance advises a client without any regard to the lawyer's economic interests or his feelings is to miss entirely a significant part of the professional relationship. Obviously, some lawyers have more character, conscience, and wealth than others. The affective factors that color objective legal advice (to the extent there is such a thing) belong at the base line of lawyering.

——— THE BASICS ———
OF CHOOSING A LAWYER

For the sophisticates, there is little problem in picking a lawyer. Constant dealings with and against lawyers educate them. The average citizen, however, has little experience with lawyers and legal matters, and quantitatively not much need for them. Often the requirement for a lawyer comes abruptly, as in a sudden death, an accident, an arrest, or other emergency circumstances.

A lay person whom the would-be client respects, and who knows of a lawyer, is a good source, except that whereas many people do turn to friends or relatives for referral, others avoid them for the sake of privacy. This is a common attitude when it comes to estate planning, matrimonial disputation, and criminal trouble. Doctors and clergymen are often good referral sources. They know of lawyers.

The seeker of legal advice who has no informed and trusted friends or associates to whom he wishes to turn may consult legal directories or local Bar Associations (listed in the local phone book), which offer referral sources. They yield a choice of names, with their qualifications. The American Bar Association publishes a lawyer referral Service Handbook, which describes lawyer referral services across the country.

The principal legal directory is Martindale-Hubbell, found in all legal libraries and in many public ones. This standard legal directory lists the age, basic education, and location of most practicing lawyers. Other directories are also available, many of a specialized nature. A particularly useful feature of Martindale-Hubbell is that in addition to the listing of individual lawyers, many law firms place display advertisements, which provide details on the background of their partners, along with mention of the aspects of law in which the firm is most active, such as "general litigation," "corporate," or "real estate." A Martindale-Hubbell display announcement reveals much about the law firm. Among other things, it points to firm size and the diversity, ages, scholarship, publications, prior government service, Bar Association, and community involvement of its members.

The very least desirable means is a random selection, a vaguely remembered name, a relative of a relative, or some other equivalent.

Years ago, in New York City, a man just in from Texas came to me as a client who had actually picked my name with a pin plunged into the yellow-page listings of a telephone book he found in his local hotel room.

For those with limited means, the growth of legal advertising is an aid in choosing lawyers. Storefront law offices, even in neighborhood shopping centers or within large general stores themselves, attract attention with legal bargains featured in the window, not unlike a supermarket. The openly quoted prices for routine transactions are a distinct attraction, since potential clients are often deterred from seeking legal advice because they fear the price. Going into an office or a store for legal services at advertised prices may shock the gentry of the law, but it fits the pattern of buying with which many people are comfortable.

No one should retain a lawyer until he has spoken with him at length. Questions that should be weighed in interviewing a lawyer include:

Does the lawyer seem to you capable and knowledgeable?

What is his experience, his training, and his work?

Does he inspire confidence?

Can you "talk" to him?

What is his cost?

Will the lawyer do the work or give it to someone else? If the latter, to whom?

Regardless of who you are or who he is, if a lawyer does not inspire your confidence or communicates with you poorly, you should express your gratitude for the interview time, leave the office, and seek another lawyer. Few lawyers charge for a consultation as to whether they are to be hired, although it is a good idea to check this out in advance. There are too many elements wrapped up in a lawyer-client relationship to start off with personal doubt. A client should remember that the cause, the cost, the responsibility, and the result are all his. Any client with a choice is poorly advised to enter into a lawyer relationship where, as some nonlegal thinkers might say, the "vibes" are not good.

The great bulk of lawyering as it touches the average citizen, apart from trial work, is generalized and fully dischargeable by good lawyers of no specialized bent. Contracts, trusts, estate administration, basic real estate, landlord-tenant, business acquisitions, general government compliance, partnership and corporate work, commercial transactions, matrimonial discord short of hostile litigation, employment rights, personal counseling, and innumerable other subjects form the common mass of general civil practice. An advantage of going to a sizable law firm is that where specialties are necessary, they are in place, serving under one roof.

If, simply to function, an extensive working body of information on a specific subject is required daily, a specialist is desirable. Federal taxation is a good example. Much of the field involves giving current business advice, often spontaneously, and often for immediate use. The stances and responses based on tax advice are often immediate and irretrievable, so that intensive current experience in the tax field, which is beset with complication and special terminology, is highly important. The overwhelming aspect of a tax lawyer's work is not in the court advocation of given legal tax positions; it is in advising on legalities or risks inherent in the numerous courses available to the client. Constant changes in the laws, regulations, and rules, along with shifting business uses to exploit tax advantage, make keeping up to the minute an essential for tax counselors. The assumption that, given enough research time, any good lawyer can do anything is untrue with a complex and volatile specialty such as tax law.

The brashest generalist I know would not undertake an overly technical patent consultation. The amount of special information necessary is simply too much. Few trial lawyers would take on the trial of a complicated patent case; to question witnesses appropriately, one would need to have extensive knowledge of engineering, scientific, and technical matters.

The common legal specialties that usually preclude generalist lawyers are criminal, matrimonial, personal injury, taxation, advanced estate planning, complex real estate, pension, labor, patents, bankruptcy, sophisticated corporate, and copyright and trademark, and some technical government-agency causes or transactions. In any of these fields, no client should retain a lawyer or a firm that is not experienced and proven.

For litigation, a client must look for experience in litigating. Capable trial lawyers with legal intelligence generally can try any number of different kinds of cases, because the important underlying skills remain the same from case to case. The ability to analyze facts, present a case, question witnesses, and argue is transferrable. The substantial law background of a lawsuit is frozen in the time of the underlying occurrences. There is ample occasion to research the law, and although the requirements of a given case may justify the invocation of unusual legal doctrines or the understanding of the complexities of some other professional discipline, like medicine, an adept trial lawyer should be able to anticipate or meet these challenges. The more pertinent question is whether the trial lawyer would want to extend himself in trial fields he deems strange, uninteresting, unappetizing, or unremunerative. While capable general trial lawyers can, if they wish, handle negligence, matrimonial, or criminal cases, most of them will not handle negligence cases, owing to distaste, matrimonials, owing to emotional wear and tear, or criminal cases, owing to the company they would keep.

Having told you all that, let me now qualify my remarks, a practice rather ordinary for my profession. There are lawyers of high ability, dedication, energy, and experience who can do everything in the law short of the more arcane specialties, and do so. Mostly they are found in operations with ample assistance for research, drafting, and pretrial activities. Some years ago a book entitled *Super Lawyers* described Washington lawyers who reportedly exercise great influence in the government. The real test of superlawyering, however, is not in governmental manipulation. The superstars are those whose capabilities run into every area in which a lawyer is called upon to function, including, I might add, proper governmental representation. Their ranks are predictably thin. Some lawyers of this rank are totally unknown except to their clients and a small circle in the profession who know of their versatility. Some are national figures.

Trust is a key client attitude. Without it, the relationship is never good and the results are often suspect. But if the client is confident of his lawyer's legal ability and couples this with personal trust, the lawyer-client relationship can be firm. Clients who do not reach this state of mind—and many clients are emotionally incapable of doing so—may shift from lawyer to lawyer, from use to use, from economy to economy.

————CONFLICTS OF INTEREST————

Occasionally, the issue of conflict of interest complicates the selection of a lawyer. Obviously, the problem exists in a contested trial matter where the lawyer being considered is closely allied with the other side by any tie that binds, be he a relative, a close friend, or a business associate. The determination is rarely that clear-cut, since common sense steers people away from such known situations, and lawyers in conspicuously adverse relationships will decline to undertake the representation.

The issue of prior representation is a more common one. Assume, for instance, a lawyer is called upon to represent an investor charged by a stockbroker with failing to pay for securities he purchased, and that the lawyer represented the stockbroker briefly ten years earlier in the underwriting of totally different securities to the public. Where there is no connection between the incidents of representation, and no confidential knowledge bearing on the investor's case acquired in the earlier underwriting representation of the broker, there is no legal reason for the lawyer's services to be refused the investor based on the prior legal representation. Of course, the lawyer should disclose the prior representation to the client so that the client may determine his ease with the situation.

The modern trend is to fortify the right of each party to counsel of his own choosing. If a client knows of a prior representation by his attorney of the other side, and chooses to proceed anyway, he may do so. The other side may, however, raise the question that his former lawyer's presence is prejudicial to him, and seek to remove him. This often happens in matrimonial cases, where unscrupulous matrimonial practitioners, simply for harassment, seize upon an opposing lawyer who may have had earlier relationships with both spouses. The burden of removal rests with the moving party. Prior representation alone is not enough; prejudice must be proven.

Conflicts in representation are not restricted to litigation. They can arise in insidious ways. Take the example of two old friends and partners, Greene and Cone, in a manufacturing business. There is no partnership agreement—there never was in thirty years of partnership. The business used one lawyer, Grey, who had close relationships to both partners. Greene himself retained Grey for his personal matters, including the preparation of his will. Suddenly, Greene dies, leaving a widow and two children. Mrs. Greene, if she is typical, never before dealt with a lawyer alone, but now a lawyer is needed to probate her husband's will, handle his estate, and to counsel her generally. It is natural for her to reach out for Grey, her husband's lawyer, the one whom he trusted. But under these circumstances, Grey may prove the worst choice imaginable. If he continues to represent partner Cone and the business, he can easily find himself in conflicting circumstances. Mrs. Greene, the widow, is interested in withdrawing capital from the business for her personal needs, including her children. Cone wants to reinvest in the business. Most usually, Cone, who got along so famously with Greene, will not have the same relationship with his widow. She draws an income from the business without working for it—a customary arrangement under the circumstances—and it is a unique partner who will not eventually resent the unearned draw and who will not ultimately conclude that he was always the more important partner and now should get more. After all, Greene is dead and the business is running fine under Cone's stewardship. Does that not prove something?

Lawyers, like other economic creatures, quickly recognize which is the buttered side of their bread. The continuing partner is alive and a source of renewed business; a partner's estate is likely to be a onetime thing of lesser magnitude. Accordingly, in counseling the widow vis à vis her business attitudes, the lawyer is under strain. Should the widow wind up selling out to the surviving partner, her lawyer's conflict will pop out into the open, since he openly represents two sides of a negotiable transaction. Unlike trial practice, a lawyer can represent, with consent of both sides, the two parties to a contract. But dual representation, even on consent, is usually a bad idea, which at least one client, and often the lawyer, later realizes. Seasoned lawyers suggest that one of the clients, usually the economically subordinate one, the one not to control any ongoing enterprise, should get another lawyer. He may even recommend one, or, better, an alternate few. The client should be sure any new referral lawyer is truly representing her independently. It is asking too much to expect that lawyers will recommend enemies, so that client caution is maximally indicated with this kind of referral. Lawyers understandably resist bringing possible competitors too close to their client relationships.

For the same general reasons of conflict of interest, a business partner is normally well advised not to name his copartner as his executor in his will.

The problem of separate lawyers is a serious one for those who form a business together. Habitually, at the outset of an enterprise, good will is abundant. Many would-be partners will, for instance, use the same lawyer, the one who will handle the business, to suggest and draw the terms of the partnership agreement. The lawyer often prefers this mode, since it best protects his own position as the ongoing legal representative of the enterprise. It also costs the partnership community the least. Experience shows, however, that it is a poor idea. Each partner should be separately represented. Similarly, a potential employee of a company should not rely on its lawyer for legal advice against the company.

Retaining a lawyer who represents another client in the same line of business may also raise conflict questions. The practice is common enough and acceptable, particularly where specialists are concerned, providing the lawyer does not involve himself in circumstances where information or status gained in the course of one representation will appear to prejudice the other. Full disclosure to and acquiescence by clients competing is always desirable.

Going into an investment with a lawyer coprincipal where the lawyer will represent the business entity presents two problems: one is the representation of the client as he goes into investment; the other is the continuing representation of the entity itself. Full prior disclosure is again the key. No client is well advised to rely on a coinvesting lawyer for his legal counsel going in. Representation of the entity is, however, less personally focused and is quite generally acceptable, with suitable prior disclosure.

It is totally unwise to hire any lawyer whom you cannot discharge gracefully. This category is a subjective one, but habitually encompasses relatives, friends, co-worker lawyers at a client's regular work place, and people to whom money is owed.

─────────POLITICAL PULL─────────

Political "pull" is legendary in client regard and rarely available to any of them. Too many political lawyers, those who trade on political influence, tend to be "fifty percenters." This means, in general political parlance, that any reasonable cause has a 50 percent chance of success even when left alone, a kind of informal law of averages at work. The political lawyer makes his fee arrangement (no guarantees, of course), and if the law of averages is not repealed, the lawyer becomes a well-compensated hero enough times.

The principal legitimate advantage of political status is an ability to communicate a problem at an appropriate level of government. Well-connected political operatives do offer this facility, which can be valuable. For this reason, political expertise is often helpful in lobbying for legislation. Moreover, a slow-moving matter may be accelerated by a lawyer with some political force. Public officials with an eye to advancement are attuned to lawyers with perceived political clout.

A big downside of hiring lawyers for politically oriented results is that you may waste your money on exorbitant fees that buy nothing but a blind item with an enforced air of mystery, which is part of the trade. Worse, your case may have suffered because of representation that is insufficiently serious or improperly addressed to your true problems. Reliance on bare political pull may deprive you of a vigorous, properly prepared, and persuasive address on the merits. A special hazard is that your politician may be not well regarded, even disliked, distrusted, and therefore a source of danger to you merely for associating with him. In addition, many civil servants, the ones who do the work, flatly resent political interference of all kinds, or hints, particularly when their jobs are fortified with Civil Service tenure. If clients have offensive political lawyers, they need few enemies in the Civil Service.

It is difficult for clients to assay the truly effective political operatives and their proper operating sphere. Lawyering ranks are crowded with false representations of political weight. Mere prior office-holding means nothing. Except for the very few unusually powerful political figures, for problems conveniently addressable by them, political pull means little, and on balance should be disregarded as a determinative factor in general legal selection. Of course, there is never harm in good political standing, and often benefit, where a lawyer of discretion holding it otherwise meets appropriate standards for retention.

COST

Expense is expectedly a factor in lawyer selection. This leads some clients into lawyer shopping, which is appropriate. When the shopping is done by corporate house counsel, an experienced user of legal talent, the buy is most likely to be satisfactory. However, the selection of lawyer by price alone can lead to most undesirable effects. Sophisticated clients understand this well enough; lawyering is a highly personalized activity. But sometimes even these veterans grade their matters as to how costly a lawyer they really need for a given act. There are, after all, differences between a murder defense and a speeding ticket, between a $700 collection and piracy of a prosperous business, between an unfair trade practice injunction and an eviction of an apartment tenant for nonpayment of rent.

There is no answer to the question "How good a lawyer do I need?" The easier question is, "How badly can I get hurt?" Its corollary is, "Is it worth enough to me to give it a quality try?"

The better-known and more expensive law offices have client-acceptance policies that preclude the less affluent. Time chargers will not accept contingent-fee payment, even for the high percentages that make it possible for other lawyers to handle even the weaker speculative cases. Noted criminal lawyers will not take traffic cases. Big real estate lawyers do not close one-family homes in the suburbs except as a courtesy. The same applies to small estates of decedents. Only some lawyers and law firms will handle small collection work at all.

Price may be lowered for lawyering at large by moving away from the bigger, better-known established legal operations to lawyers of lesser public reputation, overhead, and financial expectation. The trick here is in their identification. These lawyers maintain within their ranks a full range of talent. Such retention is often a client blessing, for smaller firms and solo practitioners may be more involved with the types of transaction at hand. These lawyers can often attack and solve the problem without the "big deal" approach endemic to large-firm mentality.

"How badly can you get hurt?" Much lawyering is routine, and calls for attentiveness and experience, not brilliance. But from time to time a catastrophe develops from a minor matter. For instance, a routine one-family-house closing is a simple legal transaction. Notwithstanding the flaming emotions that attend many of them, as, for instance, where a light fixture beloved by both seller and buyer is removed, or the garden-tool inventory is shorted, the legal part is easy, particularly where there is title insurance. Yet it is conceivable that an irregularity that should have been provided for, but that was overlooked, can cause considerable grief. The client may have sold one home and cannot move into the one he bought, which is tied up in litigation along with its down payment.

Where there is little money involved, a will need only be clear; the competence for simple wills and simple affairs is widespread. In small cases, where definite sums of money are at stake, claimed or owed, the client measures his gain or loss against the legal expense. Very few clients would knowingly pay $5,000 to collect $1,700.

Client concerns for the fee-paying arrangements should always be discussed clearly in advance, and preferably reduced to writing. A client should never accept evasiveness on fee charging, or any airy dismissals that "we'll get along." The times when lawyers suing clients for fees were ungentlemanly and perhaps unethical are long gone, and the lawyer is in the suing business. Where there is no prior or special relationship governing amount of fee and time of payment, careful lawyers send confirmatory letters or agreement forms to clients, particularly where the matter promises to be extensive. It is to the best interest of both lawyer and client that there be no misunderstanding as to fees or reimbursable disbursements.

Clients are normally more comfortable with fees billed regularly at relatively frequent intervals, monthly or quarterly. This keeps the client abreast of his costs, and prevents the unwelcome arrival of a huge lump-sum bill. Of course, there are business clients, particularly, who prefer to be billed as late as possible, the longer into the future the better. This deferral is, in effect, an interest-free loan from the lawyer. Periodic billing and prompt payment are obviously the lawyer's preferred mode, except where he is himself deferring receipt of a payment to a subsequent year for tax reasons. The last quarter of the calendar year sees a slowdown in legal billing in some law firms for just such reasons.

Understandably, clients are often unhappy with time charge billing because of its open-ended character. They often press for a dollar limit. This effort is not customarily successful with established time charging firms, unless the quoted limit is unrealistically high, or the lawyers are reaching out for the particular client. Time charging law firms in the strictest form of their fee art do not like to estimate the possible size of their ultimate fees, but under sufficient client pressure most firms will estimate a fee range. The frequent desire of the lawyer to soothe the would-be client is complicating. While the lawyer may consider that the language of the fee letter suitably hedges the flexibility and nonbinding nature of the estimate, clients steer by the estimate, which becomes part of their expectation. The rule of thumb for clients to hold in approaching time charging is: "It will cost more than you thought."

───────IS A LAWYER NECESSARY?───────

In my enthusiasm to discuss lawyer selection, I should not ignore the question of whether the would-be client needs the services of a practicing lawyer at all.

A good part of law practice involves things a client can do for himself. Going directly to a government agency for information is a prime example. Much depends on the level of complication of the inquiry and the nature of the help sought. Direct inquiry of a local development office, for instance, will give valuable information on the background of opening a business in a different state. Small-business agencies assist in the start-up of new enterprises. Internal Revenue operates an intensive outreach program for tax return assistance. Consumer-affairs agencies abound across the country. Municipal law-enforcement officials are customarily alert to citizen complaints, particularly against such publicly unpopular targets as real estate promoters, landlords, securities "boiler" shops (high-pressure sales tactics via telephones embanked in an office), and the hucksters of all kinds of products. The political mileage in righting these wrongs should be discernible.

Resorting to the government is obviously inappropriate when one is seeking advice to "get around" a blocking legal provision. Generally, the weakness in resorting to governmental advice is that there is no assurance of competence in officials simply because they sit in a government office. Their advice, moreover, is necessarily limited by levels of training and inclinations to go "by the book." The client who seeks specific advice, tailored to his situation, must seek his own lawyer.

Enforcement is a sometime thing. Public interest in a question or a crime normally must be apparent to bring the public prosecutor to an investigation. Law-enforcement offices uniformly refuse to act as debt collectors in private disputations, although they will act in cases of widespread hoaxes or swindles. Consumer-affairs agencies, on the other hand, are more willing, where mandated, to intervene in isolated or private noncriminal transactions. Their efforts are frequently circumscribed by budgetary constraints.

The belief that there is magic incantation in legal verbiage leads many people to lawyers for the interpretation of letters and documents they could otherwise read themselves. Agreements of all kinds, printed, typed, or handwritten, relating to employment, terms of sale, and use of property most often fall within this category. So do government regulations. Much of what a lawyer sells is confidence. For this reason, the demeanor of his lawyer is important to the client.

Representatives of unions, the American Legion, the NAACP, and many other organizations, as well as hospital and social workers, often give advice as to entitlement under social-assistance laws and practices. They effect referrals to the agencies, and they may call or write the appropriate government officials, either putting the client directly in touch with the help source or acting as a conduit.

Recourse to good lay books on the law is educatively useful, and may assist in identifying rights and problems, but they should not be the base for a legal course of action. Such books, whose purpose is to bypass lawyers, are known as "sue-it-yourself" manuals.

It is truly said, *ad nauseam,* that the lawyer who represents himself has a fool for a client. The lay client who has himself for a "lawyer" is in even worse shape. The most dramatic example of the lay client in action as his own lawyer is when he represents himself in court in a contested matter. This kind of court appearance is called *pro se* (for himself). In most places a corporation cannot appear *pro se*. Sometimes the action is forced by economic circumstances—the person really cannot afford a lawyer and he does not qualify for legal assistance. There are occasions, moreover, when *pro se* appearances are tactically useful. In one highly publicized proceeding in New York, a well-known lawyer personally on trial on criminal charges summed up to the jury for himself, even though competently represented by others. This procedure in effect enabled him to testify to the jury for himself, to say things without fear of cross-examination and generally to lay down circumstances of sympathy with impunity. It worked. A nationally followed Florida murder trial saw a nonlawyer wholly conduct his own defense, which resulted in his conviction. Intelligent, articulate parties, with some sensitivity to court procedure and a grasp of their case, may be able to help themselves, but strictly in terms of legal protection and advantage a capable lawyer is a better choice.

Judges look with disfavor on laymen conducting their own trials, since their participation is usually the signal for messy disruption. They must avoid seeming unfair to the represented party if they lean over backwards to help the unrepresented one. Laymen do not understand rules of evidence or the proper phrasing of questions, and they rarely pursue effectively any advantages they may have. Their temptation is to argue with their adversary when questioning him. My experience is that unrepresented parties generally come off poorly in trials. Very often their supposed inability to hire a lawyer is not really believed. The judicial suspicion, particularly of the more educated self-representers, who theoretically can do the best, is that they could be straining themselves a bit more to hire a lawyer. Their self-appearance is quickly taken, only sometimes mistakenly, as a sign of disrespect for legal procedure.

The rising costs of lawyering have promoted a "do-it-yourself" approach. Divorce kits for uncontested matrimonial actions are sold in many places. These consist of printed forms in which the party who would not be a client only need fill in the blanks. A kit may sell for $50 to $100; a lawyer's fee might be $750 for the same matter. One author published a widely selling book on how one can avoid the probate of a will on death and the consequent estate administration by transferring during one's lifetime all one's property into a revocable trust. As might be expected, a general do-it-yourself aid would not address the specific affairs of any one person. However, the risk-reward ratio between the net fee conserved and the amount of property involved is a significant equation. In uncontested matrimonial cases, if no children or property are involved, where the proceedings themselves are steeped in artificiality, the do-it-yourself kit can make sense. The revocable-trust procedure is much too fundamental a device to assume without specific legal advice.

In perspective, it must be observed that there are courts in which no lawyer is necessary or even desirable. Small Claims courts are the best example, since these forums were created for the express purpose of enabling a hearing without the expense of a lawyer. Typically, only corporations or business or commercial people use lawyers there. Domestic Relations courts and those courts hearing breaches of the peace and minor criminal and traffic violations are accustomed to many participants without lawyers.

A final recourse, taken by a growing number of would-be defendants, is simply to flee the jurisdiction, a practice so common in the matrimonial field as to be known as "the poor man's divorce." But flight is not restricted to the poor. From the beginning of time, debtors of all means have taken to physical escape. I have seen in my court a number of instances where husbands grabbed all the family assets and fled to Europe or Hong Kong, beyond their wives' effective alimony reach. The newspapers amply reflect the rich and well known who jump bail or who leave the state or the country to avoid prosecution or suit. Spiriting a child who is the subject of a heated custody dispute to another jurisdiction is becoming par for the course. And there are those who flee without the threat of any judge's gavel. They go to save taxes, avoid union obligations, or amidst a whole panoply of motives. I should like to report to you that virtue is always its own reward, but I cannot. I can only wonder at the personal damage sustained in warping a lifetime to avoid transient legal or economic hardship.

───SETTLEMENT DECISIONS───

Among the burdens of clienthood is the decision making involved in case settlements. While the lawyers are the ones with the legal expertise, in the end it is the client who must either make or agree with a final decision to accept or reject a settlement.

In commercial cases, the lawyers have a quaint expression for passing the buck; it is "a matter of business [client] decision." Actually, compromise is the client's sole affair in every serious sense, except where there is a contingent fee. But, in all truth, most clients have no real way of appraising their cases in terms of legal merit or practicality of success in court. Theoretically, if a client has insufficient confidence in a lawyer, that lawyer should no longer represent him. However, it does not usually work out that simply. Meaningful settlement proposals tend to come after considerable lawyering has already been done, and lawyer removal at that point can be costly because of the need to familiarize a new lawyer with the case. It may also prove more of an emotional burden than the average client can bear. In contingent-fee cases the lawyer is truly a partner, and disassociating him is an especially costly action. There is always the possibility that the judge will not let the lawyer leave the case in its later stages.

Acting against his lawyer's recommendations is a serious matter to a client, since the lawyer is his authority, and his odds maker. Clients who reject their lawyers' advice, and wish to speculate on a result with a settlement sum within their grasp, vary greatly in disposition. There are the hunch gamblers, the pugnacious, the emotion-bound, the infallible, the foolish, and those with different needs. There are those incapable of making up their mind, who require the authority of judicial decision. There are those with a firm sense of rectitude, who insist on a court decision, as the righteousness of the occasion, regardless of the pragmatic sense of dispositions of convenience. There are those who simply think more of their cases than their lawyers. There are those who distrust their own lawyers' settlement motives, and there are those who simply will hate themselves in the morning if they do not see it through to the end.

Sometimes lawyers are unsympathetic with what their clients are doing; they may consider their demands or desires overly selfish, greedy, or ruthless. Lack of sympathy with client objectives is perennially a factor in legal advice. Clients must know that their lawyers are not slot machines to move equally with infusions of similar coin. Clients should be aware of any nuances of lawyer reaction and discuss them frankly with their lawyers at whatever stage of their relationship they might appear, particularly when settlement is urged. Are the legal odds the forces moving the lawyer, or is his personal point of view getting in his way?

———————THE LITIGATING WIFE———————

Matrimonial litigation embraces annulment, divorce, and separation actions, as well as alimony (maintenance) and child-support proceedings. It is typically the husband who has the bulk of the money in his control and the wife who is seeking alimony and child support. Under usual practice a wife who is awarded alimony will be entitled to reimbursement from her husband for her counsel fees, which are becoming increasingly substantial as the marriage-dissolution practice (both social and legal) burgeons. In a contested matrimonial action, the judge ordinarily determines the amount of fees, if any, the husband must pay for the wife's lawyer. Where the husband's resources are particularly slim or the wife's more than usually adequate, the legal-fee award may be reduced or eliminated.

As with litigation generally, the bulk of matrimonial dispute is settled before going to actual trial, although a formal judicial decree is necessary to alter the legal form of matrimonial status. The usual practice where there is no contest is to have the case submitted to a judge, with papers or a brief testimonial scenario sufficiently grounded to enable the legal relief sought, including the agreed financial settlement.

Significantly, the voluntary financial settlement usually includes a provision for payment by the husband of some part, if not all, of the wife's lawyer's fees. Regrettably, too many of the legal profession's less shining hours take place at this juncture. Many a negotiation starts, with total lack of subtlety, with a fat fee dangled by the husband's lawyer in front of the wife's lawyer to tempt his diminished effort. Sometimes it is even solicited. The wife is not present to hear this. More often, but of little added solace, the wife's lawyer may be relatively well meaning, but weaken in litigative resolution when the payment of his own fee, without further court work and with prompt assured collection, appears in what promises otherwise to be a long and difficult case. Judicial discretion is chancy to any lawyer, and a fee in hand is worth several in the courthouse landscaping.

In presiding over countless matrimonial cases, I have always been struck by the injustice affecting women, particularly those married for some time, who came to their maturity in preliberation times. Most men who have been through the divorce court grinder (and it is just that for both sides) are convinced that it's a woman's world. Not so, as I have seen it. Apart from the woman with independent means, the average woman who in 1984 has been married over fifteen years has little occupational skill and less separate money. Today's woman may be a different story, but her mother or older sister is clearly in trouble in court. The legal bromide is that for alimony the wronged wife is entitled to maintain her marital standard of living. But in most families there is enough difficulty in that maintenance within one household. Put the husband in a separate home and take into account his separate needs and it becomes plain that two cannot live cheaper than one. Inevitably, the wife's financial expectations are radically diminished, and intensely so under our system, where the husband fights every step of the way, including threatening to seek child custody to terrorize his wife for economic leverage.

Historically, matrimonial lawyers worked for wives on credit, relying on an ultimate collection from the husband. This compounded the problem of conflicting allegiances to the client or the fee. Today, there is much more of a trend to require the wife to post a down payment, or even pay a whole or partial fee on a time basis, subject to reimbursement to the extent the husband ultimately is liable for a fee. This new charging practice is a pattern change not wholly dependent on the fact that there are now more working women. Changing social patterns have made divorce big legal business. With the great bulk of experienced lawyers now operating on this new basis, women are driven to relatives, friends, miscellaneous jobs, or borrowing to produce their lawyers' fees. Of course, if the case involves a matrimonial lawyer's classic, a very wealthy and very errant husband, and a sympathetically pure wife, the credit pattern is more likely to continue. An interesting fee is secure here, since the husband is bound to be ordered to pay sizable alimony, and certainly child support if there are minor children. In this situation, the real chance being taken by the lawyer is that the parties will reconcile. On any scale of distaste, few lawyers rank higher than the reconciled husband's recoil at his wife's lawyer. Even the wife may become hostile to the lawyer. In this case, the lawyer, not paid in advance by the wife, usually looks to the husband for his fee. His fortunes ride heavily with the wife's willingness to take a stand for him as part of the reconciliation process. Unfortunately, the wife's lawyer is a low priority to the blissfully reunited couple, and the suspicion lurks that maybe he caused all the trouble in the first place.

The housewife in court is in the most difficult of positions to agree to a settlement. In her we find a compound of fiscal inexperience when it comes to the money matters of divorce (alimony, child support, and property divisions), bitterness, a distinct and often correct belief of being very wronged, with all the normal wounds. Worst of all for her client status, her adversary is usually the one person in the world who previously made her financial decisions. His judgment became her judgment. The working husband and the housewife make an incongruous couple in court, adversary clients, yet their lives previously have been characterized by a commonality. Often, the husband's very presence dominates and subordinates her. Little prepares that housewife for her role as combative client on her own.

Her lawyer becomes her confidant and her champion. Matrimonial lawyers accept this, and parts of their fees are earned for emotional unburdening and some plain and simple hand holding. When the time sheets are totaled, the magnitude of this emotional unburdening becomes apparent. Part of the size of current matrimonial legal bills, even where court proceedings have not been extensive, is in the repeated meetings and telephone calls. Unfortunately, a number of matrimonial and estate lawyers take advantage of the personal vulnerability of their women clients and carry hand holding to more advanced physical degrees. To be sure, temptation is heaped by some women out of their need to reestablish their desirability, or for many other reasons, including, perhaps, a hope that legal attention will be greater or the fee lower. In an extended matrimonial proceeding, lawyer and client get to know each other very well. It is not surprising that more than a few matrimonial lawyers find new spouses from among the ranks of their former clients.

But through it all the essential aloneness remains with the housewife matrimonial plaintiff. Her decision to reach a settlement with her husband can be specially wrenching, for by consensual act she participates in wiping out her past. Some women cannot do that and require the grinding unpleasantry of matrimonial litigation, including its expense, through a judicial solution. Some are so passive they will take anything to get out of the painful situation, others so resentful that they assume unreal cavalier attitudes of "Who needs him?" and ask for nothing. All of these clients could be the despair of matrimonial lawyers, and thick-skinned acceptance of their attitudes becomes necessary for sanity and survival to lawyers who practice matrimonial law daily.

It is better by far to settle a matrimonial dispute consensually than by judicial fiat. Many cases are destined to go to the bitter end, but whenever possible a consensual settlement, where the parties control the terms, is to be preferred. All of the frailties of the litigative process apply to matrimonial causes, with the added burden that adversarial courtroom litigation is an inappropriate vehicle for much of it. In the highly personal milieu of human relations, where reasoning is of limited use, where interchange is all, a setting of understanding with outreach for the facts and feasible alternatives is indicated, not cross-examination to the marital death. Certainly, child custody does not lend itself to the combative "win or lose all" courtroom process. Moreover, the personal preferences and life style of the judge are closer to the surface here than in any other litigation I know. His family and personal life are basic to his own perceptions of what is taking place. Given the huge amount of personal judicial discretion in matrimonial litigation, the person of the judge looms high.

The matrimonial client must remember the judge has heard all of it the day before. The calendars are cluttered with cases with the same emotional glaze, and precious little objective measurement devising. Matrimonial cases rarely wipe out one side totally. The crushing vindication so eagerly sought is hardly ever there. Judges constantly reach for the stuff of compromise, even as they draw the inevitable hard lines they must.

So it is in litigated matters generally. Judge and juries understand that only occasionally is someone all right and the other all wrong. Where there are middle grounds, courts move to them. It must be an improvement for the parties to try to attain, consensually, the measures more meaningful for them to achieve than to reach into the judicial grab bag.

——LAWYER WARINESS OF CLIENTS——

Lawyer wariness of clients is deeply ingrained. I mean this in no morally pejorative sense, but as a notation of the state of skepticism in which lawyers habitually operate. Clients do not necessarily lie consciously to their lawyers, although some do. It is more that people are advocative by nature and they suppress unpleasantry readily. The selective feature of memory is a wonder to behold. In addition, clients often leave out of their narratives things they believe immaterial or which they simply forget. A lawyer facing a client whose case may go to litigation may view him as sitting on the witness stand, and measure the way he might stand up to cross-examination. He searches his plausibility. Any client who has a lawyer who does not question him closely and skeptically on his facts should be in the market for a new lawyer. Those who deal with trained lawyers should be on notice that no matter the tears, the number of breast beats per minute, the lawyer takes everything he hears said with a grain of salt. Lawyers learn early to be wary of the distortive potential of self-interest, and these perceptions stay with them all their days wherever their professional trails lead them.

Collecting some legal fees in advance of services makes good economic sense on its own, but it is, in many cases, reflective of the concerns the lawyer has of his client. The lawyer is oftentimes like the surgeon whose patient will do or offer anything for him to ease his pain, but, once the surgery is over, and the danger is gone, turns casual about his obligations, even to the point of minimizing his former plight. In criminal cases a habitual practice of lawyers who continue to be successful in their practice is to collect their entire fee in advance. It is downright amazing how clients who seem to be of impecunious means can come up with their fee money when pressed.

An old German lawyer, an émigré, who never practiced in this country, warned me early in my career, "Never put yourself in a client's hands." By this he meant never do anything illegal or immoral for the client, since the client then has the misconduct as a club against the lawyer. The advice is good strictly on moral grounds and should be followed faithfully. I have found an additional verity to be that most clients, however sharp or ruthless, in the end have greater respect for the lawyer who unerringly takes the high road.

——CLIENT MISCONCEPTIONS——

A knowledgeable client tends to keep his lawyer in perspective as a legal adviser. While he may use his lawyer as a sounding board for his general decisions, or be respectful of his good sense, he remains conscious of his supremacy in his own personal or business choices and of his lawyer's true expertise, which is practicing law. However, many clients look upon their lawyers as more general than legal authority. Not accustomed to the situations in which they find themselves with lawyers, they transfer to their lawyers their dependencies for guides to conduct in strange circumstance, for nonlegal advice, and often for approval. Unfortunately, this may be a mistake, because lawyers as a whole are unreliable sources of business advice and are often lacking in the interpersonal perceptions requiring the giving of ground in personal disputations. The structured vocational training of lawyers meant to minimize risk taking is at odds with the "taking a chance" aspects of life and the economic angulations of business. Many a family, an estate, a trust, or a small business has foundered on lawyers' excessive attention to legal technicality, made dreadful by their inflexibility in relating to the relevant human conditions. A lawyer is not necessarily a general expert. Some lawyers are worthy of trust in a broad spectrum of business and personal affairs, but not all lawyers, and clients must stay aware of this.

A subtle retransference is at work where lawyers are overeager to move into the clients' shoes and propel judgments based on their own likes and dislikes of the people and the situations. Lawyers who are frustrated in the scope of their own life activities may rush more easily to economic judgment for clients in playing out their own emotional needs. As in the weighing of settlements of cases that lawyers propose, clients must have confidence in their lawyers, but must remain attuned to the separation of the nonlegal nuances that may creep into ostensible legal judgment.

It is a popular fallacy of clients that contracts are enforceable only if they are in writing. This is true for certain kinds of contracts, such as the transfer of an interest in real estate, or an agreement that by its terms cannot be completed within one year, or a guarantee of someone else's debts, but is not true for contracts in general. The importance of writing in many contracts is not its enforceability, but as a memorial to the parties of the actual terms of understanding. In practice, the most general hazard of oral agreement is poor memory, not poor intentions. Given the difficulty of enforcing oral, or, for that matter, written, contracts, the client's best assurances for contractual success lie in dealing with trustworthy people. Oral agreements are enforceable providing they can be proven. As some legals wag, oral contracts are not worth the paper they are written on.

Clients put great stock in writing letters. There is a belief that every letter must be answered and that every reply begets a further reply. As lawyers know, there are times to write and, more often, times to remain silent where disputation impends. The difficulty with the long tortuous explanations and exculpations in writing so dearly beloved by clients is that they are self-serving, and can be used to damage the writer with unexpected admissions in or out of context, as well as that they open up new grounds for attacking or trapping him. These painful letters, rich though they may be in injured rectitude, are best written and torn up.

Perhaps the most harmful client illusion is that during a trial he will be able to fence successfully with the opposing lawyer on cross-examination. He may even try to beat the other lawyer. This is the poorest of ideas. Clients refuse to accept silently an inevitable feature of trial work, that the other side takes its own turn and scores its own points. Practically no witness is a match for an experienced cross-examiner. Questioning can be done only by the lawyer; that examination is his thing. The witness's sole position is to respond to questions put to him by the lawyers and the judge. He has no assertive right of his own. Cross-examiners delight in the cantankerous witness who strikes out against his oppressor, because usually he comes across as evasive, argumentative, arrogant, or testy, none of which are traits that raise endearment in judges or juries.

I remarked earlier on the instinct of some clients to focus excessively on political "pull." The reverse side of that pattern is rampant paranoia when an opposing political figure of any silhouette is detected on the scene. Losing clients are amazingly ready to believe the worst, including the fact that the judge was "reached." To me, it is an unfailing wonderment that grown people, otherwise decent, go so readily to accusation of despicable felonies on the part of judges. Is it because they think of judicial misconduct not as really criminal but as somehow forming an inevitable part of an omnipresent political process? Or is it such an ingrained righteousness that the only possible explanation for their rejection is corruption? It is naïve to assume that no judicial corruption takes place anywhere, whether for money or for political accommodation. The evidence of history is too plain. But like Mark Twain's death, the many reports are greatly exaggerated.

CLIENT HANDLING

To be a client is also to be handled by a lawyer. Client handling is a separate art of the legal profession, not featured in the curriculum of any law school; probably its only courses are given in the school of hard knocks. Some lawyers never learn it.

Litigators seem to lean more heavily on a dispassionate professional approach. In their work, day-to-day client contact is unusual, except when actually in court or preparing for trial. Unless there is corporate house counsel working with them, pleadings, briefs, and other litigation papers, except personally sworn affidavits, are rarely subject to critical client review. Where the client is not a continuing one, such as might be the case with an insurance company, bank, or self-insured public utility, for whom litigation is a commonplace part of the regular business, there is typically little concern for ongoing relationship. The litigator is used to being in charge. While litigators vary in their willingness to reassure clients, in their patience with them, and in their toleration of suggestion, good trial lawyers insist on the continuity of their own best judgment. Since litigation is out of their hands, clients have little choice but to go along. Clients participate in grand strategy, but usually are guided along even here by the trial lawyer. It may be correctly inferred from all of this that a suitable store of determination (stubbornness) is useful to a trial lawyer.

Lawyers in business and personal affairs as opposed to litigators work in a different client context. Their activities constantly place them alongside the client at a negotiating table, and in constant touch by telephone and meetings. They draw contracts that embody clients' specific instructions as to the essentials of a proposed transaction. They counsel clients in face-to-face sessions, with personal interaction effecting constant shaping and reshaping of advice and alternatives. Necessarily, the so-called business and personal "office" lawyers must take the client into more daily account. Office lawyers are keener on keeping in touch with the client. In larger law firms, where a corporate partner, for instance, turns a client over to a litigating partner to run a contested lawsuit, it is most often the corporate lawyer who calls the client, or hounds the litigator to call to keep the client posted. Obliviousness of many litigators of the need to handle the firm's clients, to touch them, is the despair of many of their commercial and corporate colleagues. In a loose sense, the trial lawyer sees himself as the soldier, and the office lawyer as the politician. The problem becomes particularly acute when office lawyers refer a trial matter to an unaffiliated trial lawyer. Not only is that trial lawyer unlikely to extend to the client maintenance courtesies, but sometimes even the referring lawyer is lucky to hear from him. Naturally, the client complains to the referring lawyer.

Lawyers who are important business getters understand full well the necessity of steady client contact, and maintain the practice. Litigators, on the other hand, may receive their principal business by referral from other lawyers, and entertain fewer thoughts of bedside manner towards the people they represent. The vestigial barrister-solicitor dichotomy from English mores finds some counterpart here.

Client expressions that always interest me run along these lines: "I want a lawyer to tell me what I can do, not what I cannot do"; "There are lawyers who are deal makers and lawyers who are deal breakers." A client who searches long enough will find a lawyer who will advise him that he can do anything. He can also find lawyers who will go along with virtually anything the other party wishes, so that he will not be in a position of displeasing his client by seeming to hinder the deal.

Emphasis on what cannot be done connects to the essential negativism of many lawyers. The safest legal course is to say "No." Medals are not awarded for legal heroism; it is an unappreciated trait in the end. Lawyers prefer to err on the side of caution, and to point out that there are degrees of risk and that their assumption relates to the rewards to flow from taking them. A certain negativeness is healthy in lawyering, to counter client exuberance. Lawyers get paid to stand their ground.

Extreme caution in guiding a client is not, necessarily, a function of personal insecurity, although it may be. Bear in mind that legal training inculcates the safest course. Lawyers who render opinions used to induce third parties to act, such as bank lenders or buyers of securities offerings, are becoming increasingly cautious because of the possibilities of their own personal legal liabilities. Specialists tend to run to the overly cautious, since their training is narrowly but intensively focused to a relatively small field compared to law as a whole. They become so immersed that they see shadows that outsiders, including the Internal Revenue Service, would never contemplate. It is a marvel to see the number of angels that can be made to dance on the head of a tax lawyer's pin.

Legal caution must be laid alongside the practical urgencies of the client who needs the loan or the proceeds of the stock sale and who can ill afford for business reasons a tax position that is urged. Some professional courage must be sprinkled on the scene. When is the lawyer being too cautious in his honest insistence that the client disclose more information or that he should stop the trading in the securities? Or that a voluntary disclosure of facts not strictly required be made on a tax return? Obvious frauds or abuses of public interest prompt easy answer. The real problems come from the close judgment calls of uncertainties engendered by such fuzzy legal concepts as "fair" disclosure, "reasonable" man, "material" event, "willfulness" of intent. All things being equal, the safest course is the most conservative thing to do. But all things are not equal where the client will be unfairly injured by overly cautious lawyering. Here, there is a balance of risk; business harm to the client, normally palpable, against legal risk, often unquantifiable, that grave penalties may attend the client if he follows a certain course. Here, perspective is king.

Making deals rather than breaking them involves the lawyer's own personality inventory, creativity, intellect, expressiveness, flexibility, and grace of demeanor. There are definitely creative lawyers with superior talents in formulating and closing transactions. Patience, persistence, and persuasiveness are the prime virtues here. Many lawyers could not close a difficult deal if their lives depended on it, and a client disregards at his own risk his lawyer's limited capability. This is an area where a client's instinct must serve him, since it is his deal that has to be done. If he slouches behind his lawyer, who is recognizably deficient in negotiations, he alone must take the blame for a failed transaction.

Litigators are generally poor negotiators of business transactions; too often they stumble over their own combativeness rising to win unnecessary points. Litigators have ingrained tendencies to press for more and to resist concession. They may not know when to let go. Their training makes them suspicious of opening up their positions too early. Their trials are structured events, which shape their time frames, and their judges provide a fulcrum around which they work for cash settlements. The more free-and-easy styles of commercial negotiations are strange terrain, in which they become lost and unduly hostile to the natives.

Before leaving the subject of clients, I must comment on the two extreme positions of client handling. As with all extremes, most real cases fall somewhere between the polarizations. Among lawyers, there are the "terrorizers" and there are the "soothers." As might well be imagined, the terrorizer trades in dire consequences; he scares his clients out of their wits to enlist their engagement and to ensure their adherence. The soother takes the opposite tack; he urges that everything can be handled to satisfaction. The soother alarms the client as little as possible; he feels clients fare better on assured tranquility. Even soothers, however, must be careful in pending litigation to hedge adverse outcome, for they risk early egg on the face. Litigative results may become apparent too fast, right out in the open courtroom. Terrorizers flourish in the arena of government regulation, since government administrators hold such a conspicuous lock on the lawyers who specialize in their agency. Soothers flourish more where transactions are bound to pan out, or where no adverse consequence or court action immediately overhangs the recommended action.

The soother is usually more successful at attracting clients, since he infers that all will go well; he assures the client of his interest in the case and his belief in it. Clients like lawyers more if they think the lawyers like their cases. It reinforces their own belief, and they feel that a lawyer who believes in a case will fight harder for it. While a truly professional lawyer can take either side of a case with equal zeal, it surely does not hurt, clients reason, that the lawyer feels good about their side of the case.

9

SELECTING
JUDGES

The greatest single blemish on our legal system is the way we choose our judges.

The ideals of justice for all, regardless of color, religion, ethnicity, or economic or social station in life are bound up with a participating judge who is, we would have it, wise, fair, firm, dignified, knows the law, and applies it without fear or favor. The common law is what its judges say and do.

Yet our system of judicial selection, which is no system at all but a potpourri of varying appointive and elective devices in fifty states and the federal jurisdictions, is essentially political and largely indifferent to assuring a regularized flow of qualified judges.

Politics constitutes the prime threat to judicial quality, but "politics" is a misleading word in a democracy; it points to both high and low roads, but it cannot be denied that we have a nation which has thrived for over two centuries with these same underlying political methods, and no other country has done better. The judiciary is part of government, and, inescapably, partisan politics are part of the price paid to relate the people to the courts, where the sense is generated that justice is being done to the governed.

Political training is not necessarily contaminating for service on the bench. It may, in fact, be excellent training, particularly for trial work, where sensitivity to the interaction of people is an essential. Since the trial judge is a presiding officer, much like a chairman of a meeting, political background can be an asset. The "street smarts" that go with climbing the political ladder are useful in handling difficult people, in measuring witness credibility, and in appreciating the true factual picture as it happens in ordinary life to ordinary people. It helps in judging crime and punishment. On the other hand, even aside from the more insidious implications conceivable, political training may be harmful for irretrievably damaging the will to do unpopular things, for indelibly imprinting the desire to give something to everyone, and for fostering an undue regard for the appearance of things. The instinctive lesson of politics is to protect yourself for a later day. Even appointed judges, without prior partisan political investment, quickly learn these lessons when ambitions of their own set in for higher judicial office.

——SELECTION OF STATE JUDGES——

Elections by the people are common judicial selective devices in the states, unlike the federal judiciary, which is wholly appointive. Critically, state court vacancies occurring between elections by death, resignation, retirement, or the creation of new judgeships are almost invariably filled by appointment, and those who are appointed are later generally seated permanently by election.

Where judges are elected, their terms vary for lengths up to fifteen years in Maryland and the District of Columbia, fourteen years in New York State, and down to six years in many states. Generally speaking, a judicial candidate appears on the Election Day ballot as a party's nominee, in the same fashion as the party's nominees for all other offices. Sometimes the judicial candidate receives his nomination by a regular party nominating convention, sometimes by a distinctive nominating conclave called a "judicial convention," through petition, and sometimes in a primary election. A few states use a nonpartisan voting approach.

State judges who are appointed are designated by a governor, mayor, or local governmental executive, depending on the particular jurisdiction, and are customarily subject to confirmation by a legislative body.

Picking judges by election has deep historical roots. The original New York system, for instance, vested all judicial selection in a Council of Appointment, a legislative committee of state senators. In 1821, the appointive power was transferred to the governor, subject to confirmation by the state Senate. Because of great inequities in real estate laws and practices, and public pressure by tenants, with open hostility to landlords, whose "control" of the courts was thought to be related to their influence in judicial appointing, the New York selection procedure for state judges was changed to direct popular election in 1846 and has remained largely so until today. Only the New York Court of Appeals, its highest court, is now appointive, although judges are appointed to intermediate appellate courts from the ranks of popularly elected trial judges. The New York turnabout and the populist appeal of election fostered in the United States by Jacksonian democracy in the second quarter of the nineteenth century established the early predominance of the elective procedure.

The advocates of election of judges urge that courts discharge governmental functions in which the people should have their say. Since judges often make law themselves, they should be responsible directly to the people. Many who favor election of judges point out that election is the American way.

Basic to the proelection stance is a fear of the "elite" and its dominance of the common man. The unmistakable philosophical backbone of elective proponency is that appointing results in favoring the rich and the powerful. Bar Associations, led by economically preeminent lawyers, so active in judicial recommendations, are felt to place undue stress on property rights.

On the other hand, the view favoring appointment of judges is doubly hinged. One part is the seamy underside of the political process. It turns the political argument against the elective adherents. Appointive proponents argue that electing judges brings to the courthouse all the undesirable attributes of the clubhouse. In the more affirmative part, they argue that better judges come from an investigative and selection process of responsible and informed people who know about judges and lawyers, and that professional merit can be suitably recognized only in the appointive process. Judges are professional and technical people who should be chosen for skill and knowledge. Public accountability is satisfied in that the appointing official is elected by the people and answers to them on Election Day for all his conduct, including his appointment of judges.

A surprise in assaying the whole controversy over electing or appointing judges is probably that most of what both sides say about their own position and the other is true. The controversy can be reduced to an issue of conflicting value judgments. But experience demonstrates, as we shall see, that there is considerably less practical difference than meets the eye in whether the selection system is elective or appointive.

JUDICIAL CAMPAIGNING

Judges nominated to run for judicial office are very different from other candidates. Their campaign conduct is impossibly limited by the Code of Judicial Ethics, the ethical precepts devised by the American Bar Association (generally opposed to electing judges in the first place) and ratified by most states. Even where not formally ratified, the Code serves as campaigning ground rules.

Canon Seven of the Code of Judicial Ethics is captioned "A Judge Should Refrain from Political Activity Inappropriate to His Judicial Office." It deals with political conduct and is designed to keep judges out of politics, except when they are running for judicial office. Unlike other political candidates, a sitting judge cannot run for a nonjudicial public office.

Under the Code, a campaigning judge must be dignified and encourage his family to equal dignity. He cannot pledge what he will do in office. He cannot state his position on controversial legal or political issues. He can describe his qualifications.

Standard judicial campaign fare includes a few jokes (dignified, to be sure), family references, educational material, and some general proposal for court or legal reform, which the nature of the office customarily renders the candidate powerless to accomplish in any event. Occasionally, if the crowd is right, and the media missing, a genuine point of view filters through, either that or a raunchy story.

Some years ago, I was a contender for a Democratic nomination for position of associate judge of the New York Court of Appeals. My schedule called for a speech at a largely Spanish-speaking political club in a New York City basement. The room was crowded with Puerto Ricans. The meeting itself was well run, with great skill and dignity, by a Latin woman in her late thirties or early forties, and the large crowd was most respectful to her and quietly receptive to the candidates. Later I found out that a good number of the audience spoke little or no English and were essentially there for the body count. My turn to speak came sandwiched between a local legislative aspirant and a would-be United States senatorial candidate.

Campaigning can be good for the soul and for the perspective; I learned a lot that night. It was early in the campaign and I was struggling to stay within the Code of Judicial Ethics by spinning an artful Cardozo-Holmes construct about the significance of appellate opinion writing that went over big with the intellectual clubs of Manhattan's East Side, but was visually becoming a Spanish omelet in that basement. As the audience fidgeted a bit, a hand shot up and an old man arose. "Judge," he said, "forgive me, but if you had a case between a landlord and a tenant, who would you favor?" I said, "Well, sir, that is not an easy question. Cases cannot be decided in advance. Results depend on the actual facts of each case." He digested that for a moment, and as I renewed my talk, he got up again. "But who would you favor, the tenant or the landlord?" "It all depends," said I. After two more interruptions like this, the chairwoman spoke to him rapidly in Spanish (of which I understood nothing) and he subsided.

I will never forget that chairwoman then turning to me and saying quietly and gently, "Judge, how could you possibly know what it is to be a poor Puerto Rican in this city?" The stark earnestness of her question drained all my stock answers. I thought of telling her of my own schooling in Coney Island, my own problems, that no one knows another's suffering, and that she could not know the special prejudices felt by my own people. But I could not bring any of it out. She was right. What did I know of the grinding poverty, the language barrier, the color discrimination, the educational deprivation? My own troubles were yesterday, and they were mine. Their troubles were raw and bleeding and were theirs. I could think to say only that we are all human beings, and to pick our judges we must figure what kind of person is before us. "You are hearing me, you have my record in front of you. I am standing before you answering all your questions the very best way I can. Vote for me only if you trust me as a person who will try to do right no matter who is standing before me." And I sat down. I can report that, happily, I received the overwhelming endorsement of that club, although I suspected, Holmes and Cardozo notwithstanding, my earlier promise to work for a Spanish translator in night court was my most effective offering. While I was thinking Holmes and Cardozo were important in their appellate nuances, those club members knew nothing was important unless that Spanish translator was in the only court most of them ever reached.

One postscript. It grew late and I was quickly shaking my way out from one hand to another when that same old man materialized at the door, blocking my exit. He grabbed my hand and squeezed it, then whispered in my ear, "You can tell me now—you got my vote— who would you favor, the landlord or the tenant?" I glanced around and, seeing no one else near, whispered in a low tone into his ear,

"You know," and winked at him conspiratorially. He winked back.

Election campaigns may have their faults as appointive adherents argue, but out among the people you learn important truths that are not in the casebooks. Months later, I reflected on this old man's concern with tenants' rights and remembered that the New York switch in 1846 to direct election of judges was the result of action precisely by tenant-oriented forces. *Plus ça change, plus c'est la même chose.*

There is obviously something peculiar when you tell someone to run for judicial office and then tell him for ethical reasons that he cannot really say anything controversial or political. If one is to ask the public for votes, he should at least be able to distinguish his candidacy. While cases must be judged with fairness on their particular facts as they unfold in court, judges do have social outlooks and they are continually called on to exercise them in the course of judging. Surely no one can be oblivious of the significance of a judge's personal views on welfare and criminal sentencing, his attitude on trade unionism, draft evasion, and sexuality, his perceptions of civil rights, affirmative action to aid minority groups, abortion, obscenity, marijuana usage, and a myriad of other legal causes. There must be ways devised to unlock the vital elements of personal philosophy.

Generally, judges are not excused from their court calendars to campaign, quite unlike legislators, who manage to adjourn their sessions, and executives, who can delegate their work. This is a practical restriction of no small moment.

An evil of electing judges is "ticket balancing." The conventional wisdom of politicians is that campaign tickets must be balanced for religion, ethnicity, and geography, and, more lately, for sex and for color. The balance wheels turn ceaselessly. Party leaders are not greatly interested in the caliber of the judiciary. They are more interested in the political concerns of greater job opportunities and the happier times made possible by such connections.

Ticket balancing by judicial fodder is even more atrocious when you consider that nominations for, say, the fourteen-year terms of New York's Supreme Court are habitually traded for the two- or four-year terms of local offices, sometimes even party offices. The campaign of the moment is the thing, and the fourteen-year judicial commitments are shrugged off. After all, there will be more judges, and what does it mean to the party anyway? One town leader actually told me at a meeting the time-worn bromide that "these judge appointments [*sic*] are nothing but trouble. Each one you make leaves you with twelve enemies and one ingrate."

——POLITICAL ''APPOINTMENT''——

In point of fact, judicial selection by election is today largely illusory. Aside from sporadic primary activity, which breaks out now and then, the election of judges flows from judgeship nominations handed out by party leaders. While elective political office in general is at the discretion of party leaders, judicial office is particularly so because of the use of judicial nominating conventions with party-selected delegates and the low number of primary races for judgeships where that option is available. Aside from ethical restrictions in campaigning, the nature of the office does not seem to attract the in-the-righters or the issue idealists, who are drawn in great numbers to challenge the existing political order.

In many political places, there is an aberrant feeling that sitting judges, or even potential judges, should not be involved in political contest for judicial office, and so the parties agree on these judges as "bipartisan" nominees. This means both parties agree to run the same candidates as part of a political trade. Since the bipartisan nominees of principal parties have no real electoral opposition, they are elected automatically. Truly, they are appointed by the party leadership.

This was the route by which I ascended the New York State Supreme Court bench in 1968. A trade was engineered in early summer for the fall general election, when several sitting judges and three new ones were to get bipartisan (Republican and Democratic) endorsement in the fall election. Notwithstanding my Democratic enrollment, I was appointed to the bench by the late Republican Governor Nelson Rockefeller in August to fill a vacancy occasioned by the resignation of a judge originally elected on the Democratic ticket. In early fall, those of us bracketed by the bipartisan fates received the Democratic and Republican judicial-convention endorsements unanimously. As a lifelong Democrat, I must say I felt a bit strange (and pleased) to be sitting on the Republican convention dais, staring out at a thousand Republicans, and getting every one of their votes without saying a word. I later received a third-party endorsement without appearing anywhere at all. In the general election some months later, I was gratified to note that three-quarters of a million of my fellow citizens opted for my candidacy, notwithstanding the fact that I spent no campaign money and did not make one single speech or conduct any electoral activity whatsoever.

With wry amusement, I recollected my earlier try at judicial election, for a lower court in 1953, when I had the Democratic nomination and nothing else in a suburban Republican stronghold. It was an exciting time for the whole family. The morning following Election Day, my daughter Andrea (now a lawyer but then a precocious tot) bounded down to the kitchen and asked, "Did we win?" When I told her that I had lost the election, she stood quietly, and then declared, "It's all the fault of those darned Republicans." But I guess "those darned Republicans" made up for it in 1968. Many times during that 1968 general election I reflected that if you are going to run for judicial office, bipartisanship is the only way to go.

Let there be no mistake, the appointive, as opposed to the elective, systems are themselves laced through with politics. Political considerations are constantly in the minds of officials who appoint judges. A decision by a governor or a mayor alone is in the hands of a person who maintains his career by significant political accommodation. The added requirement of legislative confirmation of an executive appointment is an improvement, but not much. Elected officials are intrinsically political in their workings, and, overwhelmingly, there is legislative acquiescence, with or without a brief show. Rejection arises only when the appointing executive is caught way off base in a newsworthy setting. It is the safe candidate, not the extraordinarily well-qualified one, who is the ideal.

One United States senator was quoted as saying of the federal appointive process: "I fear the Brandeises and the Carswells alike will be screened out and a high level of mediocrity will be enshrined in the judiciary." He refers to the bitter 1916 hearings, which led to confirmation by the Senate of the legendary Justice Louis D. Brandeis, who came to the United States Supreme Court directly from a lucrative private practice, leavened by great social activism and innovative legal methods, as well as being too Jewish too soon, and former federal District Court Judge Harrold Carswell, whose nomination to that court by President Nixon was scorned and rejected in more modern times amidst a great media outburst.

Unfortunately, a judgeship is in too many places simply considered a reward for past political services. Whether elective or appointive, no judiciary constituted on that basis can be very good. There is simply no legitimate place in our system of law for this attitude, because judging, properly done, is no sinecure; it is hard and demanding work. If a judge regards his position only as his reward, he is not likely to exert himself as he should, for what kind of reward would it then be?

Politics can be hard and cruel, and after a while the temptation to take a reward becomes an offer that cannot be easily refused. The battler for survival in political life, if he has no economic sustenance of his own to fall back on, is in a grim position. He knows no one stays in favor indefinitely. The dignified office of judge, prestigious, well paying by municipal standards, and often in relation to the actor's own prospects, secure, without endless night meetings and banquets, without late hours, without the constant wooing of people, becomes more attractive as life wears on. Those like him, who understand, are all around him on his same political scene. They want to help him from friendship or feelings of its being the right thing to do. Some day they may want that help themselves.

Can anyone guess how many judges got their positions by being "kicked upstairs" by executive appointment or by party nomination? How many political trades have been enabled by judicial bait? For the health of the judiciary, this part of political activity nurtures a painful infection.

THE FEDERAL SYSTEM

The all-appointive system for the federal judiciary is generally considered to yield higher-caliber judges on average than do the state systems. These are difficult measurements to make, since there are obviously some very poor federal judges and very superior elected state judges. Unlike all state judges, who have specified terms, federal judges are appointed for life.

At the rarefied United States Supreme Court level, the President's staff and the Justice Department consult in order to screen nominees, who are tried by balloon in the media, cleared by the FBI, eventually submitted to the American Bar Association for endorsement, nominated, and thence sent to the Senate. The same general procedure is followed for the more numerous choices for the Circuit Courts of Appeal (the regional appellate courts), but with less White House involvement. For the even more numerous federal District (trial) Courts, the White House profile is even lower. The overriding exception is always there for a favorite of a political favorite. The processes historically involve political negotiations with senators and other politicians from the areas affected. The statistics tell the story: according to a 1976 *New York Law Journal* study, over a fifty-year period, 90 percent of the appointees were of the same political party as the President.

Today's senators are more likely to confer with Bar Association leaders or to use their own screening panels, who gather names, screen, and report before making recommendations for District Court judges. Some senators exercise strict personal control, others relate to varying degrees to screening committees they constitute. Generally speaking, each of a state's senators of the same party trade turns in initiating District Court nominees, but eventually the other must concur. Traditionally, a senator of a party out of federal power may get some judicial recommending opportunity, perhaps 25 percent of the available judicial openings.

The role of the Justice Department in the federal appointment procedure is a disturbing one. The President must use his staff if he is to work successfully and efficiently; and, to him, his own professional corps of lawyers, many with high talent, is best equipped to assay would-be judges. On the other hand, the Justice Department is a major litigator in federal courts. Unlike the normal lawyer-client relationships, where the lawyer is purely representative, the Justice Department is part of the government, and in many ways is as much principal as lawyer. The thought of one side, already powerful enough, having a major role in the selection of the judges before whom it appears wars with the usual concepts of fair play. Too, it is not only appointment that relates to Justice Department favor, but also the promotion of the very judges before whom department lawyers appear. Ways must be found to discharge the federal executive selection function through an organ that is not itself the major federal litigating force.

While some federal judicial appointments arise entirely from reputation, largely in government legal employment, or the fortuity of having performed well in the direct vision of a recommending agent, it is clear enough that to get to be a federal judge you have got to know someone. The old bromide about who you know and not what you know recurs all too frequently in judicial selection, whether it be appointive or elective.

In judicial selection, the test should not be whether the judge will be good enough, but whether he will be very good. The federal bench, considered superior to the state judiciaries as a whole, itself has too many judges who are no better than marginally qualified, certainly when measured against the standards of accomplished lawyers.

The heaviest proportions of elected judges are in the trial courts, where the least social policy is set. The appellate courts, particularly the highest, make laws and establish public policies, but are more generally appointive. This seems a doctrinal inversion; yet the trial courts deal with the people and for all practicality dispose of most cases, whereas the appellate courts hold more need for professional competence in lawyering skills.

Appointment of judges, as opposed to their election, does not remove politics from judicial selection; it merely shifts it from one political place to another. However, it is a more benign political approach, somewhat more responsible, and yielding higher-caliber judges where there are meaningful merit-seeking initiatives and where media coverage focuses public attention on what the appointors are doing.

The constantly drawn federal analogy of the presumably higher caliber of an appointive bench is unpersuasive, since, court level for court level, the higher-prestige federal judiciary is more attractive as an institution and thus more of a magnet to better-qualified judicial aspirants. The state court stress on cases of negligence, matrimonial dispute, and street crime understandably leaves lesser judicial scope than does the more exotic federal legal gamut. An irony is that part of the prestige of the federal bench is its ostensible separation from politics, which, although not wholly true, is made believable because the clubhouse connection is more remote.

While my own inclination in governmental affairs is to trust the people, and to maximize the popular election of the significant policy makers, my unremitting perception is that the popular election of judges does not, under existing premises, work out sufficiently well. On present terms, appointment works better in the balance.

──────BAR ASSOCIATION ROLE──────
IN JUDICIAL SELECTION

There are many Bar Associations, of varying kinds and sizes, in all states and principal counties, cities, and among certain religious and political affinities, from the ABA on down. They speak from different vantage points and embody countless personal rivalries and conflicting ambitions for leadership positions and committee assignments. Most are called upon to make judicial-selection recommendations in some context.

The participation of Bar Associations in judicial selection has a mixed desirability. On the positive side, Bar Associations consist of lawyers, those who supposedly know the legal system best. They are informed people, holding relevant information for the selection task, who have demonstrated an active interest in the legal community.

There are problems, however, that call for perspective in any Bar Association role in judicial selection. Bar Associations are not truly representative of lawyers generally. While any one association can speak for the majority points of view of its own active constituency, it cannot speak for lawyers who are not members. For that matter, there is an inactive majority in most associations which retains dues-paying membership out of propriety, of an interest in receiving publications and announcements or occasionally hearing a lecture, of desiring eligibility for good insurance programs, or, perhaps, simply to have a convenient luncheon facility.

Bar Association leaders essentially act out an oligarchal pattern of succession. With the exception of maverick groups, they are the establishment personified. Economically successful lawyers as a whole become that way through association with people and corporations of means. They personify the white propertied elite of society. Moreover, the major city and metropolitan associations, which share dominance of the nation's Bar Association scene, typically feature those doing the "big-time" legal things—corporation law, securities, taxes, trusts and estates, important (big-fee) commercial litigation, real estate, and work in other financially fertile fields. Large and middle-sized law firms have great Bar Association influence because of the continuing influence of participating firm members on newcomers, and because their lawyers tend to have the time for the activity. A certain social respectability is seen to attach to Bar Association upper crusts. To be fair, there are educative and experiential functions to Bar Association activity, and participating lawyers are in the best position to take advantage of them.

General Bar Associations are not crowded by criminal or matrimonial lawyers, by those doing landlord and tenant work, by negligence lawyers, or by small-claims or consumer-oriented practitioners. Indeed, such types are relatively uncommon in larger Bar Association upper echelons. So, the Bar Association representative, presumably a spokesman of the legal profession and a watchdog of its service to the public, is not quite what he seems. The kinds of lawyers with which the vast majority of individual Americans deal do not readily boil up through the Bar Association processes, and the typical Bar Association representatives are unlikely to represent their views. Yet the work of the trial judges to be passed upon most significantly involves the fields of activities of these lawyers.

Bar Associations do not deserve their near monopoly of the nongovernmental role in judicial-selection procedures. The point is important not only in the federal appointment procedure, which makes a large unofficial grant of power to the American Bar Association, but also in the various "merit" schemes of judicial selection in which Bar Association participation figures prominently. Excessive reliance on Bar Associations tends to result in excluding the input of broad segments of the legal profession and of society itself. Unions, civil-rights groups, other organized legal groups, including poverty and public-interest lawyers, and educators, among others, should be able to convey authoritative meaningful impressions when it comes to qualifying judges, and should share that role with Bar Associations.

——————————MERIT SELECTION——————————

The trendy catch phrase of judicial selection through both the appointive and the elective routes is "merit selection," and this applies to both federal and state courts. This development is important for what it is and for what it is not.

Reformers have sought for years to introduce merit, not reward, as the judicial touchstone. But now that merit is "in," the rankest political scoundrel and most unscrupulous appointing executive wraps himself deep in some cloak of merit selection when talking about picking judges. It is now impossible to tell the sinners from the preachers.

The simplest and least effective screening method is the classic committee, communally balanced, appointed by a governor or mayor or political leader to advise on the merits of proposed judicial candidates whose names he publicizes with the solemn assurance that he will be voluntarily "bound" by the committee's decision. But so long as the committee is chosen by the appointor, it will be in his image and at his service. Political figures are not known for appointing enemies to do their work. I do not call these excursions "merit selection."

While competent judges have emerged from such mild screening processes, a process that narrows the field to a politically acceptable few remains suspect. Friendly committees do not distinguish between well-spoken personable people with professional papers; most every applicant who is not evasive, offensive, or some kind of horror will pass minimal muster. The worst feature of this light kind of screening is that it shields the deciding authority from the personal responsibility that is his in making the choice; and in practical effect it allows him to do his political dealings under the committee's virtuous mantle. In the shade of this simple screen, he may be fooling the public.

"Merit selection" is, strictly, a traditional phrase in reform judicial circles, derived from American Judicature Society initiatives in 1914 and a later and more effective sponsorship in 1937 by the American Bar Association. The approach to judicial selection posted by these organizations is the pioneer "Merit Plan" for our time.

Three elements are essential to the so-called merit plans: first, the nomination of candidates by a commission designed to be non-political; second, judicial appointment by an official (governor or mayor) elected by the people, sometimes subject to ratification by the legislature; and third, provision for a relatively short beginning term of office, subject to reappointment or a noncompetitive referendum of the people with some kind of question like "Shall Judge X be continued in his judicial office?"

Obviously, different methods are conceivable under these headings, and some states use different elements in different ways. Easily, the best-known merit plan is the 1940 Missouri Non-Partisan Court Plan. The Missouri Plan features a seven-member nonsalaried commission; three are lawyers elected by the bar, three are laymen appointed by the governor, and the chief justice of Missouri serves as chairman.

The commission gets publicity, and the bar and the public are invited to submit nominees. The commission considers suggestions from every source, and encourages interviews. After deliberating, the commission submits a list of three nominees, one of whom must be appointed by the governor. After the appointed judge has served a year, at the next general election his name and the names of judges whose terms have expired and who wish renewal are placed on a separate judicial ballot with no indication of party affiliation. The ballot is worded: "Shall Judge———of———Court be retained in office? Yes. No." There is no opponent; the voters simply vote "yes" or "no" for each sitting judge.

The Missouri Plan has many enthusiasts. While the nominating-commission feature is thought to be excellent, the referendum election is dubious. The "yes" or "no" plebiscite really is not a meaningful public expression; it appears to be a deep bow to democracy—in fact, it is nothing more than a clever intellectual sop. The fact of the matter is that in all the years since the plan's adoption, only one judge has ever been recalled by Missouri referendum, and he was, it is understood, a central figure in a notorious state scandal at the time.

A weakness of the referendum trumpeted as a virtue in one *American Bar Association Journal* article occurred in Missouri when several labor unions opposed some judges for their philosophies. In the referendum campaign, the judges ostensibly did not campaign at all, but the Missouri Bar Association roused the electorate, who presumably spontaneously routed the prounion forces and retained the judges thumpingly. While the Bar Association created the voter interest necessary for the judges to win, the article carefully refrained from suggesting that the Bar Association took any position on the issues. Yet the Bar Association carried the day, and the judges became indebted to the very class of people who made their living appearing before them. Indeed, in Missouri, the Bar Association is known to sponsor regularly secret polls whose results are publicized so the public may know how the lawyers consider the judges. Combined with the three nominating-commission members elected by the Bar, it would appear that the Missouri Bar leaders maintain a relationship of maximum comfort with their judges.

A real danger of judicial recall by referendum is that judges can be thrown from office on single-issue campaigns, such as tenants' rights. This was the case in Florida. Explosive issues such as abortion, homosexual rights, and school busing can blow a judge out of office, unrelated to his general judicial performance, but strictly as a vote in principle for or against the posed issue in the abstract.

The nominating commission is at the heart of true merit plans. As we have seen, if the appointing authority dominates the commission, the process is mostly a game for the public's entertainment. Merit procedure can realistically work out, free of political edge or favoritism, when there is a meaningful separation between the proposer and the selector.

The commission should have a civil-service staff capable of developing full information, and should generate its own applicants using its own procedures. The commission should be charged with making a limited number of preferred choices. The appointing authority, who must be popularly elected, must pick from among the commission's choices. Finally, the commission should combine a strong mix of lawyers and nonlawyers, with suitable community diversity.

The need for a separate staff relates to the independence of the commission. The ability of the commission to attract its own candidates is a safeguard that the pool will sufficiently be stocked with nonpolitical, nonfavored applicants. The dual points, of the commission setting up a limited choice, from which the appointor must pick, are vital, since a difficulty with most screening panels is the absence of meaningful limitation on the appointing executive.

While "highly qualified" is the highest cachet in merit ratings, it has no apparent appointive weight. For instance, in New York, where there are executive-constituted screening committees, the governor feels free to appoint anyone from a large field minimally designated as "qualified." When a long list of legal hopefuls is submitted by a shrewd politico, it is inevitable that the lukewarm appraisal of "qualified" will yield an assortment of eligibles to satisfy the appetite of the most political or personal of appointors. In other words, a real act of choice must take place at the commission level, a narrowing of substance that leaves the appointing authority leeway only among those the commission deemed the best. That is the only way to derive a collaboration in pursuit of merit.

The participating presence of lay people leavens the technicality of legal evaluation. Personality, character, and temperament are essential to judging, and those unencumbered by ritual drill, strangers to the fictions and posturings of the law and its procedure and operations, may see things that lawyers miss. Or perhaps see them differently. After all, the ultimate court consumer is rarely a lawyer; he is a lay person, one who must leave the courtroom with the feeling that, win or lose, he was in a place where a fair attempt at justice was made by a judge he respected.

──BLOCKS TO JUDICIAL QUALITY──

The expectations that people have of judges are very high, maybe too high. Different levels of talent are tolerable, and perhaps necessary. A modern-day Oliver Wendell Holmes, Jr., might be an ornament to a traffic court in Dubuque, but the failure to recruit him will not be devastating there.

The qualities that contribute to judicial goodness, such as character, intelligence, legal knowledge, patience, objectivity, diligence, compassion, dignity, courage to do the unpopular, resoluteness, and morality, are parallel to those that create sainthood, and there are precious few saints among all of us, let alone those in the ranks of judicial applicants.

Even the raw numbers are instructive. Assume there are over 600,000 practicing lawyers in this country, who form the entire pool for judicial selection, a quarter of whom are not in private practice. A *Time* article of some summers ago, captioned "Judging the Judges," and accurately subcaptioned "An Outsize Job, Getting Bigger," reported there were then 28,000 state and local judges, nearly 700 federal judges, and about 1,000 federal administrative law judges. This added up to 29,700 judges, or about one judge out of each twenty lawyers. The qualities of aggressiveness and ambition that drive many to the law often war with the requisite saintliness for the judiciary, as does the monetary lust overtaking so many of the legal brethren. When you dig deeper and separate out those of more moderate intelligence, of poorer character, of indifferent qualification, the political hard-liners, and those just not interested in the judging life, the stock of saints runs thin.

A high proportion of the most able lawyers of the country, those who appear to combine with their legal skills the desirable traits of character, never get into any position where anybody will call them to the judicial colors. The distaste of many of these lawyers for politics and for what has to be done to make headway in it ensures their obscurity.

Money, of course, is a big judicial deterrent. Although judges may make good salaries by public standards, experienced lawyers of high ability are accustomed to earning several times those sums. Well-qualified judges regularly leave the bench because of their inability to maintain their desired standard of living. But government service could never match private practice in money. The pricing structures of government and private sectors in our times preclude from public service lawyers who steer their legal courses by the money constellation alone.

Yet there are those lawyers, both those already financially secure and those willing to adjust to a judge's pay scale in the interest of personal challenge or in the fulfillment of a judicial career, who disregard their superior economic opportunities in private practice and opt for service on the bench. Their numbers seem, unhappily, to be diminishing. Judging is hard work for the conscientious, the loads are heavy, public gratitude is in a deficit position, and such a choice is not easy for affluent lawyers. This observation is notwithstanding Finley Peter Dunne's Mr. Dooley, who commented in "The Law's Delays": " 'If I had me job to pick out,' said Mr. Dooley, 'I'd be a judge. I've looked over all the others an that's the on'y wan that suits. I have th' judicial timperament. I hate wurruk.' "

In measuring the willingness of qualified lawyers to do the work, a true appreciation of what judges actually do is an important insight. Not all judges do the same things. There are marked differences between higher and lower courts, trial and appellate courts, and specialty courts. A lawyer with a judicial opportunity must factor the particular court opening available. Most lawyers who respect their profession and do not reasonably harbor higher prospects would put aside their practice for an opportunity to serve for life on the United States Supreme Court. But that is only nine at a time. The prestigious federal and state benches are greater attractions than the lesser ones, and down the line. Each private-practicing lawyer who really wants to be a judge, not the "wouldn't it be nice" variety, has his own crossover point of level of court lure against the sacrifice of giving up his practice.

For these reasons, many, perhaps most, of the fine judges come from municipal-law backgrounds. They enjoy public service. They spend a good part of their working lifetimes as district attorneys, county attorneys, corporation counsels, United States attorneys, and lower-court judges. Their salaries as judges may be the highest income they have made or, for that matter, to which they aspire. They are more accustomed to staying put occupationally and geographically. Their life styles have values different from those of the huge economic producers of the law. Law school professors may also fit into this category.

Younger lawyers of ability who come to the bench early, before their practices mature and become sacrifices too great to give up, form a distinct talent reservoir, for they grow up professionally as judges. The time other lawyers devote to building a practice, they spend building judicial resources. Unfortunately, this category is the most susceptible to the temptation to leave the bench in order to bolster their income. Many of them have significant vested pensions just at the time their usefulness in private practice is at its height. Their time on the bench may leave them judicially jaded, or weary of it all, while still relatively young as lawyers go. Given a good alternative, they move on, with the feeling they have sated their judicial appetite.

Prejudice, plain and simple, diminishes the judicial pool. This is wrong not only on moral grounds, but also on the pragmatic basis of building a better judiciary. A bench overly preponderant in middle- and upper-class white males of traditional "American stock" is unsatisfactory. The widening of the pool of available judicial selectees makes more good people available. Moreover, courts have a group characteristic in that they show an institutional face to those seeking justice before them. The necessities of judiciary confidence, respect, and awareness compel attention to representative factors for women, blacks, Hispanics, people of divergent social and economic background, and even for geographic diversity. Nonetheless, a black litigant may appear before a white judge, or a downstater before an upstater, and only the individually assured traits of the judges can be protective of fair process. No system can ever assure every litigant a judge "of his own kind." Sometimes, the last judge a litigant wants to see is one who is likely to know him best or who identifies with his status but would feel disgraced by his action.

A mixed judiciary gives confidence to litigants individually and to society as a whole that the law is being rightly applied. Confidence in the courts is fundamental to a justice system, which must propound not only justice, but its apparency as well. A court with enough blacks is at least not a big white machine. The meaningful recognition on the bench of minority aspiration is a concrete sign of interest, which tends to foster confidence and respect. Too, judges issue opinions for others to note, and then judges have educative effects on each other. The presence of reasonably representative persons of different backgrounds and perspective works to enlarge the informational input of judges and lawyers.

Temperament is a factor in deterring judicial candidacy. Laymen fail to perceive that judging is an experience different from lawyering in many significant respects, in nature of work, and in necessary emotional equipment. The differences affect the appetite. Judicial work requires neutrality and objectivity, while some lawyers trained from professional birth to the promotion of the one side they represent thrive only on involvement. Judging is sedentary, and many lawyers seek out the activity of practice, with its challenges, rewards, and shifting locales. The bench is not a place for the restless.

A prime current discouragement to lawyers from seeking judicial service, and to sitting judges to continue so, lies in the increasing disrepute of the court system throughout the country. Where once being a judge was a hallowed affair, the goodness of holding the office has eroded alarmingly. Much judging is now administrative routine, or personally harassing, especially in the areas of great trial-calendar congestion. Much has been written about crumbling institutions in society, the courts among them. Whatever the cause, the effects are apparent. There is a great defensiveness in the judicial ranks; I can tell you that from my own career and familiar association with judges. The feelings are most acute among able and dedicated trial judges, the front-line judges to the population, who absorb unjustified abuse in enormous quantity simply as a matter of station. The good judges, for all their efforts, are pilloried along with the bad. All the ills of the criminal-justice system, the shortcomings of municipal finance, and the vast disorders of society are unfairly laid by irresponsible commentators at the doorsteps of all judges. It matters little whether the reckless mudslingers are politicians, policemen, journalists, or literary critics; it is open season on judges, who have no effective way of defending themselves, and in many places the question becomes "Who needs it?"

Irresponsible destructive accusations against all judges and all courts by demogogic governmental officials and politicians or by sensation mongers of journalism are eroding the very foundations upon which all our expectations of justice are based. Unfortunately, tearing down sells more papers than building up, and seems to get more votes; mindless resistance to change by judges and lawyers alike fuels these processes; and public disinterest finds its own reward.

CAREER JUDGES

An alternative approach to judicial selection that is rarely heard, and when the point does arise it is pointedly ignored, is whether we should have a nonpolitical career judiciary of professional judges trained from the beginning to be judges, who rise from assistant judges to full judges and from lower courts to higher courts. This is the practice in most of the free world outside the English-speaking world.

France, Germany, Belgium, and Italy, among others, have career professional judiciaries, which work well for them. These countries are not common-law countries, where case analysis is the key to legal rationalization, but, instead, stress statutory codes with rather rigid construction modes.

Could there be a supreme national court, as there is in Japan, made up of designees of the career judiciary itself, the organized bar, and the legislature, for popular input of elected representatives? Things can be done differently from the old ways.

There is a reflexive reaction in opposition to the notion of an American career judiciary. There is a rooted suspicion of an elite corps of judges presumably not responsible to either the executives or the legislatures, or, more fundamentally, to the people, although they could be made so. There is also the concern that sheltered career-ists would lack the life experience of private legal practice necessary to judicial qualification.

Yet no particular experience accompanies any new judge to the bench today. New judges may come directly from the ivy-clad cloister of law school faculties, government service, legal-aid societies, the political clubhouses, minimal law practices, narrow specialty practices, large law firms with limited ranges of exposure, as well as the ranks of the classic general practitioner. It is unclear why a career judge is socially deficient, particularly where he is specially educated for the precise function of judging. His training can even include social internships or work release periods. Career judges have families, circles of friends, membership in veterans' organizations, money problems, health worries, civic responsibilities, and perhaps jog two miles every morning. What kind of mill is prescribed for incipient judges now?

Does total concentration on judging as a separate process lead to judicio-technocracy in the overemphasis on rules and techniques to the exclusion of the intuitive, compassionate, and common-sensible factors that later arrivals to judging may have picked up en route?

It need not, although exclusive indoctrination in the authoritative stances of judging may unduly unbalance a person in the graces of humility. But many judges show signs of overappreciation of their importance without going to school for it.

In effect, the judges who rise exclusively through government law offices are careerists in an unbroken skein of public service, though, to be sure, they see the wrong side of the bench for some time. Federal judges are now placed in judicial orbit quite beyond popular control for life.

American tradition is such that a career judiciary has little chance of implementation in the foreseeable future. It is hard enough to lay four bricks in a judicial line, let alone a whole new court structure. But that does not negate the ideal of special training and education for judges, or the creation of organized mechanisms that will contribute to the regular flow of qualified judicial candidates.

Specific academic attention to judging would be useful training for law practice generally, and would benefit potential judges or even induce the aspiration. The best time for special judicial education within existing institutions seems to be postgraduate, starting with a basic course, which would then be extended by continuing-education requirements. Studies should cover the substantive and procedural aspects of judging, but also cover such relevant studies as economics, use of statistics, psychology, penology, and sociology. These would be too extensive for law school, which should give priority to basic lawyering skills in the time available. The postgraduate course of judicial study as a significant requirement of its own would work a marked screening effect in detecting strong judicial interest. A prerequisite course of study, conducted full- or part-time, day or evening, could create a base of qualification and thwart those strategically located politically but lacking in proper background from receiving judicial designation at the spur of a moment of political truth.

Special educational qualifications, which offer current institutional practicality without significant disruption, fortify the assurance of professional quality in any panel parade for judicial selection. It stocks the judicial selection pool so that a specially nourished fish must be caught. With a genuine certification as an entry qualification, the subsequent political or personality exercises of the panels, committees, or commissions not only become less damaging, but also actually gain a more beneficial flavor in shifting their accents to outright assessments of character, bearing, attitude, philosophy, and the other traits laymen all come to gauge in their daily lives. If that pool of eligible judges is sufficiently stocked and protected, the political pollutant can be reduced to safer levels.

10

VIEW
FROM THE BENCH

My view was from the bench of the New York State Supreme Court, on which I served as a justice for almost eight and one-half years. Notwithstanding its "Supreme" imprimatur, that court is actually the basic trial court of general jurisdiction in New York. I learned there not to be misled by hierarchical terms, for it is the trial court where the people gather personally and present their personal petitions for justice. A relatively small number of cases is appealed, and only a tiny fraction persists to the highest court. Of the cases that do go to appeal, a significant majority of appellate decisions give credit to the trial findings and affirm them. While it is habitually denied that lower-court legal decisions are presumptively correct, it happens that way in the great majority of appealed cases. This is because the fact-finding role at the trial level is primary, and appellate courts usually accept these factual findings unless they appear arbitrary. In addition, a certain amount of inertia attaches to decisional habits. Finally, although rules of law are very much susceptible to individual variation of interpretation, there are in many instances common understandings of the ways things should work out that are shared by judges and that stay in place unless some element triggers a departure.

ORDER IN THE COURT

Trial courtrooms are clearly no neighborhood social rooms. Their decor, featuring highly polished wood with governmental crests and flags, is a reminder that this is a hall of authority. Various people move officiously about, popping in and out of side doors. If any doubt persists, it is challenged by the entry of the judge, an ordinary man but cloaked in a ceremonial robe and a solemn look, to the fanfare of the bailiff's announcement: "All rise. Hear ye, hear ye, this honorable court is now in session, Judge Bruce M. Kaplan presiding. All draw near, give your attention and ye shall be heard. You may be seated." Something very official is afoot, and caution comes to mind quickly. This seems like an easy place in which to get into trouble.

Aside from criminal trials, where armed officers may be in the courtroom and occasionally their defendant charges may be manacled, courtroom decorum is maintained by respect for the institution and no little awe. The witnesses walk unescorted to the witness stand, the lawyers normally question in courteous tones, answers are similarly given; objections are made by the lawyers to the judge, ruled upon, and accepted with nothing more than a courteous explanatory interchange, or an occasional exasperated objection by a lawyer.

In matrimonial disputes, there are times when an embattled husband and wife may erupt into a shouting match, but order is customarily restored by a simple admonition from the judge. However, in the corridors of courthouses, between sessions, more than one wife's lawyer has been the beneficiary of a punch in the mouth by an irate husband. The veneer is thin, to be sure. In courts like Family or Domestic Relations, which proceed on an informal-hearing basis, with all involved family members standing before the judge for a summary disposition, often without lawyers, the noise volume is notably higher and considerably less dignity surrounds the domestic happenstance.

The key to maintaining order in trial court is the personal dignity of the judge. A shouting judge, florid of face, or snidely accusatory, encounters fewer tranquil scenes than do his steadier colleagues. Unfailingly courteous judges, who eschew humor or sarcasm, run the best courtrooms. Black-robed, elevated in height above the courtroom floor, neat, serious, well spoken, surrounded by flags and governmental seals, personifying the respect our citizens have for justice, the judges hold great presiding advantage. Those judges with quiet but firm bearing, who stay within their pocket of advantage, are self-generators of the respect they command.

The slamming gavel is a popular hallmark of judging—"Order, order in the court." But many judges rarely, if ever, bang a gavel. I must confess that the handsome mahogany gavel my brother Joel gave to me as a gift on my own judicial induction has never been used except as a desk ornament; and although the gift speaks for our mutual fraternal affection, its weight holds down only unruly piles of paper.

Nothing impressed me more in my view from the bench than the orderly trial scenes duplicated in the fifteen or so functioning courtrooms of the Nassau County Supreme Courthouse. In each case, every day, a civil trial would be conducted as if it were a calm and ordinary meeting, despite the charged emotions underlying it—

without guns, without troopers. No barrier or shield protects the judge, who is at the fulcrum. The judge simply presides; the lawyers take their turns; the clients, the witnesses, the jury, and the spectators are all appropriate actors in their turn. Here is the ultimate testament to the consensual nature of our system of justice: that people, in great numbers, are willing to submit their disputations peacefully, and to accept the results with equanimity if not joy. If every courtroom required force and tension to maintain order, we would require many times the court facilities and personnel we now employ. The implicit social contract in the cooperative resolution of disputes, by procedures of talk and response, would be impaired; it would shift from the democratic flavor of a contract between private persons to more inflexible tribunal imposition, where the will of the inevitable third party, the state, would be more intrusive.

The effectiveness of uniquely American, democratic case presentation can be credited in major part to lawyers, whose training and responsibility, as "officers of the court," enable the even flow of disposed cases. If every point, however immaterial, were fought, if every obstruction, however unrelated to the merits, were put in issue, if the laws of evidence and procedure and professional discipline were not effectuated, if all emotions were indulged, every whim given its way, our system would crumble. The procedures and the substance merge subtly in justice democratic-style.

Here, too, lies one of the dangers of the so-called political trial, where the end result pursued by the lawyers, and sometimes their clients, is not relief for the client, but publicity. This is sometimes sought by means of disruption, which comes easily to our trial mechanisms, based as they are essentially on consent of the parties to orderly procedure. Unfortunately, personal publicity for the lawyers seems to be an end in itself in a number of these cases. I admire the courageous lawyer who fights for unpopular clients with all the resources he can draw from his personal legal repertoire but not the "look at me" lawyer who, on television or a picket line, exploits social injustice for the sake of his own ego.

Where a client has either committed a crime or civilly abused the rights of others in pursuit of his own conception of "true" social justice, to which he is deeply committed, an atypical situation in court arises. The client may expect to be penalized, but is more interested in the cause than he is in his own disposition. He may even welcome the martyr's role and believe his sympathizers will cherish it. This client, and his lawyer, may legitimately generate publicity, which by itself is unobjectionable and constitutionally guaranteed. But the disruption of trials, with judge baiting, violent outbursts, and all the sordid rest to which the newspapers and television eagerly treat us, is inexcusable. A lawyer's obligation is to stand up to an abusive judge in responsive courtroom dialogue on the record. He must do so. But, in meaning to provoke reversible error in the trial by insults or disruptions, his conduct is sabotage of the system that affords his clients and him the very rights on which they stand.

There can be no justification for blowing up a university laboratory and killing an innocent student inside in the name of antinuclear protest. The murdered student is as dead as a mugger's victim in a deserted subway station. On the other hand, we must have access to demonstrations of protest in a civilized and open manner, and we must accept the consequences commensurate with the offenses. Here there are nice questions of social balance on which true democracy poises. Dissent is one of our prime American values.

Those who would murder and steal and wantonly destroy under a banner of social justice choose to forget that in a legal system of justice victims have the rights of their own lives and properties, and society as a whole has expectations of peacefulness. Those who argue that the system is hopeless because social justice will never flow within a propertied class structure, regardless of internal attempts at change, show an inability to devise an alternative system that offers greater promise. Their liberal use of every device the system affords them in order to mock it remains a silent irony.

——HOW JUDGES DECIDE CASES:—— THE MOVING HYPOTHESIS

Cases, as they unfold in court, run the gamut from genuine theater to tedium. Every judge will agree. After enough experience, no sitting judge is surprised by anything he hears. The exposure to recurring court testimony develops a healthy respect, in responsible judges, for hearing out the whole story, from everyone, and avoiding pre-judgments until all the evidence is in. I think it not sophistry to suggest that judges believe all and nothing of what they hear.

Judges develop their own personal adjustments to their roles. Seasoned trial lawyers study their judges and approach them in ways best calculated to reach their mentalities. It has always surprised me how few lawyers really take the trouble to study their judges as prospects to be worked on, to be sold an argument, as it were. Judges are not fungible; they hold varying personal traits. Some judges are more receptive to the plain text of statutes or cases; others, to their policy bases. Some are more interested than others in the intrinsic fairness of an occurrence. Some judges are better able to understand oral argument than others, or to act upon it. Some judges are deemed so intractable that lawyers try to avoid them by "forum shopping," or seeking to choose their own judges.

When it comes down to cases, how do judges decide? I call the process "the moving hypothesis." No judge comes to a case empty-headed. Somewhere in that judicial mind lurk innate beliefs of law content and sensors of receptivity to stimuli of the kinds that arise in courtrooms. As soon as the case comes to the judge's attention, and he learns, even incompletely, the competing claims and contentions, inevitably intimations of conclusion begin to coalesce as to what happened and what should result. No one should suppose that a judge picks up a trial with a virginal thought stream and maintains pristine mental purity until the very last instant, when he utters in open court a decision that suddenly comes to him in a blaze of revelation.

My theory is that as soon as a judge gets his first inkling of a case, usually from a review of the pleadings or a pretrial conference with lawyers, he cannot help but form an impression. This is not to say that he then decides the case, although the initial impact has a greater lasting effect on some than on others. Rather, he reacts spontaneously to the case and the manner in which it is presented. At some preliminary point, the judge hypothesizes a decision based on told and apparent "facts" and innate legal judgment. This is one reason why lawyers should always be circumspect with their judges in pretrial conferences, and never imply weakness of their clients or their cases, regardless of the informality of the intercourse. Judges are accustomed to hearing lawyers praise their causes, that is part of the language. But the cause that is criticized by its champion has special symptoms. Lawyers must remember that judges never see their people or their cases as fully as they do, and that the judges constantly monitor discussions for decisional aids. The most fully presented case does not disclose all that a lawyer knows of its circumstances. Careless judicial feeding at early stages has caused fatal legal ingestion in many a case.

Good judges may have bad days, but bad judges have few good ones. The good judge, deliberate, unemotional, patient, keeps his mind open constantly, but starts hypothesizing his decision at some mesne point, and moves it along as input gathers. Much depends on the clarity or complexity of the case. The trick is to keep the moving hypothesis just that, until all the evidence is in and the law is sufficiently considered. Only then should hypothesis turn to decision.

The lawyers open their cases in court with oral arguments, which, while not evidence, temper the moving hypothesis. The interchange of oral argument is a critical point, since the judge assumes each lawyer is making his best case. Holding back on oral argument, for fear of alerting the opposition to particular points, is an occasional but risky courtroom ploy, since in the process you may lose the judge or the jury for good. When the evidence begins, the plaintiff is the first to present his case. As the testimony proceeds, more input tempers the judicial hypothesis. By the time the plaintiff rests, his case may impress the judge as strong, or at least sufficient in absence of rebuttal; or it may seem as meritless as to warrant dismissal on motion for failure to prove even a prima-facie cause of action. If the case proceeds, the defendant's witnesses now must bear up against the plaintiff's proof, and the judge's hypothesization of the case attends a new state of refinement. He may now have, for instance, a diametrically opposite hypothesization to one he entertained earlier. With the proof completed, and the summation done, briefs may be submitted. The impressions of the open-minded judge may fluctuate until the case is fully submitted, and can continue changing during the course of his own deliberation until he feels confident of his grasp.

Perhaps the best analysis I have ever read of the way to decision is found in Cardozo's remarkable *Nature of the Judicial Process* (1921), in which that famous justice wrote:

My analysis of the judicial process comes then to this, and little more: logic, and history, and custom, and utility, and the accepted standards of right conduct, are the forces which singly or in combination shape the progress of the law. Which of these forces shall dominate in any case must depend largely upon the comparative importance or value of the social interests that will be thereby promoted or impaired. . . .

If you ask how he is to know when one interest outweighs another, I can only answer that he must get his knowledge just as the legislator gets it, from experience and study and reflection; in brief, from life itself. . . .

I have spoken of the forces of which judges avowedly avail to shape the form and content of their judgments. Even these forces are seldom fully in consciousness. They lie so near the surface, however, that their existence and influence are not likely to be disclaimed. But the subject is not exhausted with the recognition of their power. Deep below consciousness are other forces, the likes and the dislikes, the predilections and the prejudices, the complex of instincts and emotions and habits and convictions, which make the man, whether he be litigant or judge.

The moving hypothesis of decision means, in effect, deciding the case as you go along. Knowing this, the advocate must order his case to put forward his best foot at the earliest time, before the moving hypothesis stops moving and sets in against him. In addition, all the elements of submission, the pleadings, the pretrial conferences, casual banter at the bench, the trial, the arguments have an effect on the decision.

Fine judges hold the final decision making until the submission is complete. It is not uncommon for such judges to tear up a proposed decision, even a signed one, before filing it officially and replace it with a brand-new one that would contradict it. But I believe that many judges close their minds along the way.

Judges approach their cases with varying degrees of wisdom, experience, and self-confidence. In too many cases, the latter attribute is inflated; intellectual humility is an attractive, but not overstocked, judicial attribute. The burden of decision must rest heavier on some than on others. Some agonize over a decision because of a personality malfunction; some, because they are intellectually keen and have acute senses of responsibility. And there are those, regrettably, who do not consider cases in any depth and habitually rely on the work of their law secretaries.

A phenomenon seen most clearly from the bench is the case that seems airtight on the law but cannot be won. Inexperienced lawyers and those whose efforts become calcified in logic often fall into the trap of believing that the operative facts, those pertaining directly to the transaction, and the rules of law governing those facts in the abstract line up perfectly for a predictable win for the plaintiff. But the plaintiff cannot win. Some examples: children evicting a parent from a home originally the parent's; wealthy sophisticated parties who take advantage of impecunious, less-educated associates in transactions where the associates were not represented by counsel; the location of a wall of a large apartment house that is two inches over its proper boundary line; cases that will set a precedent for others on too broad a scale. Where the conduct involved is sufficiently outrageous, the result so grossly unfair, some legal snag can always be uncovered by a judge to thwart the excessively unpalatable result. The absolute unacceptability of some legal positions is known to experienced judges and lawyers. Recognition of such a situation, even some probability of its existence, comes with legal experience and alertness to the human condition. It is but another reminder of the personality of law.

———THE POWER AND PERSON——— OF JUDGES

Assessing judges as a whole is an uncertain enterprise; there are so many working under such diverse circumstances. The process from which judges evolve is not calculated to yield—and does not yield consistently—the best judging talent the legal profession can offer. The promotional processes from lower to higher courts take insufficient account of good work and effective service, although in appointment and promotion the federal courts appear to recognize judicial merit and responsibility more than state courts do. The mixture of merit and politics in the state courts contains a higher dose of politics, maybe too high for the stability of the solution.

Yet, with all that, judges are much maligned. In my experience, judges are generally conscientious and hard-working. Their compensation is incommensurate with the earnings of many of the lawyers before them, and with the responsibilities they bear. A hard-working judge earns his salary and then some. Whichever way they come to the bench, once there, most judges do their best, which in a surprising number of instances is considerable. Whether it is that the bench is ennobling or that, once freed of the needs to maintain social positions on political grounds or to toe the political line, true qualities show up, I cannot say. Some judges learn a lot on the job, and others get their first real chance to expose their natural ability to the serious practice of the law.

For the average personality, judging can be too much to absorb without shock. The personal power and the movable prestige of judgeships are so seductive that they can affect even the most adjusted individuals. The judge is monarch of all he surveys. From the time the bailiff bellows his arrival, he is in charge—of that there is no doubt. Perched high in his paneled redoubt, he rises physically above all in the courtroom; not unlike the royal presence ministering to sundry petitioners from his throne. The absolute power of the judge in the courtroom is not readily understood by laymen, who are accustomed to more free-and-easy ways in their public congregations. While there are general guides to courtroom practice, the judge's latitude is virtually untrammeled. If a losing litigant wishes an appeal to higher authority, he must go elsewhere. If the decision is reversed, it is done by another judge. Essentially, no one can order a specific judge to decide anything in court that day.

The individual power of the judge is real. Legislators act in large groups to adopt the resolutions that provide laws. Except among his own staff, or within an unusual delegation, no single legislator has the personal power to order anything done. Even mayors and governors do not wield the awesome personal powers of the man in the robe.

Almost a decade ago, as I mentioned earlier, I campaigned

briefly for election to the New York Court of Appeals, which is now an appointed bench. When you are running for an office that epitomizes fairness and objectivity, and you must address an audience of varied political belief, good speech material that people will listen to comes hard. Sitting on a dais in a huge hall crowded with candidates and political people, I hit upon these words to single out my candidacy:

> Do you realize that of all the candidates in this room, for Governor, the United States Senate, Attorney General, Comptroller, and all the legislators, only one here [that was me, then a Supreme Court justice] has the power by a simple stroke of his pen or sound of his voice to have you put to death, to cage you up like an animal for the rest of your life, to take your child away from you, to order you to pay out enough money to bankrupt you, to foreclose your home . . .

The congregation fell silent; I had their ears.

While some judges, with the passage of time, fall into irascibility and impatience with the views of others—and develop an absolute passion for the sound of their own voice—most judges acquire added dignity and patience in hearing out controversy. Career satisfaction, the serenity in judgment that experience brings to those who can accept it, and good basic character can tell in the long run. Unfortunately, a judgeship can also grant a person the license to act out character defect.

There is a great loss of human perspective in being a judge. In their courtrooms and essentially in all their working days, judges set every pace and tone. When they talk, everyone listens; if not, attention can be compelled. They talk without interruption as long as they like, yet they feel free to interrupt others at will; this, incidentally, is often necessary, given courtroom proclivities of lawyers and clients alike to self-serving legal oration. If judges are contradicted, it is in careful, respectful terms. Many learn that ascension to the bench sharpens their wit, for their every sally is greeted by laughter. It can be disconcerting, since one never gets an objective measure as to whether the humorous material is really any good. Judicial humor is edgy to the extreme. A deft touch is helpful in moving things along without tension, but a good judge rarely will make parties or lawyers the butt of his humor.

Judges take different views of appellate reversal. Many judges accept reversal as official recognition that they were wrong. Given the sense of infallibility their position fosters, they feel some personal affront or shame at reversal. Many feel that the tenure of their very position becomes threatened by appellate reversal. Trial judges of higher caliber feel no challenge, although they may be outraged. These judges, secure in their ability, may consider reversals with care to see if indeed they did miss something or if there is profit in some nuance, but I suspect most of them write off reversals as inevitable manifestations of disagreement among judges. After all, the appellate court is entitled to blow one now and then. The fact that rises in judicial rank only sometimes accord with legal perspicacity understandably propagates these sentiments.

A surprising number of trial judges take uncommon personal interest in the appeals of their cases, seeing their reputations at stake. A lawyer friend once told me that on the eve of an appeal that he was scheduled to argue, the trial judge phoned him at home and entreated him to do his best to "uphold me."

WITNESSES

Lay people are usually apprehensive in court. Testifying under oath is a wrenching experience for many, even those who are only peripherally involved in the case, with nothing tangible at stake. The judge sitting alongside them sees the handkerchief crumpled in sweaty palms, the restless movements of the limbs, the tightened jaws and spastic swallowing, the body tension. Some loosen up as the testifying continues. One of the prime duties of the lawyer who summons witnesses is to put that witness at ease as quickly as possible. Most all witnesses are briefed sufficiently in advance to know that the first lawyer to question will be friendly. He is the direct questioner, who has usually met the witness before and given him some idea of his questioning. This same questioner also has warned the witness previously that the opposing lawyer will cross-examine him and try to trip him up.

Even the most honest witness who testifies at any length will not have a perfect story. There are always inconsistencies and omissions for the cross-examiner to explore:

Question: Miss Rich, you testified earlier that you are office manager of Abel Leasing Corporation, and that you have worked for the company since its inception twenty-eight years ago.

Answer: That is right; I started as a file clerk.

Cross-examining style varies from honeyed inquiries to entice the witnesses to harsh staccato meant to break them. Usually the cross-examiner starts slowly, goes over the witness gently, and then moves in.

Question: Your progress is certainly commendable. You are a conscientious worker, indeed, staying late every evening to be sure all the mail is out, are you not?

Answer: Well, I try to do my best. Mr. Dwyer, my employer, is a very inspiring man to work for. He has been very generous and understanding to me.

Question: Do you like Mr. Dwyer?

Answer: Very much.

Question: I can well understand that. Now, tell me, did you mail a letter of May 24, 1978, to the Solid Insurance Company?

Answer: Yes, sir.

Question: That was two years ago, was it not?

Answer: Yes, sir.

Question: I show you plaintiff's Exhibit 1. Is this a photocopy of the letter?

Answer: Yes.

Question: What does the stamp in the upper right-hand corner mean?

Answer: It is our regular office stamp, to show the time we mail out a letter.

Question: I would imagine you are a very busy person, and handle an awful lot of mail.

Answer: Yes, I am. I mean I do.

Question: How is it you can recollect so clearly a letter to the Solid Insurance Company of two years ago?

Answer: Well, I remember Mr. Dwyer emphasizing its importance. We had this big fire, and we worked hard to get up an inventory of what was lost.

Question: Did you discuss your testimony with Mr. Dwyer before coming here?

Answer: No.

Question: Do you mean to tell this court and this jury that you never discussed with Mr. Dwyer until today the Solid letter of May 24, 1978, from the day he claimed you mailed it?

Answer: Well, no, not exactly.

Question: You did have some discussions with him? Did you not?

Answer: Yes, I guess I did, after the company claimed it never got the letter. But I remember the letter.

Question: Did Mr. Dwyer tell you what to say here today?

Answer: No.

Question: But he did tell you to mail the letter?

Answer: Yes.

Question: Would you do anything Mr. Dwyer asked?

Answer: I would.

Question: You like him very much?

Answer: I certainly do.

Question: Would you testify you mailed the letter if he asked you to, even if you had no recollection of mailing the letter?

Answer: Certainly not.

Question: Even if he asked?

Answer: Not at all.

Question: Did you not just testify you would do anything he asked?

Answer: I did not mean anything wrong.

Question: Did you place the letter in the mail yourself?

Answer: No.
Question: How do you know it was mailed?
Answer: Well, the stamp on the right side means it went
           to the mailing room and one of the boys stamped
           it, dropped it into the mail cart, and carried it to
           the post office that night.
Question: Did you see the envelope dropped in the cart?
Answer: No.
Question: Did you see the cart taken to the post office that
           day?
Answer: No.
Question: You cannot tell me as fact, can you, Miss Rich,
           that the letter was actually deposited in the post
           office?
Answer: No.

A scenario like this is repeated regularly in every civil court-house in the country. An insurance claim is said to have been filed, but the insurer denies receiving it. Letters mailed from large busy offices are subject to a processing order in the ordinary course of business. When Miss Rich said she mailed the letter, she was actually saying she put it into the firm's regular mail process. To her thinking, when the letter went to the mail room, it was mailed. Mailing is usually established in court by proof of a regular customary practice. Someone familiar with the practice need only testify as to regularity. The possibility that a letter could fall behind a cabinet and never be mailed exists, but the probabilities favor dispatch in the ordinary course of business.

Naturally, this witness discussed the insurance claim with Mr. Dwyer, his lawyer, and others. The fire caused a major business loss. The lawyer's inference that she had been coached threw her, as it does most lay witnesses. In fact, many witnesses mistakenly try to cover up prior discussions of the case, even though any judge or jury would find some discussion natural. In absence of other damaging circumstances, Miss Rich's story would stand as proof of the mailing. Yet many Miss Riches would leave the courtroom feeling that they had hurt their Mr. Dwyers, and that they had not been candid on the witness stand. Actually, the opposite is often true, and it is usually the cross-examiner clutching for straws and innuendoes who is hurt.

The fears of seeming foolish, of being thought, even innocently, a conspiratorial knave, or of being overly nervous upset witnesses. Flights of tears, uncontrollable shouting, and bizarre behavior on the part of witnesses under pressure are familiar to all judges. Testifying can be stressful: I actually saw a witness die in his witness chair during his cross-examination. He never even slid to the floor. That was the case of a defendant debtor with a bad heart who had insisted on testifying after several medical delays. In another case, the complaining witness in a criminal prosecution, a housewife with no prior coronary history, was afflicted with a seizure in the course of her testimony and had to be rushed by emergency ambulance to a nearby hospital.

Lawyers who must reconstruct events for trial are well familiar with those people who are so confident that they can stick to a fabrication or that old Jones wouldn't dare say a word. These clients lack an understanding of cross-examination and court processes—indeed, the investigatory processes generally, both public and private—and fail to appreciate how readily their concocted tales can be unraveled. In the final analysis, "making up" a story is lying under oath, which is perjury and a felony; it takes a hardened and clever liar to persist. Honesty is not only the best policy; in court it is the best tactic.

The end goal of parties to a trial is not the truth; it is to win. The cross-examination method seems the best procedure we have for attacking lies, for separating fact from fancy and testing memory, for giving opportunity to observe the witness testifying to the events and to check his seeming credibility. Yet the cross-examiner is more interested in tarnishing a harmful truth than in establishing it. For him, there is no truth, only shades of advantage or disadvantage to his client. If a witness launches into the awful truth about the circumstances, the cross-examiner tries to trip him up, attack his person, and add irrelevancies to distort the picture. Anything is acceptable to him but the bald truth staring unchallenged at the jury. If he can prove that the witness cannot even remember what he had for breakfast last Saturday, perhaps the jury will believe that this person can scarcely be trusted to remember the details of a contract signing a year ago. The bag of tricks into which a skilled cross-examiner can reach is deep and useful to his purposes. Most of his craft is directed at lay juries, unfamiliar with the tricks of his trade.

In many cases, there are no truths at all, only relative human feelings and effects. The spectacle of a ten-year-old child being cross-examined in a custody proceeding is at once ludicrous and depressing. The custody of a child, where there is volatile parental conduct, depends hypothetically on his best interest. The child's present emotional state and what is best for him cannot be measured by any cross-examining engine. The professional methodology of doctors, social workers, and other understanding professionals is called for in search of the truth here, not sophistry in the cause of winning, which typifies so much cross-examination. Similarly, a divorce can be so complex a matter of accumulated hurts—real and supposed, and no less real for being supposed—that a more responsive fact-finding process than court trials seems indicated. These long petty examinations of who did what to whom and when, of insults to my mother, and coldness to your aunt, of all inconsiderate statements are among the most aggravating of court litanies. In these, there are no winners, only degrees of losers. In these family disputes there may well be relevant information available that does not fall into the realm of admissible evidence.

The need for searching out the truth is not restricted to family disputation, however. It applies to labor controversy, offenses of the very young, medical malpractice, civil-rights vindications, and all the areas where a narrow yes-no adversarial questioning is simply inadequate. Here, the shades of truths are more important than cut-and-dried affirmation or negation.

It is regularly argued that courtroom questioning should be directed only at getting at the truth, without obfuscation. Cross-examining proponents reply that their method is in fact the best way to get at the truth, even with its potential abuse in a disputed matter. While my heart is with the former, I know the latter is usually closer to the mark. When you sit in court for any length of time and realize that a goodly number of those pillars of the community—elderly ladies, white-maned businessmen, red-blooded young American boys—testifying earnestly are doing so falsely, you become increasingly skeptical about voluntary direct statements standing unchallenged.

When friends accused me of being overly cynical about human nature, I would tell them that 50 percent of the people who talk to me every day lie to me. This is, of course, an overstatement made to establish a point. But it is so that half of the parties who appear in court, equally righteous, lose their cases—their stories either are not believed or are seen in a different light from what they had hoped for. This does not necessarily mean they are deliberately lying, although there is enough of that. They may be confused, mistaken, poor communicators, or perceive things differently from others. Mostly they blend what they *wanted* to see into what, in truth, they actually saw. It is axiomatic that there are as many versions of an occurrence as there are people who witness it.

——THE SLOW PACE OF TRIALS——

An effective judge must maintain absolute control of the proceeding; if not, the orderly trial can dissolve into a maze of confusion that is likely to be recorded incorrectly. A chaotic trial incurs a double default: the parties are unable to present their cases in their best light, and if the written record, as taken by the court reporter, is inadequate, there can be no proper basis for appellate review. Sometimes observers feel the pace of trials is too slow, and lacking in drama. But the courtroom is not theater.

There are a number of principal trial procedures that work mostly at a snail's pace. In commercial cases and those involving white-collar crime, for instance, the lawyers must introduce voluminous documents in evidence. A suitable explanation must be offered for the authenticity of any document or thing made an exhibit in evidence. This is called "laying a foundation" for the exhibit, which may be a letter, a contract, a ledger sheet, a book, a picture, or anything demonstrable. By rules of evidence, painstaking questions establish the admissibility of the exhibit: the witness must study it and be questioned about it; then the judge may read it if its admissibility is questioned. Once the judge rules, he hands the item to the court reporter, who marks it as part of the record with an identifying stamp. When a record is forwarded to a reviewing activity, all of the exhibits in evidence are attached. A court attendant may make a supplementary entry in a control ledger. The item is then circulated to the judge and jury for reading. In the most heated centrifuge of passion, there must be painstaking care to maintain a cool record.

Another delaying factor of trials is implicit in the question-and-answer format. Narrative statements, in which a witness simply tells his whole story, are not made unless special permission is granted. Narrations are usually allowed in cases where a lawyer in the trial is also a witness, and rather than have him question himself, the court permits a narrative statement. The general question-and-answer routine is maintained with good reason. The fear in trial procedure is that inadmissible evidence will get before the court and hopelessly prejudice the judge or the jury even though they may be advised to disregard it. Presumably, questions and answers prevent that. One question is put and one piece of information is extracted. If the question leads to an inadmissible answer, a timely objection can forestall the answer, and, in turn, a whole line of otherwise offensive questioning. It builds up the witness's testimony in a way that signals his position and his ability to know what he says he knows.

A pernicious habit by unscrupulous lawyers, and a sore point in keeping trials under control, is the deliberate trick of putting improper questions before a jury, knowing that the question will plant prejudicial seeds. For instance: "Question: Mr. Kelly, is it not true that you were arrested for crimes three times since January 1st?" Immediate objection follows that question because an "arrest" is only an accusation and not the proof of a crime. Moreover, the crime, even if there was one, may have no real bearing on whether the acts charged in *this* trial were committed. Yet, even though the judge sternly admonishes the lawyer and instructs the jury to disregard the lawyer's question, the jury is cued that Mr. Kelly may be a criminal, and it is only for technical reasons that the question of his criminality cannot be discussed in this case. If a man was never arrested, why not say so? What is he hiding?

Another example is this question addressed to a woman whose automobile has hit a pedestrian: "Question: Is your husband a millionaire, Mrs. Koeppel?" Obviously, the question is improper, since the only issues legitimately before the court in an accident case are whether the woman was negligent in hitting the pedestrian and the extent of his injuries. The husband's wealth is obviously prejudicial, since it implies he can pay plenty. And anyway, would not a rich man have a big insurance policy in force? And, oh, that poor boy who had both his legs broken! The prejudicial remark has been made, the damage is done, and no order to strike and disregard the statement can erase it from the minds in that courtroom.

THE JUDGE AS A PERSON

One must always remember that the judge is a person, and reacts to headaches, sleepless nights, bores, rudeness, the opposite sex, and financial pressures as other mortal humans do. The classic error is to mistake the body within the black robe for an automaton who will respond predictably to any stimulation. While some judges have greater personal qualities than others, every judge has peaks and valleys.

The judge's personality relates directly to the way he will handle courtroom distraction. Few lay people understand how well the judge can see the courtroom from his perch. The average courtroom does not exceed sixty feet, front to back, and unless the judge is myopic, he can monitor it all. Facial expressions, fidgeting, whispering, and a variety of "looks" are all observable. Many lawyers know this and, in an effort to sway the judge, will feign shock, dismay, or surprise during their opponent's presentation. Experienced judges are rarely taken in by these dramatics; many are offended by them, and will rebuke a lawyer for them, even in the jury's presence.

Many judges work on unrelated papers during a tedious trial, particularly one without a jury. Some of the distinguished public letters of Mr. Justice Holmes were written from the bench during dry argument. With modern time pressures on judges to produce, perfunctory orders to be signed and drafts of proposed opinions often find their way onto the bench as the dreary questioning and argumentation grind on. Most judges are loath to cut off long questioning forays of conceivable relevancy. There is a normal desire to permit everyone to be heard out to the fullest. One should feel he has had his full day in court, regardless of result. Moreover, tangential questioning is sometimes profitable, and judges, in charting lawyers' courses, have few guides to help in deciding in advance whether the questioning will come to have worth. The impatient judge who cuts off lawyers may expedite the cases, but in doing so runs the risk of injustice through impinging on full and fair hearing. When a judge has decided in his mind against a party and is merely listening out the rest of the case, he is likely to give the loser-elect much more leeway than the winner. He becomes graciousness personified as he eases the loser to the chute; this is for appellate hygiene. Most clients are exuberant when everything flows their way from the bench, but it may be time for mourning.

The notes that occasionally pass from the judge on the bench to an assistant often puzzle onlookers. It is generally assumed these are important communications. However, as often as these notes may call for a book to check a point, or for research, or for information on the state of the backed-up calendar, they may be lunch orders, requests for personal errands, or even facetious comments. Alert judges do not miss much from their perched aerie.

Yes, all on the bench is not jurisprudential. I am reminded of one of my experiences. During my second month as a judge, I sat in my heavy leather chair, which stood on four bulky round casters, and leaned forward to charge a jury. As I shifted my weight, I felt that the skirt of my robe was caught under one of the wheeled casters. While continuing my charge, I shifted my body to roll the caster off my robe. Unfortunately, the maneuver worked in reverse, and I felt my robe pulling me to the floor. I moved again and was pulled even farther down. Now my chin was barely above the desk. All the while I kept charging the jury in as even and serious a tone as the circumstances permitted. Finally, desperation set in, and abandoning my subtleties, I put one hand under the front of the chair, the other low on the robe skirt, lifted my body and the chair, and yanked the robe free. The jury seemed not to notice, and I finished with aplomb. Once off the bench, back in my chambers, I examined the robe and found to my horror, a large tear about six inches from the hem. Here I was in the second month of a fourteen-year term, and my expensive robe was already torn. Was I destined to ply my judicial career with a patched robe? The epilogue took place some weeks later, when at a meeting of judges I noticed that their robes varied from ankle to knee in length. Mine was ankle length, since I had taken the robe salesman's offer uncritically. I instantly saw that my sartorial salvation was at hand, and had the robe shortened to knee length, eliminating the patch. Those were the days of mini-skirts, and I joked about my mini-robe.

The robe is a necessary symbol. Much as a judge may be respected (a common attitude) or revered (a rarity), his ability to maintain order and acceptance of his rulings is linked to the image of authority that he embodies. The black robe is a reminder of the extraordinary role the judge plays, a visual sign that in court he is different from other men. The ritualization of justice, as formalistic as it may seem, contributes to its viability; in a way, it is a visual invocation of unconscious conditioned factors. You do what the judge says because he is the judge, not because he is wise or persuasive. In the end, personal respect is never woven into a bolt of black cloth, yet that cloth is a constant reminder of the force the wearer represents.

In my almost nine years on the trial bench, I had only two occasions to rebuke litigants for wearing improper dress, and, ironically, they came on the same day. Both were women plaintiffs, separately seeking uncontested divorces; they were unknown to each other. The clerk called the name of a case, and a party stepped forward, and immediately silenced the cacophony normally in the background of that crowded courtroom in which uncontested matrimonial awards were being processed, so much so that I looked up from the papers I was signing to see what was happening. There from the middle of the room came a young woman, perhaps in her early twenties, on very high heels, wearing short shorts (of the variety then known as hot pants) and a brief halter that shielded a minor portion of her ample bosom. Her appearance on the beach, I had no doubt, would have been noteworthy; in a courtroom, she was nothing short of a sensation. The eyes of the clerks and a number of the lawyers up front darted from me to her and back. That is, those eyes that could be torn away, so sensual was her appearance in so incongruous a setting. The pressure was on me now. What would I do about her? Rallying my wits, I called her lawyer to the bench and made some inquiries. He apologized for his client, but said he had no control over her actions. I asked him whether she had another garment, a sweater or a jacket, with which to cover herself; he spoke with her, and she shook her head, insisting loudly she had a right to be dressed as she was. With the gauntlet down, I told her that getting a divorce, even if uncontested, was a serious matter. I advised her on the record that I considered her costume a deliberate affront to the court and contemptuous. I refused to let her take the witness stand and directed postponement of her proceeding until she returned suitably attired. With that, she turned sullenly, but without a word, and marched back across the courtroom floor to the corridor door and departed, I was later advised, not to return.

So be it, I thought to myself, although I was conscious of annoyance that perhaps I might have reacted out of some antediluvian prudishness. I thought of my three college-age children, who were not slow in teasing me about old ways, and I wondered. About an hour later, the chief clerk was there, clearing his throat—his way of signaling a dire development. "There's another bare midriff, your honor, next case." I peered out into the spectator section, where a lawyer was escorting a slight blonde woman, who from that distance appeared to be in her early forties, immaculately groomed and wearing an off-white costume consisting of a brief cropped jacket leaving a few inches of bare midriff above a nicely tailored narrow skirt. Had it not been for the first woman, it would not have occurred to me to balk at this second woman, who was actually quite elegant. "What should we do, your honor?" whispered the clerk. My thoughts were swarming. The second woman was turned out in a style I subsequently discovered was then enjoying some vogue. But was my aesthetic judgment a proper guide for deciding whose case is heard? As the clerk pointed out, a bare midriff is a bare midriff; but I was not entirely convinced. Would my children taunt me for favoring the older establishment lady? In the end, I opted for the apparency of equal justice and decided to keep the witness stand untainted of even those few inches of older skin. When I told the lawyer I could not let his client proceed in her current attire, he was accepting, since he had witnessed the earlier episode. Fortunately for all concerned, the woman agreeably produced a white cardigan sweater that reached below her midriff and rendered her sufficiently demure to receive her uncontested divorce.

A young editor, now a lawyer, read this chapter and commented to me that I really had two subjects here, one the serious substantive aspects of the law, the other the human asides in discharging judicial duties. She failed to realize that they were one: that legal substance and the human foibles of those who apply the law are bound together as the law.

——EFFICIENCY VERSUS JUSTICE——

Court reform is an elusive goal; everybody agrees that it is desirable, but few can agree on what it is. In New York State, and elsewhere, a high priority of court reform is disposing of as many cases as possible, particularly the old ones that started way back. This process is known as "clearing the court calendar," which is the inventory of cases to be heard. In other words, it is cleaning up the backlog. The point would be banal and scarcely worthy of special comment except for some of the means used to accomplish it. The very phrase "expediting justice" sets my teeth on edge, even though I recognize that delays in disposition of cases on the court calendar may themselves work injustice. The Magna Carta (vintage 1215) declared in its paragraph 40 that to "none will we deny, or delay, right or justice"; its modern abridgment is "justice delayed is justice denied."

I do not mean to imply that I am against court reform. I am not. I do believe that court-reform programs that strive to increase the number of trial dispositions by forcibly imposing settlement and by overly rushing lawyers during trial war with the interests of justice, which should require a deliberative conduct and ensure an opportunity to be heard. The elements of justice are plainly missing where the judge is constantly on top of the lawyers, urging expedition, cutting off argumentation and questioning alike, and generally harassing all in sight.

The word "efficiency" has come to judging to stay. In administrative statistical sheets, I have seen uncontested matrimonial cases lasting ten minutes count as "one disposition," just the same as a three-week contested trial. I saw an administrative guide put out by a New York judicial administrative agency that ran for twenty-six pages and never once mentioned the word "justice."

Nor should compulsory rules of bench time be expected to accomplish anything beyond a minimal framework that ensures the judge's presence in the courtroom. Judges may sit on the bench and try cases when the material is available, but sometimes it is not. The use of chambers, rather than the courtroom, may signal conferences with lawyers, deliberative time, legal research, decision writing, correspondence, and telephone calls. There are also administrative chores assigned to many judges. Judicial discretion is so great and its activities so cerebral that all the monitoring in the world is not going to reach those judges operating below their potential, either in time spent or in personal diversions. To be sure, courtroom monitoring picks up the absent, the abusive, maybe even the infirm; monitoring may pick up excessively free-and-easy adjournments granted to lawyers. But the only guarantee of judicial performance is in selecting a good competent person as judge in the first place.

To me, justice and efficiency do not relate. In fact, justice is automatically inefficient when free opportunity is given parties to prove their cases, to discredit their adversary's proof, and to allow the kind of argumentation that may go beyond traditionally accepted rules of law to social-policy consideration. It is true that most trials could be streamlined in questioning and argument. In a trial of justice, however, the benefit of the doubt must always favor a full opportunity to be heard, and the assurance that the parties believe they were given the opportunity. Beware of the man with the chart outside the courtroom counting cases as a numerical index of judicial efficiency and virtue. When responsible officials put pressure upon judges to meet quotas, as if they were giving out tickets, justice inevitably is sacrificed on the altar of statistical efficiency.

Pressure to use settlement as an expeditive device in case disposition is mainly directed at negligence, matrimonial, and criminal cases, since that is what is largely in the state courthouses. "Settlement" means an agreement between the parties to end their dispute in some kind of voluntary compromise. It is essentially a contractual disposition by the parties themselves that takes the case away from the judge and jury. Negligence cases do not seem to worry the judges who force settlements with a heavy hand and implied threats, because these cases are frankly considered a commercial enterprise, sort of a Levantine rug bazaar, not at all like real legal matters. The fundamentally pragmatic nature of the activity is clear to all concerned. Similarly, matrimonial cases do not have the jurisprudential aura that impresses all with the need for full hearing. The endless and largely irrelevant petty complaints in testimony have to be cut off anyway. Since by trial time it is apparent the marriage is dead, most marital litigation comes down, not to the question of whether divorce should be granted, but to an inexact shuffling of family income and assets to resolve alimony and child support. If the parties cannot agree, the judge's rough cut is called for, and again the court venture is seen as a variety of economic enterprise. Criminal cases seemingly should be considered apart, for these are classic judicial occasions. But the immense number of essentially uncontested narcotics and petty theft cases, involving clearly guilty parties, lends itself to bulk-processing procedure. Plea bargains, which are essentially settlements of criminal cases, are necessary to keep remotely current in criminal disposition, given existing facilities. If every criminal accusee were to receive a full trial, the court system for criminal justice would grind to a halt. Here, the conundrum is: is justice done in the processing of these dispositions, or is the processing of these dispositions elevated to appear to be justice?

JUDGES SETTLING CASES

The glorification of judges who dispose of the greatest number of cases is adjunctive to the trend to expedite case disposition. If the parties wish to settle their cases between themselves, that is fine. But it is not so fine for the judge to impose a settlement upon the parties to avoid conducting trial. Yet this, too, is a daily occurrence in every principal courthouse in the country. A curious feature of all this is that, on balance, trial lawyers like judges who settle a lot of cases, regardless of their methods. While the clients may howl, the practice is good for the law business. In fact, the greatest compliment most trial lawyers can pay to a judge is that he settles cases.

There are two kinds of cases, jury and nonjury. In a jury case, where the jury will decide the issues, judicial interventions have an arguable place in the settlement process. But where there is no jury and the judge is to try the case, his settlement role is entirely different. If settlement discussions are extensive, the trial of that case really begins in his chambers, and if there is no settlement, it is frequently decided in the judge's mind before the first witness is heard. Indeed, it is common in nonjury trials to dispense with opening statements, largely because the judge learns so much of the case in the off-the-record pretrial conferencing.

Extensive settlement discussions plainly contaminate judicial ministrations that are later expected to be impartial and objective. Normally, in court procedure, nothing happens unless at least counsel for both parties are present with an available facility for a written verbatim record. But settlement talk is mediation and negotiation. The classic ploy is to send one party out of the room so that the other can let his hair down to the judge, confide his minimum demands, and define his possible concessions. Then the lawyers reverse. Of course, only the most naïve fail to recognize that the judge will work the minimum against the maximum, and seek to trade concessions off to find a middle ground. The lawyer who reveals his rock-bottom figure to the judge too quickly soon lives to regret it. That trustworthy man in black robes, with the grey hair and serious face, is not the judge of common-law fame; he is the dealer in the legal blackjack game called "settlement."

During the course of these settlement discussions, particularly when the parties, by their own consent, are dealt with separately by the judge, many unchallenged things are said. No rules of evidence here. All kinds of hearsay, opinion, and even slander (which is oral defamation; "libel" when it is written) ricochet from the mouths of counsel off the walls of the chamber. Granted some judges are better suited to filter out the sales talk than others, it is a rare judge who is not affected in some way by an extensive failed negotiation. There may have been simply too much intimation of the case even for the most levelheaded jurist, and most judges are not mentally equipped to hear that case again from scratch with total objectivity. The situation worsens when the judge invests too much time in the case, for which he will have nothing to show the statisticians if the settlement fails. The judge takes on an interest in pursuing that settlement, if only to maintain his own disposition quota. There are judges who take personally, as affronts to their wisdom and clear insight, any refusal to follow their settlement advice. When we find a judge walking into a courtroom with a grudge against one side, for being unreasonable in not settling, no really fair trial can take place.

Unfortunately, there are judges who overtly threaten parties with harm in their case if they do not settle on the terms he urges. Parties are hard pressed to resist settlement blandishment of a judge who will decide the case without a jury. After all, he has the virtual unfettered power of decision; all that can be done to him if he reacts vengefully is to seek a reversal on appeal, an uncertain enterprise of certain expense. Skillful judges can bury a party in a beautifully laced-up record. As lawyers will assure you, it is harder to win a case if the judge is against you, even where there is a jury. There are too many subtle, and not so subtle, ways judges can influence juries.

Many courts have pretrial settlement-conference procedures before judges to encourage settlements and thus move the calendar. However, where the conferring judge is not the trial judge, the usefulness of a conference is limited. The judge who is going to sit on the case holds a whip; the judge who merely confers is a respectable figure who may bring the parties together and who can be handed polite declinations without fear of recrimination. Many lawyers like this phase, because it affords a formal settlement opportunity and may open the direct lines of settlement communication between the parties that they should have done themselves long ago. Trial lawyers for the defense, working on a per-diem charge basis, always love a session with a judge. There is no vice in using judges as settlement mediators unless it is overdone to the extent that the trying of cases becomes affected by the unavailability of judges.

Settlements are constantly occurring and being discussed from the inception of a case to its final court disposition. In the war of nerves that is part of settlement practice in more lucrative situations, a large number of cases are settled only when the trial judge receives the file with instructions to start the case. This is brinksmanship by the parties, when both become satisfied that the other is not pulling back. Since one or both want to settle anyway, and the judge is not averse, a tremendous pressure to settle is built up by the morning of the beginning of the trial. This is a variety of the expression "settling on the courthouse steps," except that you have come up the steps and are now inside the courtroom door.

The most dramatic settlement confrontation I ever saw involved a deliberating jury deadlocked for two days in an accident case. At about 9:00 P.M., I asked the bailiff to sound out the jury on whether a verdict seemed feasible that evening. Then the lawyers came into my chambers from my courtroom and said the parties had reached a settlement. Just as they finished talking, the bailiff returned and told me that the jury had reached a verdict, which was in a sealed envelope he handed to me. Without opening the jury's envelope, I asked the lawyers whether they wanted the settlement or the verdict, and after conferring with their clients outside, they returned to announce they preferred to let the settlement stand. At their request, I tore up the verdict and threw it into my waste pail. We all returned to the courtroom, assembled the jury, and I explained to the jury the development and excused them with thanks. The jury never knew the settlement figure, and, by further agreement, neither side was to talk to the jury, and none of the parties ever knew that jury verdict. I suspect I could have gotten it from the bailiff, but the long wisdom of judging is to put the case behind you the instant your role is concluded. Never poke around with the jury; trouble finds the judge soon enough without fishing for it. Questioning the jurors only brings up such bad news as that they did not really understand the case or the judge's charge of the law. Maybe a bailiff was in the room when he was not supposed to be. This puts the judge on notice of developments where a mistrial decision may then have to be considered, and no judge likes to start a completed trial all over again.

In my opinion, trial judges should not engage in settlement efforts for cases pending before them. Many lawyers are waiting for the trial level to work their settlements and they rely on it. If lawyers knew there would be no judicial intervention for settlement at the trial level, the serious settlement levels, by interparty consensus, would be reached earlier. Removing settlement discussion from the trial parts of the courthouse would expedite trials dramatically. Trial judges are there to try cases, and lawyers should not count on them as settlement adjuncts. Unfortunately, and unbelievably, many trial judges do not like to try cases, or at least certain kinds of cases; they much prefer to talk around the settlement route. They may not be confident of their abilities; they may recoil at the tediousness of many trials, or bask in the sociability of settlement talks; and they may be too aware of the fact that settlements bring better disposition statistics than trials. In many courthouses judges brag about their settlement ability, and some even derogate those who wind up trying their cases.

TRUSTING JURIES

Some judges trust juries more than others, and this affects their evidentiary rulings. Judges are more liberal about admitting testimony into evidence when there is no jury, on the theory that they, as experienced listeners, can sift out the offensive testimony. But the population at large has more good common sense and innate intelligence than many judges and lawyers think. A rising awareness, encouraged by media coverage and by improved levels of education, has lifted juries from the low estate in which they were held in English common law. Personally, I leaned to liberality in admitting evidence. I do not believe in selling juries short.

Juries are too often underestimated. They hold no legal knowledge except the common notions that laymen have about the law. Typically, juries are not made up of the well educated, the business sophisticates, or the professionally trained. In the courtroom, their appearance is unprepossessing: they are ordinary in dress, and they move in a herd. It is only in the closed quarters of the jury room that they come into their own.

Many lawyers, even while radiating courtroom charm, regard juries with condescension, and they sometimes unwittingly project these feelings of superiority that are often held by the supposedly educated towards those less schooled. The expression "You never know what a jury will do" serves double meaning. On the one hand, it denotes the fortuity of trials, the inability to predict or produce results with certainty. On the other hand, it suggests jury irrationality and inconsistency. However, this latter meaning may, in fact, be a way of saying that jurors do not think the way lawyers do, which of course is precisely why they are chosen.

The jury is designed to bring into the courtroom the conscience of the community. In its small cross section, its communal microcosm, the jury constructively speaks for society. Here is the trial by one's peers so classically described through the legal ages.

That juries respond through their own strengths and weaknesses as people should be hardly surprising, since on different levels the same applies to the judges and the lawyers. Actually, juries work under more distinct handicaps. All they can legitimately know of the case they learn within the confines of the courtroom. They do not have the advantage of long familiarity with the facts, nor do they have any intimacy of detail. The judge's charge on the law pours over them in an avalanche of dry, carefully hedged verbiage. Their ability to take notes or to ask questions is limited. If technical material is placed before them, they rarely have the expertise to cope. If lengthy documents, studied by the parties and the lawyers for years, are handed to them, they must read them quickly and hand them from one to the other in open court, as everyone stares and waits. The longest documents waft through whole juries in less time than it took to type them. Even if the jurors were capable of deliberative reading, the jury box affords little time for it.

To me, the wonder is not that juries do so poorly, but that they do so well. Most jury trials are either criminal or negligence and other tort (assault and battery, trespass, defamation, fraud) cases—ones that present factual situations of human conduct that can be readily grasped. The object in such cases is to fix a punishment or derive a money award for injuries; such subjective judgments (except where prescribed wholly or partially by law) are best dealt with by communal response. Since guilt and retribution in criminal and tort cases are primarily social judgments, jury action is most appropriate here.

Conversely, I have always felt that present jury submission forms are inappropriate in cases involving technical expertise, special training, or extensive knowledge of institutional affairs. These are largely civil cases: business, property, financial, and technical torts of medical malpractice or faulty product manufacture. The complexity of these questions may place an enormous burden on jurors. Similarly, cases that are largely documentary seem better left in professional legal hands. Generally, I would stress jury performance in criminal and personal-injury cases, separating out in the latter instance parts of medical malpractice and products-liability cases. In these two special situations, the technical findings of faultiness of procedure or product should be made by a panel of experts, suitably constituted and using reasonable procedures, and given to the jury for any remaining issues, including damages.

In the main, juries are remarkably sound. In their quietness, in their relative anonymity, they are misleading. If a case is well presented, the juries will understand. Much unanticipated jury action stems from the failure of the lawyers to communicate their position effectively. It should never be forgotten that the only thing a juror knows of a case is what unfolds before him. This underscores the need for total concentration by lawyers in their trials, and a constant awareness of "how their case is going in." There is no substitute for a good case, but lawyers cannot sit back and assume that the merits they believe their case to have will be so obvious as to bowl over the jury. Sometimes it does; more often, in the presence of a skilled adversary, it does not.

I can recollect only one negligence case in which I took serious issue with a jury. It involved a large truck slamming into the rear of an automobile standing still at a red light. The two passengers in the rear of the auto were seriously hurt, the two in the front escaped with minor injuries. Liability for the accident was admitted by the defendant, and the trial proceeded only on the issue of damages. The ultimate damage award was so outrageously inadequate that I, as the sitting judge, set it aside, and was promptly reversed on appeal. The insurance company's lawyer was superbly articulate and energetic; the plaintiff's lawyer not so. The large and obvious disparity of trial presentation unmistakably warped the jury outcome, but from its vantage point of only a written record the appellate court saw a different happening.

I believe that in appropriate case classifications jury trials are best, and disagree with those who would import the English system, which largely does away with civil juries. To be sure, the plethora of civil jury trials congests court calendars, but the courts are there to give all the people their days in court. Courts are for cases, and if there are too many cases the remedial action should be along the lines of effective procedures and enlarged facilities, not at the expense of the jury system so traditional to American notions of justice.

One last observation seems pertinent. That juries only find facts and not law is another of the fictions that flourish in the law. Once the jury goes into the jury room, it is gone from view. If, as a group, it did not understand the judge's charge, which is usual in a complex case, given the impossibly intricate way some judges charge orally with both eyes on the stenographic transcript for their appellate overlords, the jury decides the case the way it wants to. It is only if the verdict departs significantly from the parameters of a conceivably reasonable result that jury verdicts are set aside. Indeed, many verdicts are reached on some basis apart from the charged "law," and this is never detected.

The use of the famous weasel words promotes independent jury action. Was the defendant "temporarily" insane? Did the defendant act in "good faith"? Did the plaintiff exercise the care for her safety that a "reasonable" person would have "under the circumstances"? Since the ostensible legal rules may be phrased in such vague terms, the jury essentially can do what it wishes; it has a lot of leeway. Judges are fond of saying that the "reasonableness of conduct" is a matter of fact, when in reality it is an opinion, and one on which the jury may act to effect legal results.

—ARE JUDGES SOFT ON CRIMINALS?—

The basic proposition of American criminal justice is that every person is presumed innocent until proven guilty. A host of constitutional rights restrict the ways the state can go about proving guilt. United States Supreme Court cases, in past decades, have put procedural safeguards around such conduct as confessions, police search and seizure, right to speedy trial, police wiretaps, rights to counsel, self-incrimination, and identification. Trial judges are bound by high-court rulings in the protection of constitutional rights, and in following them cannot be fairly taxed for malfeasance or softness. If changes in fundamental constitutional guarantees are thought desirable, either the United States Constitution must be amended or the United States Supreme Court persuaded.

Shortcuts across constitutional rights are dangerous ground, since the freedom of all of us is linked together. Those who would trade liberty for security must know that all the clichés about vigilance being the price of liberty are true, for what the government can do to one it can do to another. People become lulled where violent crimes are involved; after all, how many such criminally accused does the average person really know? It is only when civil-rights deprivations strike home that most people become alert to their personal significance. Just as the national will to continue the Vietnam War crumbled as the military draft began to cut heavily into the middle classes, the criminal involvement of "nice" youngsters with drugs and "nice" adults with white-collar crimes has driven to unlikely homes the reminders of freedom's necessities.

Impatience with due process and other legal rights may also be ill-concealed manifestations of racism or ethnic hostility. There is an unfortunate tendency to aggregate guilt by class of person, particularly among racial and religious minorities, and the disadvantaged. The rights of these, and of the unpopular, are more apt to be forfeited when the panic is on.

Trial judges often take the blame for sloppy police work or poor preparation by the prosecution. If an acquittal results from a failure of evidence, the judge is likely to find himself blamed, particularly if provocative journalism has formed public opinion in the belief of guilt. The basic point, often overlooked, is that the accused person may simply not have been proven to be guilty. In plainer terms, the judge or jury found the accused "did not do it." The public, innocent of the actual facts of the trial, starts from the immediate assumption that "he did do it." The public often assumes guilt based on the mere fact that a person was arrested. Even if the arrested party is never charged in court—as most felony arrestees are not—and even if he is discharged by the police or the prosecution without trial, the judges are still blamed by the public. Parole deficiencies that result in the premature release of prisoners (a function normally beyond the control of judges) and any violence these paroled prisoners may commit are often attributed to the trial judge. He is culpable for all the ills of the criminal-justice system; he takes the "rap" for the malfunctioning of society. A particularly ironic quirk is that judges are universally blamed for treating criminals too "softly," when it may have been the juries who actually mandated the protested verdicts.

"Judge" is a good active headline word. A story appeared in the *New York Times* (scarcely known to be a rabble-rousing newspaper) describing the judicial release of a teen-age gang member accused of involvement in a subway violence incident, which had earlier attracted considerable public notice:

A GUARDIAN ANGEL IS SET FREE BY JUDGE
A Brooklyn judge has dismissed assault charges against a 17-year-old member of the Guardian Angels accused of

fighting with two Transit police officers who had accused him of smoking in a subway station.

[Name deleted], a member of the volunteer group that fights subway crime, was cleared by Judge Alan I. Friess in Criminal Court *after a grand jury had declined on Wednesday to indict him on charges of assault and resisting arrest.* [Emphasis added.]

The charges stemmed from an altercation that took place Oct. 5 in the BMT Pacific Street station in Brooklyn.

While the headline plainly accuses the judge, it is mentioned only in passing that the dismissal of charges actually resulted from a grand jury's refusal to indict the suspect.

But are judges too lenient? Does judicial leniency result in so-called revolving-door justice, under which criminals are brought before a judge and then released to the streets without going to jail? The questions are critical, because there is obviously considerable activity around that revolving door in the nation's urban courthouses. Before the judiciary is condemned, critics should note any inconclusive police and prosecution work that fails to support the charges brought, the glut of the court calendar, the number of prison cells available, the lack of effective penal rehabilitation, and the relative seriousness of the crime charged against the numbers of more serious crimes imminently pending on the court docket faced by understaffed prosecuting offices with understaffed police support. Can the public accept that a shortage of typewriters in a district attorney's office may work a criminal processing bottleneck?

Some judges are doubtless too lenient as a result of sheltered existence and inexperience in criminal reality. Criminal law invokes tough decisions, with punishments to match, and there are judges who simply cannot stand this gaff. A mayor of New York City made an interesting observation in commenting on his city's crime difficulties. He questioned the value of merit selection of judges, and indicated he would go back to political recommendations for his appointees. He felt merit selection yielded scholars and theoreticians, but the political leaders would send street-smart judges more attuned to criminal realities. But my own observation is that, taken as a class, judges are harsher, much more inured to meting out punishment, than average citizens.

Another force is at work; it is called humanity. The greatest calls for Draconian sentencing come from afar—from the society at large that seethes outside the courtroom. In the courtroom, judges and juries alike see the defendant as a person, not as a photograph. The sympathetic emanations for mercy are strongest in the courtroom and fade out beyond. The most vivid analogy I can make of that contrast is the difference between an infantry soldier killing an enemy with a bayonet, close up, where he can smell his body and be drenched with the spray of his blood, and an Air Force bombardier dropping his bomb from tens of thousands of feet in the clear air, without challenge, on people who will forever be unknown and anonymous to him. The kill at the bar of justice is an infantry kill, infinitely harder than the one pressed by the bombardier at the bar of the local saloon.

Average citizens go to great lengths to avoid giving offense. Civilization operates on the assumption that other peoples' feelings must be accommodated. But judges and jurors must make and deliver in open court hard decisions over people they will come to know. Is it wholly unacceptable that they act with compassion when they see the defendant up close and become fully aware he is a person? Critics say that judges are paid to be objective, and if judges cannot stand the heat, they should get out of the courtroom. But judges are people. And the jurors, the conscience of the community, are not really paid at all, and they are conscripted into the courtroom.

A necessary social factor in the scheme of criminal punishment is the belief that it works. On this rests the average person's confidence in the system, and his sense of security. The courts can and should do more than they do to inform the public of their activities. Cases of high public interest, particularly, must be explained in some meaningful manner. I was freshly reminded of this need when a Westchester County Court judge in New York State set aside, as contrary to the weight of the evidence, a jury verdict of guilty of arson against a young Hispanic man accused of setting a highly publicized hotel fire that resulted in the deaths of more than twenty people. Indeed, the newspapers had all but convicted the accused before the verdict. The public clamor against the judge was high, as might be expected, and no little bewilderment was evident. Why was a "guilty" man being set free? Why did the judge allow the issue to go to the jury if he was going to set aside a guilty verdict? The apparent answer is that the judge believed that if the appellate courts reversed him, no new jury would be required, since a jury had already spoken in the case, albeit unsatisfactorily to him. Right or wrong, the judge's action was courageous. In view of public interest and indignation, I felt the court system owed some explanation to its sponsors and supposed beneficiaries. Media accounts of trials are notoriously distortive, particularly through the trouble/action-oriented television camera, which tends to condense trials into a few unrepresentative seconds. Cases can never be judged from any media vantage point.

There is, at times, excessive preoccupation with the rights of the accused—often in neglect of the rights of the public and of the victim whose person or property has been violated. It is unquestionably in the public interest to arrest and punish criminals. The point must be made, obvious though it may seem, that criminal law is neither a game nor a contest. Judges must know the governing rules of fair prosecution, but they must also understand that the idea is not to throw out as many cases as possible on mechanical or farfetched applications of constitutional principle. They must shun legal gamesmanship and seek to understand the reason for the rules: to do justice for all. It is easier said than done.

SENTENCING

Once an accused is found guilty (convicted) of a crime, his punishment is later set by the judge, who receives, in the interim, a background report on his record and his family. In some states, the punishment is fixed by the jury. In either event, the punishment is the "sentence." Criminal-sentencing guides in the form of maximum and minimum jail terms and ranges of fines are customarily established by legislation. However, there are always those who call for achieving more uniformity in sentencing through the use of automatic sentences, which are mandated by statute, with no variations once there is a conviction. A conviction for stealing goods valued at over $500, for instance, might call for two and one-half years of imprisonment if it is a first offense; and this would hold for everyone, regardless of the circumstances.

But in automatic sentencing, the law loses an elasticity that is essential to justice. The criminal's motivation, past criminal record, previous life history, and the circumstances of the crime are all important in meting out appropriate punishment. While general conformity to standards should be the desired objective, there must be room for variation in individual cases. If mandated penalties are overly severe, prosecutors will hesitate to bring forth maximum charges, and, more damaging, jurors will simply not convict.

The best hopes for maintaining levels of consistency in sentencing are insistent judicial education and the same careful appellate review that characterizes the conviction itself. When sentencing, judges should state their full reasons for the record, in order to facilitate this appellate review. Jury sentencing is more the voice of the people of the community, and there is much to say for it. However, jury sentencing does tend to lessen consistency from case to case.

Some hold the view that criminal sentencing should not be done by judge or by jury, but by a totally detached panel of social workers, penologists, and psychiatrists. Presumably, these are the experts. I believe it is undemocratic and sociologically unsound to take the task of punishment away from the tribunal that heard the whole case— prosecution and defense—and to substitute a panel of "experts." It is naïve to wrap criminal conduct in a sociomedical cocoon. The vast bulk of improper social conduct is not sickness, nor are social ills excuses for certain among us to transgress the rights of others. No one sits in courtrooms for too long without learning of these experts' inexpertness when it comes to criminality. This is particularly true in those who hail from the social-science and psychiatric fields. Sentencing judgment is best in those who hear the whole case as it unfolds, who receive the maximum presentation by both sides and thus can weigh all the circumstances. If professionalism in sentencing is a good goal, the judge is the best professional to address the sentence. Parole, reclamation, rehabilitation, and penology are separate and subsequent social affairs.

Of course, the general principle is true that one thief should not get a suspended sentence if another who has committed the same crime is put in jail with his key thrown away. But theoretical principles, when applied, are subject to variations. The repeat offender, the hungry boy, the hardened criminal, the vicious psychopath, the penniless parent with an ailing child and an otherwise unblemished record, the provocative victim, the incited crowd—each of these may provide distinct reasons for committing the same crime, and thus sentences should speak separately to each set of facts.

In theory, criminal punishment is designed to serve various purposes. One is deterrence of the defendant from doing the crime again, and, more widely, to deter others from doing the same thing. The second general purpose is called "arrest and incapacitation," which means putting a menacing person out of circulation, presumably while he can be rehabilitated. Imprisonment itself provides an endless controversy in view of the conspicuous failure of our prison system to rehabilitate prisoners. It seems now that the best that can be hoped for is that some culprits learn their lesson, although by objective indices that is not likely to occur, except perhaps for the young.

The role of retribution in our society is controversial. Yet in ignoring the relationship between retribution and crime, criminal-justice savants miss something quite important. The victims of crime, or their families or friends, and society at large are not supposed to take the law into their own hands to seek revenge. The state is responsible for finding and punishing the culprit; that is part of law and order. But while vengeance may be the Lord's, victims and the public may want some of it, too. The apparency of adequate punishment, it is hoped, satisfies the victim and the mob and reduces their motivation to do anything more drastic.

BAIL

Bail, too, provides a regular opportunity for critical assessment of judges, although here the function of bail is usually misunderstood. Bail that is not excessive is a constitutional right. The purpose of high bail is not to punish, but to ensure attendance of the accused at his trial. The theory is that forfeiture of a significant sum of money will make trial attendance more likely. The amount of bail should relate only to the likelihood of flight, and if that prospect is sufficiently strong, bail may be denied.

Bail fixation is not designed to keep the criminally accused in jail and out of harming way in advance of trial. Deliberately keeping a prisoner in jail before his trial by unreasonably high or denial of bail is often called "preventive detention." Since innocence is presumed until guilt is proven, the specter of a police state arises wherever people can be kept in jail on mere suspicion. However, it often works out that way because so many people cannot make bail of any sum; $2,500 is considered low bail, but it might as well be $1,000,000 for those who cannot afford to post it. Actually, many question the efficacy of requiring bail in most cases, since the likelihood of court appearance is so high in relation to the great majority of crimes. Its principal effect is discriminatory against the poor, and it does not affect those with wealth or organized-crime affiliations.

The ghastliness or magnitude of a charged crime is taken into account in fixing bail, because the more severe the crime, the more severe the penalty, and the greater the temptation to flee. Reference for mental examination is another retaining device. Conversely, the probabilities of innocence, of little punishment, and of strong communal ties are seen as favorable factors, and, with their appearance, bail may be fixed low or not required at all. When judges release prisoners without bail, the latter are said to be "in their own recognizance." In actual practice, the bail most judges fix becomes standard by local rules of thumb. Most judges do not like to look bad by enabling flight with unconventionally low bail.

IN REQUIEM

My personal view from the bench will always include the image of Burr Hollister, who was my law secretary until September 1974. Sometime during the last weekend of that month, Burr, his desk awash with books and papers, was shot to death while working overtime in my courthouse chambers. His murder, as may be expected, caused a huge public stir, penetrated me to the core, and left me scarred. A court found the crime to have been one of personal passion and temporary derangement. In time, the notoriety ebbed and then disappeared entirely.

Sometimes I think of the formidability of the processes of justice in all the functions and complexity that make it up and I think of Burr. I had visualized the courthouse as part of society's barricade against lawlessness. A tiny metal pellet ended his life in the courthouse, without due process, without legal pleading, no jury, no citations. It could have happened anywhere, but it happened there. A courthouse, I learned, is more than marble, is more than a forum for rules of law; it is a harbor for human beings setting about their important causes. And it is, itself, no sanctuary from crime.

11

EQUAL/LEGAL/
SOCIAL/JUSTICE

Critics of the legal profession, of whom there is no shortage, suggest that the system has utterly failed to bring justice to society. They say lawyers are interested simply in money and power and not in society. Rich corporate lawyers control the American bar through their prominent Bar Association positions and the force of their clients. These lawyers, the critique proceeds, are nothing more than gunslingers for hire by the propertied interests. They are united in their efforts to protect the social status quo, because of both their own professionally ingrained resistance to change and their desires to perpetuate their clients' domination of society. The ideals of their economically dominant clients become their ideals without inquiry into public interest; they take no initiative of their own to reform society.

This dimmest view continues that lawyers have professional mores that justify to them their representing any client without inquiry into or concern for the social values of the client's conduct, and since they only work for the rich and powerful, their so-called professional detachment really works to perpetuate their clients' unworthy places in the social order. The famed legal willingness to take any side is not redemptive, for it only masks the fact that the major legal effort is on the side of the privileged. The adversary system of justice is prejudicial to the disadvantaged, since on balance their lawyers, if they have them, and they often do not, are outweighed by the resources of the lawyers for the rich and the privileged. The insufficiency of public outreach of effective legal services to the disadvantaged works the ongoing inequality of justice.

As gloomy as the critical outlook may be, the view for the defense is excessively rosy. There comes the claim that its legal profession, unsurpassed in the world, is a glory of America and owes no apologies to anyone. This argument is that lawyers are well-trained public-spirited professionals of high commitment, who by the nature of their profession represent all clients without endorsing their clients' views. The defense points to prominent lawyers throughout American history and enumerates the considerable social contributions they have made, in both government and private sectors. They fear that big government will threaten the independence of the bar. And they fear for the continued ability of lawyers to serve the best interests of their clients without any dilution of loyalty. Their view is that a lawyer should be able to decide which clients he should represent and how he should do it. The lawyer has no individual obligation to serve the public if he does not wish to do so; his obligation is to conduct himself ethically within the adversary system. Their belief is that existing programs make ample provision for representation of the disadvantaged.

In a real sense the legal profession itself is to blame for this dialogue, because it is unwilling to recognize that private lawyering is most often a partisan act oriented on behalf of a client more interested in getting what he wants than serving any abstract ideal of justice. For too long, lawyers in professional conclave have heard themselves lauded by themselves as anointed servants of a higher calling; but their actual activities rarely warrant such praise. Skeptics of the law have been quick to note these sociojudicial gaps.

——SUPREMACY OF SOCIAL JUSTICE——

"Social justice" is considerably broader than the legal variety. It is an overworked phrase, to be sure, which I use to relate to the distribution of the benefits and burdens of society. It encompasses the distribution of money and goods, equal opportunity to participate in the economic benefits of society, and personal liberties. In concrete terms, these are expressed in such factors as jobs, housing, education, and civil rights. Inevitably, there will be competition for social awards; the competitors will resort to political pressures; these, in turn, will affect the fundamental institutions of society, which work (or fail to work) social justice. These institutions may be called capitalism, communism, the political system, social-service assistance, compulsory health or education programs, the court system, the currency structure, housing programs, free higher education, and countless other things. The other side of benefit is obligation; social justice requires social participants to take on responsibilities that enable their society to function.

Law as it is used in court and by our lawyers and their clients is only part of a larger social design. Many indictments of the legal profession fail to take into account its truly limited scope in effecting social change. They ignore the social realities of crime. The essential power in democratic society rests with the people and with their elected representatives. The political process in this country is vastly more significant to social justice than is the legal profession.

────LAWYERS IN POLITICS────

The syllogism that since lawyers control the government and since lawyers equal the legal profession then the legal profession controls the government fails in its first premise. Lawyers do not control the government. As involved as individual lawyers may be, the great bulk of lawyers are not active politically. Even if they were, insufficient homogeneity among lawyers disqualifies them from controlling anything under the banner of their profession.

Individuals who are lawyers do hold prominent policy roles as legislators and as executives, both elected and appointed, and may also hold indirect policy roles from selective discharge of enforcement positions. Their legal training and conditioning does affect their conduct. However, elected officials who are lawyers survive at the will of their constituency, to whom they answer. Appointed lawyers answer to their appointers. There is no organized lawyers' constituency to whom lawyers are responsible. Political positions within the ranks of lawyers are as disparate as they are through the middle and upper middle classes generally.

Ironically, the lawyers who take personally active roles in party politics and elective public office are only rarely from the ranks of the so-called elite lawyers of the "establishment." The major corporate firms, to the extent there is a consistency demonstrated by experience, seem to discourage their lawyers from partisan politics. In New York, for example, the capital of the corporate bar, the major law firm partners truly active in advanced partisan political levels can be counted on one's fingers, and perhaps on a few toes held in reserve. The reasons vary from the disrepute of political activity, to inability to give it enough time, and to the concern of business clients, who rarely appreciate politically controversial lawyers on their general retainer lists.

It is only a small minority of lawyers, when compared with the profession as a whole, who are retained by the major corporations. The majority of lawyers identify their financial interest with negligence, criminal, estate, and matrimonial affairs. Their real estate and commercial transactions are not habitually of the proportions maintained by the corporate law giants.

The explanation for the heavy preponderance among politically participating lawyers of nonelitists rests primarily in economics. Lawyers who have to make their way without family money or resources, without pertinent acquaintanceships, without early outstanding talent, without good law school introduction, and without any other leg up on success must seek out ways and means to draw attention to themselves. In fact, the political road has been so commonly traveled that many take it without reflection, as a matter of course. Political appearance has always been deemed effective advertising by many, and remains so. Politics gives exposure at low out-of-pocket expense. Moreover, success in political action has the obvious virtue of leading to secure prestigious government employment at pay levels many lawyers find to be within their ambitions. Lawyers on the major law firm career ladders have no need for these presumed economic advantages; to the contrary, politics may be a hindrance to them.

But straight economics are not the whole story. There are numerous lawyers in political activity seeking facets of personal satisfaction. For instance, some aspire to the kind of work that exists only in government. Those who aspire to state judgeships go into local politics. The same applies to those who would prosecute major crimes in the district attorney's office. Others follow into politics on the undefined but generally held premise that a lawyer is helped by being in politics, if only for the useful friendships (connections) generated. Still others feel politics afford a good personal development ground, and, to boot, may throw off an economic side benefit like court appointment as a receiver or a guardian. Lawyers come to politics with confidence because of a culturally encoded belief that common skills relate, and in important part they do. A major contributory factor to political involvement is the ego booster of successful politicking, the media publicity, the being known and recognized, the ultimate power, which all become ends in themselves. There is even the thrill of the game, which comes to political buffs who are lawyers.

———NEED FOR SUPERMAJORITY——— CONSENSUS

There is a new national learning that majority vote is not always the answer where attention to significant minority needs are conditions of social stability while preserving democracy. This is changed thinking in the United States, impressed on the national consciousness by Dr. Martin Luther King, Jr., in his tragically brief years in the civil-rights movement. His was an effective movement for change worked entirely apart from partisan politics of the traditional kind. His conception of civil disobedience, accepting legal consequences for his acts, but working dramatically effective obstructing measures, exposed plainly the need for supermajority consensus if our society is to avoid unmanageable disobedience and to work effectively.

But from nonviolent ground grows violence. Today we are treated to the spectacle of rioting and all manner of social disorder as calculated political weaponry. Here is flagrant violation of the law, outright, without gloss. In one major city after another, we see rioting by minority community segments as a way to attain social justice. Worse than that, it works. Recognitions not forthcoming under regular democratic processes become activated when society's order is held ransom by violence. Some would dismiss these occurrences as black-inspired and therefore a special situation to be tolerated. But this is not the case. The end of our country's tragic Vietnam involvement was initiated, not by regular lawful means, but by street demonstrations and campus riots largely of whites. Environmentalists occupy nuclear-energy generating sites, much as labor legislation decades ago grew from sit-in strikes and picket-line violence; labor organizes boycotts of goods; housewives block access to a disputed road; truck owners barricade the highways. They get their desired attention, ofttimes results denied in courts of law and ignored by legislators and executives alike until they kick over the social traces.

All this makes thoughtful lawyers skeptical, for it erodes the foundations of respect for legal process. And it shakes up ordinary citizens, who see in it malfunctions of legal process, when actually legal process is irrelevant to political failure. Before their eyes social results are obtained, not by lawful means, but by illegal means. Sometimes the uncomfortable feeling intrudes of sympathy for the social miscreants, a recognition that their just causes may not be acknowledged any other way. Then farther down in the thought process, the awareness dawns that a determined minority can accomplish a good deal by social resistance that is technically criminal or civilly wrong, such as trespass; after all, in a democracy you cannot go around shooting every dissenter, and the indiscriminate jailing of masses of people has its own self-limiting problems.

A sad commentary on violence is that once unleashed it tends to become boundless. Sympathizers of demonstrators disapprove when police beat and manhandle charging or rock-throwing students, workers, or blacks. They fail to understand that those individuals enforcing the law who are themselves assaulted react with self-protective instincts not measurable nearly as nicely as the commentators do in their studies months and years later. Violence and tension are terrible energizers of physical passion not readily limitable in the heat of deadly struggle. Unexpectedly fierce counterviolence is a risk voluntarily assumed by those who would do violence against those who are particularly equipped, willing, and sometimes even anxious to fight back. It seems sad but fair to observe that the promoters of violence often value the police overreactions, upon which they can capitalize. Martyrs, exploiters, youngsters, idealists, innocents, hustlers, sadists, masochists, armed police, and agents of malevolence are explosive elements in social confrontations of a physical nature.

The ominous shadow is anarchy, an unleashing of destructive forces that threaten all governing consensus. It is the ultimate danger in condoning extralegal pressures, which in the end amount to social extortion. Violent action begets violent reaction, and brings out the worst in human nature. A democratic government can tolerate only so much disregard of its law, however labeled, before it ceases to function effectively. Under democracy, the answer can never be to suppress by force all those who disagree with the government. Its only alternative is to honor constitutional rights, to identify the legitimate claims of aspirants to social justice, and to fulfill them to the maximum practical extent, balancing all competing social interests.

In democracy, government rests on the consent of the governed. A democracy could never maintain sufficient police forces, with laws fierce enough, to compel obedience by terror. Necessarily, this calls for reconciliation of a practical maximum of those who do not share in the benefits of social institutions, those who are disaffected by want or prejudice, who are ill-informed and resentful. Majority votes do not inhibit minority activity in the streets. The rebellious minority, if it is of sufficient size and bears recognizable moral messages, must be given consideration lest society's equilibrium founder in the oscillation of its pervasive disorder.

The need, for effective democracy, is a consensus of its principal constituent elements, including its sizable minorities. This puts burdens of cooperation and responsibility in their group conduct on both majority and minority holders of relevant positions. It calls for opportunity to be heard, recognition that social coin is for the giving as well as the taking, and belief in human equality. The consensual process in a huge cumbersome democracy is, to be sure, an inexact thing in the working of social justice. But working consensus must be derived, starting, in our society, from the basic political unit, the individual citizen.

———PUBLIC RESPONSIBILITIES——— OF LAWYERS

Lawyers have public duties beyond their individual citizenship. Lawyers are given an extensive public franchise; they are trusted with the operation of the entire system of civil and criminal justice in this country. It follows that lawyers are trustees of the public interest in matters touching that justice system. Lawyers should be of public help because they can be. Like the doctor with the emergency patient, the man on shore with the life preserver, the lawyer is equipped for social rescue. The ability to help carries a moral responsibility to fellow human beings who need that help.

In determining the effective measures lawyers can take to discharge their continuous obligations of public responsibility and legal reform, it is naïve to overlook, when all is said and done, that lawyering is the way lawyers earn their living. Activities that, in an important way, impair relationships with clients or legal associates may be taken at significant risk. There is not only the concern of the stigma of an unpopular cause; there is also the question of tolerating time away from regular vocational duties. Working lawyers cannot go lightly to the ramparts.

There is, again, the limited effect the bar as a whole has on social change, as significantly modified by the realization that within the law some roles are better suited than others for the discharge of social responsibilities. Quite obviously, the Chief Justice of the United States Supreme Court and a lawyer who simply closes titles in Chicago have different expressive, and indeed implementing, opportunities; and different social implications attend defending the polluting of a lake as compared with drawing a will.

In choosing career directions, lawyers can orient themselves towards the public or other social roles. Obvious public-career models arise in government office-holding, including judging. The higher the office, the greater the scope. Elected executives and legislators of government plainly have the power to work at social justice within their geographic realms. Appointed officials, while normally responsible to elected ones, may, according to their office, hold important policy roles, either directly or through legal opinions or enforcement activities that implicitly carry their own value judgments. It is a fact of governmental life that experts of all stripes bootleg value judgments with much of their professional pronouncement. Teaching in law school, while not a bulk source of legal employment, is nonetheless a significant one for those who would seek to reform the law or implant social values through their classrooms, publications, studies under grant, and governmental consultations.

Lawyers devoted to labor causes can orient themselves exclusively to labor practice, and represent only the unions. Those who feel totally hostile to the service of monied interests can pursue associations that stress civil-libertarian defense or the representation of controversial figures, even social outcasts. There are lawyers and firms who survive on this legal diet, and have no need to seek sustenance from frowning clients. Or they can direct themselves to the legal outlets that represent the poor or the disadvantaged, and to public-interest law firms. All these career expenditures may align directly with commitment to cause or to principle as the individual sees it. The lawyer with the twenty-four-hour social conscience plays

Hamlet when he throws in his lot with law firms of extended commitment to major corporations.

For those who really seek, there are a number of useful alternatives that involve only partial time commitment. Part-time public office, such as counsel to legislative committees, is useful and interesting. There are professional groups that work to recommend reforms in the law, the expedition of ways to end procedural snarl, and the adaptation of old rules to new times are also useful. Changing rules on divorce, new ways of approaching judicial selection, and the negligence dilemmas illustrate important legal topics in current transactions before legislatures country-wide. Lawyers organized as an advocate force can have a marked effect on legislators; unfortunately, too much of this forensic activity is limited to the special interests of lawyers. *Pro bono* cases can be undertaken individually.

Courage in identifying with causes is admired, or at least tolerated, by more clients than lawyers think. Whether the issue be nuclear-energy safeguards, pollution of streams, school busing, location of housing for the elderly, drug-treatment facility expansion, or whatever, most clients, I have found, respect lawyers who combine their idealism with active community leadership. Clients will accept more than the traditionally safer aspects of community leadership, the prestigious ones, of school board, hospital, charitable funding, or religious involvement. For those with energy and the courage of their convictions, private practice affords a surprisingly solid platform for social crusade.

Sometimes questions come up as to whether proposed representation is appropriately *pro bono*. For instance, some time ago the corporation counsel of a major city organized a program for major law firms to supply associates to reduce the backlog of his large municipal law office. There were substantial issues raised in that program: whether the backlog was caused by inefficiency or by the unwillingness of some of the staff to devote enough time to their official duties; whether funding inadequacies were not the result of political decisions to give less pressing causes spending priority. Whether government itself is philosophically a worthy recipient of nonprofit aid in affairs that should be routinely discharged in the regular course of business is another significant matter. That particular program was tainted in my mind by the conflict-of-interest apparencies, since many of the participant firms had clients who dealt with the city. I also wondered how much of that so-called *pro bono* zeal sprang from desires to put the corporation counsel's office in debt or to make promising acquaintanceships. It struck me that the overflowing willingness of numerous major corporate firms to help here with substantial time offers was indecent when compared to the paucity of organized effort in their precincts to aid the poor, the defenseless, and the damned.

Lawyers in private practice have fine opportunities to help save the world. Whether they try is a matter of their own choice; the elements are plainly there for them. Weighing conduct against disapproval of clients or associates may occasionally be grinding, but it tests the depths of conviction. The sad fact of the matter is that, like citizens generally, most lawyers do not feel deeply about social justice. The only thing that grinds at them is the wheel nearest their nose. Here, critics of the legal profession miss a critical part of lawyering and the social interest. It is not that lawyers are scheming or plotting to protect the old order by their every move; it is that most lawyers do not care; they are only making a living. They just do not know their critics are alive, and if they did, their dialogue with their social critics would be as between people of different tongues. This cannot be prideful to either the critics or the lawyers.

——— SOCIAL CONSCIENCE ———
IN LAWYERING

What should be the conduct of lawyers troubled with the social implications of a client's conduct? Should they take the case? Classical views are that everyone is entitled to a lawyer, and that a lawyer offers services without taking to his mind or bosom his client's doings. These views are becoming increasingly troublesome, not only to lawyering initiates, but also to many experienced lawyers, who begin to question their work values. Of the latter, many are trapped by economics or simply impaled on their circumstances, without the energy, imagination, or courage to free themselves. Lawyers, as others, get older, raise families, pay mortgage installments and college tuition, and even taste of life's luxurious niceties; fundamental changes come harder as the years go.

The youngsters of the law hold more life-style options, facilitated in many cases by the growing phenomenon of liberated female consciousness, the working professional couple with double income and fewer children than the traditional husband-as-breadwinner family unit. Later marriages enable budding lawyers to take more time in feeling their way towards career satisfaction. All new lawyers owe themselves a careful analysis of their priorities before long-term professional commitment. Some law places are more likely to test conscience and conviction than others, and this subsumes the desire to be a lawyer at all.

The point never arises, however, for those who maintain rigid prejudgments or are unyielding class warriors. Legal justice is an irrelevancy for those who believe every tenant and worker is, per force, correct and must be supported in any dispute with his landlord or his employer, for those who believe every black person disputing a white is entitled to victory for his blackness alone, and for those who believe all dissenters in the street should be shot where they stand simply for being there in possession of unpopular views.

Lawyers who knowingly put themselves in loaded situations should be honest with themselves about whether the money, the power, the challenge are not their real things, and whether the inner reservations are only a sop for the conventions of social appetite. Few appearances on the legal scene are more comical than that of the big corporate lawyer willingly taking down the big-dollar draw and moaning all the way to the bank while deprecating the system for submerging his real self.

When it comes to taking unpopular cases, there is an obvious distinction between criminal and civil misconduct predicated on the primacy of personal liberty as a social value. Criminal trials are imposed by the state, acting for the people, while civil disputations largely flow from voluntary transactions between private people.

Where a client is accused of committing a crime, most lawyers who feel confident to try a criminal case would accept his representation as untroublesome. This is because of the general attitude that everyone charged with crime is entitled to a lawyer and a trial. This seems correct. While those inexperienced in criminal law being asked to take on a criminal case may be more queasy and reflective for fear of being professionally unequal to the task, there should be no taint of association with the client's purported antisocial activity. People accept that felons require lawyers. The gulf between the accused's conduct, especially if it is violent crime, and the understood pattern of lawyers' activities is typically so great that no chain of affinity will come to mind. For lawyers this kind of conduct is plainly "safe."

But sometimes a crime is so beyond the tolerable limits of anticipated conduct that getting a lawyer may be difficult; especially is this so if public ire is high. Those charged with treason, for instance, are particularly liable to widespread condemnation, even in the jailhouses among intranational criminals. Treasonable accusees may have difficulty in attracting representation from the general bar, including criminal lawyers. The essences of their crimes seem uniquely obnoxious. Where political implications or community morality are at stake, experience shows that a diligent defense lawyer can unfairly become tarred with his client's activity. While it is clear to me that accusation of any crime should not stop a lawyer from defending an accused if he feels competent to do so, I also feel no lawyer should be faulted for declining to assume voluntarily any criminal defense he finds offensive to his own conscience or even his economic best interests. Even though criminal defendants are entitled to counsel, they cannot foist themselves upon an unwilling lawyer. There are normally enough lawyers around ready, willing, and able to assume unpopular criminal representations, even many who are eager, for their publicity values. If none suitable will serve, the courts may appoint defense counsel. Under court order, absent some specific conflict of interest, such as relationship to a victim, or specific hardship, such as illness, a lawyer then becomes obligated to accept the representation. The judicial appointment makes a telling difference. The accused defendant must be represented by counsel under our system, and the only recourse where voluntary means fail is to conscript a lawyer. The burden here, including best efforts, comes with the franchise.

Civil clients do not pose the overwhelming issues of deprivation of personal liberty that attend criminal cases, although civil representation can sorely test the conscience, too. It may pose the uneasy senses of "How am I spending my life and energy?" and "Was this why I went through the deprivations of law training—to assist in the sale of questionable securities (or the toxic infiltration of ground water, or the discriminatory denial of employment, or the overcharging of consumers)?" It is simple to conclude that you should not join any office that will give you such problems of conscience. But this cannot be totally shielding, for it is difficult to foresee what may come into a busy law office, or even how a case will develop. It is in the nature of an open law office, whether it serves the capitalists or the poverty stricken, or those in between, that it represents at times those who may be doing something morally wrong, whether it be evading a just debt, cutting the corner of a governmental rule, treating badly a wife of twenty-five years, or squeezing out the best deal. For some lawyers, the only troublesome implications are those that affect the public generally, and the individual concerns are passed over. One thing above all is clear: if you cannot bear ever to side, even professionally, with a course of conduct you believe morally suspect, law practice is not for you.

An amusing paradox afflicts many of those who criticize hired-gun lawyers, urging that lawyers should only represent those to whose cause they are personally committed. These same critics would probably also criticize the same lawyers for failing to rally to the defense of politically unpopular defendants, even though the lawyers may violently disagree with the clients. A distinction can doubtless be drawn that in the latter case the exercise of constitutional liberty is the cause served. Another distinction depends on the side of the street being worked.

Should a lawyer counsel his client as to the likely adverse public reaction to his proposed action, or as to the gross unfairness of his action with respect to his adversary? My answer is affirmative in both cases, on moral grounds and further. It is invariably good lawyering to advise a client of the elements that can hurt his case, no matter how sound it appears technically. Adverse public interest and palpable unfairness are two bad forces to find opposing your client in seeking to win a case. The conscience bind becomes tighter when you consider endorsing your legal and tactical advice with your value judgment that the client should desist on moral grounds. Few clients are appreciative of what they deem preaching by lawyers, but some do listen with genuine interest, and a smaller number even heed the recommendations. The ultimate crunch, of course, is whether you accept retainers from clients or you drop them if the clients do not adhere to your goodness advice and do things you find markedly offensive to your personal convictions. But once you are into the case, it is not always easy to get out, for judges may hold you in. Moreover, if you are in a law firm, there are other people's clients who must be serviced, and that gives rise to a different kind of obligation. Lest anyone smother in the cloak of his own virtue, let me emphasize that a difficulty in sifting among us paragons who may reject unconscionable causes is our differing thresholds of conviction, fortitude, and, not insignificant, ability to resist further monetary temptation. Lawyers are the best of rationalizers.

Whatever may move the socially conscious, the majority of lawyers plainly believe their clients' motivations and actions to be immaterial. Clients are entitled, they believe, to lawyers, and they will supply their services to any lawful endeavor. To them, social implications are political questions and purely personal matters of client conscience, both unrelated to lawyering.

─────────── INEQUALITY ───────────

Inequalities of justice haunt our legal system, and remain high priorities for reform. These should be matters of concern for all lawyers, and that they are not is unflattering commentary. The perspective of equality is deceptively complex, for there is no such absolute as equality of all people, never was, and never will be.

This seems a sufficiently challenging statement in these United States to warrant a prompt explanation. We must reckon with the proud boast of American jurisprudence that "all men are equal in the eyes of the law." If this be so, the law must be myopic indeed, for men are conspicuously unequal by genetic endowment, by economic status, by education, and by all the other human things that enable one to do better than another. Can it be doubted that some are intelligent, pleasing-looking, rich, white, Christian, native-born, college-trained, or articulate? Others are ignorant, ugly, sullen, poor, Jewish, black, Hispanic, atheistic, foreign-born, uneducated, or tongue-tied. Some are useful citizens, others are repeated criminals; some command respect, some sympathy, some hostility; and some are more powerful. No one could ever have overlooked such obvious truths; so equality before the law must mean something else.

Equality before the law must refer to an equality between men based on their essential humanity. Each man bleeds, laughs, cries, sleeps, and wants. His legal rights are as important to him as others' legal rights are to them. Equality before the law must, then, connote that no man is either more or less entitled to the benefits of law than any other man. It is more a matter of equality of justicial opportunity.

But is everyone adjudged in an equal fashion simply by means of the availability of the physical setting of one judge, one jury, one lawyer, one courtroom per customer? As we have seen, law is not a fixed body of written rules for easy reference, but, instead, a loose body of principles, rules, and impressions unevenly perceived and judged and lawyered by countless people, with their personal imprints, in different social climates, and places, set in litigative processes subject to all manner of fortuity. How could all litigants receive an equal process? Who could reasonably expect equality of result derived through all those processes? "Justice" comes, if at all, diversely to people, in time, place, and station.

The adversary process of lawyer against lawyer in open court further militates against the concept of equal opportunities for justice. A significantly superior lawyer gives a better chance of winning a case. Those who can afford this assistance have advantages over those who cannot. Superior representation takes in more than native ability and training of the individual trial lawyers in question. It also includes more backup lawyers, more investigators, more clerical facilities, more pressure on the adversary, and all the things that money can buy to maximize opportunity. Indeed, the abilities of major corporations to defend themselves are so renowned and the purses of their would-be adversaries so relatively thin that, commonly, opportunities to dispute strong cases with these behemoths dissolve in compromises born of practicality. It seems an unacceptable answer that everyone has the same right to reach into the grab bag, when some have bigger hands and longer reach.

Where one party has no access to counsel at all, or cannot identify his rights so as to approach a lawyer, an inequality of justicial opportunity for him is all the plainer. People who cannot afford lawyers fall within this classification, as do those who are outside the mainstream of social communication and therefore do not understand, or even suspect, the availability of lawyering mechanisms for upholding their rights.

Outreach of legal service and information to the poor and disadvantaged is a legal priority today. Under the impetus of the famous case *Gideon* v. *Wainwright*, 372 U.S. 335 (1963), indigents in felony accusations are entitled to counsel as a matter of law. This principle has been extended to lesser crimes and to costs beyond lawyers' fees, such as court records. Thanks to the constitutional imperative, great attention is now being devoted to providing legal counsel for the criminally accused poor through public defenders, which are governmental agencies, and private legal-aid societies, and Bar Association programs, which often enjoy government support by contract or grant. The disparity in resources in criminal prosecution stacks against the defendants, but is significantly balanced by the heavy burdens of proof the states must carry to convict defendants swathed in constitutional protection.

On the civil side, the help outlook is much worse for the poor. Here, there is virtually no constitutional requirement of legal assistance. While the poor do not have the same broad vistas of civil legal difficulty found among the more affluent, they do have concerns— such as landlord-tenant, family, debts, consumer grievances—that are very important to them. Legal-aid societies, for all the good civil work done by some of them, are benevolent activities often smacking of charitable works, inadequate in uniform national outreach, and often timorous about the cases they will handle. In some places, these societies are not permitted to assume representations thought to be attractive to private practitioners, largely contingent-fee cases of negligence or debt collection. Many local Bar Associations maintain panels of lawyers for less affluent persons; they perform services at greatly reduced rates, sometimes for no fee at all. Bar Association responses, however well intentioned in the few areas where they are effective, are spotty and not available in anywhere near the requisite depth.

The only way effectively to fortify programs of legal assistance to the poor in civil matters in heavily populated urban areas is to augment regular and substantial national funding, through a National Legal Services Corporation or some counterpart, to provide more lawyers, at more places, with better support facilities. It is not inconceivable that part of the funding could be recouped by enacting legal rules requiring, under appropriate standards, overreaching defendants defeated by government-funded poverty lawyers to pay some defined costs.

A frequently articulated alternative, which is not an alternative so much as a supplementation, is a genuine legal-profession initiative, which would give the bar an opportunity to demonstrate that it can exceed itself, a process that, experience says, has a poor outlook. With urging, incentives, and perhaps some official muscling, the legal profession could be encouraged to adopt regular clinical service programs for the problems of those unable to pay, where young lawyers particularly and some supervisors should be made fully available for significant periods of time, six months to two years. This could be done in central neighborhood offices or the lawyers' own offices. The important things are regularity and continuity of the service. The encouragement of financial contributions from, or even regular assessments of, practicing lawyers could help finance poverty outreach programs—in effect, substituting or supplementing lawyers' *pro bono* service by funding. In any event, voluntary private *pro bono* assistance can never be mounted on the scale needed, even if the largely invisible private appetite for it were to materialize. Whereas in lightly populated rural areas, part-timers can suffice, in big cities full-time paid poverty lawyers can be the only reliable base of service.

The necessary definition for adequacy of adversarial legal representation must center around experienced lawyers who are intelligent, soundly judgmental, with client loyalty, who will be allowed logistical freedom to handle the case within reasonable limits. Counsel with these attributes are the adequate counsel upon whom is based the assumption of fairness in the adversary system. Accordingly, fairness for the poor lies in assurances, by selection and ongoing training, that their lawyers meet the standards of lawyering adequacy generally. Poor people with minimal lawyers are into the system only by tokenism, and they know it.

Unfortunately, many opponents of civil-law assistance mistake the implicit social tensions, and do not see civil lawyering for the poor to be in the public interest. They see civil lawyering for the poor as luxurious and mischievous. Some of their feelings are no more complicated than racism. While I do not share the belief that government spending is the end panacea for all social ills, I believe it singularly appropriate here. Our very government rests on consent of the governed; the willingness of the vast population bulk to obey the law enables the law to be enforced in democratic fashion. Traditional concepts of able, knowledgeable citizens fighting their own legal battles with the aid of lawyers known by all in their communities are casualties of the modern urban complexity. Population size, geographic diversity, educational disparities, economic inequalities, ethnic and racial intricacies in degrees previously unimagined, all these repeatedly underscore the need to make equality of justice a reality for the nation's millions now beyond effective participation in its processes.

Ongoing institutional adaptation to current needs is a key to social progress. Those who believe they are without a stake in society will not be willing social participants, nor will they respect the existing order. Unless our society acts to bring within its organic body in meaningful ways the millions of citizens who now feel excluded, disinterested, distrustful, or disenchanted, the danger must persist that these citizens will fall prey to working their resentments and redresses into unacceptable channels of obstruction of violence. The justice system is, after all, a safety valve of society.

———PREPAID LEGAL SERVICES———

The not so poor and the not so rich are also experiencing difficulties with the mounting costs of hiring lawyers. The programs now being developed for prepaid legal services and for legal-fee insurance are both constructive attempts to ameliorate cost, while still enabling people to have the lawyers necessary for them to reap the full advantage of their legal system. Under both the "closed panel" system, where an in-house staff services a group, and the "open panel" system, where group members are enabled to make their own choice of counsel, the effort is to minimize cost by group purchasing-power advantage. The prepayment of legal fees resembles a monthly or annual insurance premium. This group development, actually fostered by Supreme Court authority protection, is in its infancy, and in its maturity is bound to have important economic effects on private lawyering.

The prepaid group plan, funded by annual or monthly premiums, or by employer contribution of payroll withholding, is a way, it is hoped, of making lawyers available for the kinds of help people of small-to-moderate means and affairs typically require. The lawyers who service business clients of substance, or who have clients of sophisticated affairs, are not now threatened by either of those group systems. Both legal advertising and prepaid plans by nature reach out for limited low-cost legal involvements. While the faces of prepaid groups vary, they usually entail only a certain number of specified consultations, one legal "checkup" annually, and exclude contested litigation.

I suspect, in time, more sophisticated prepaid plans will arise and nibble away at the lower rungs of high-level legal practice. The major clients know how and where to reach out; they know about payroll lawyers and they have the volume to use them. Their own retainer arrangements and volume discounts with outside lawyers are now realistically the upper end of the scale of price preference for bulk legal usage.

AGENDA FOR LEGAL-SYSTEM REFORM

There is an ongoing agenda for legal reform. The professional literature is filled with suggested proposals, of both philosophic import and technical change in the processing of law-related affairs. A prime reformative hurdle persists in the pieced-out nature of the problems, with remedial measures being required in all the states and the federal government, and action in all branches of government, judicial, legislative, and executive, not to mention the legal profession itself. Yet, to paraphrase Eleanor Roosevelt, and all those who have paraphrased her already, it is better to light a candle than to curse the darkness.

The emerging patterns of necessary improvement within the legal system itself are becoming increasingly clear. When the customary mourning fog seemingly inevitable to all substantial legal innovation burns off, I believe certain shapes will increasingly take form. A brief inventory, although not comprehensive, may nonetheless be useful to note.

Improvement of Judges and Lawyers

The highest priority is improved judicial selection, with adequate incentive provisions to attract and retain good judges.

For judges and lawyers alike, there should be systematic requirements of continuing professional education and periodic recertification of professional fitness.

Increased Availability of Legal Services

Broader outreach of legal services into the lower and middle economic groupings is desirable. Augmented poverty services assisted by government funding, facilitation of group legal-service programs, prepaid legal plans, and legal insurance are needed.

Cost Containment

Legal costs are being priced out of reach. They can be reduced by simplifying the legal process, both in and out of court, and by the greater use of paralegal personnel in fields such as Social Security, Medicare, Medicaid, and social assistance.

Fee Reforms

Winners of civil cases should have the right to collect their legal fees from those losers who did not act within established standards of right conduct. Victims of government prosecution and civil suits should be reimbursed for legal expenses where they vindicate themselves. Contingent fees should increasingly be regulated as to limits and responsibility for bringing suit.

Court Reorganization

Court unification, including support services, is a priority item in most large metropolitan concentrations.

Court Administration

There should be greater use of the potentialities of modern electronic technology in court-calendar control, and of television and telephone communication for adjudication of motions, the conduct of conferences, and pretrial discovery; encouragement of standardized short forms for pleadings; reduction of undue pretrial discovery and procedural delays, as well as decisional delays by judges; and penalizing of dilatory tactics.

Narrowing the Appellate Apparatus

Procedural and discretionary rulings should have more limited appealability; multiple appeals should be sharply reduced to the most important substantive issues; and more summary appellate procedures should be emphasized.

Getting Cases Out of Court

This approach is today's darling. It involves establishing and encouraging alternative out-of-court forums of dispute resolution, such as arbitration and mediation, and community forums.

——OVERLOAD OF SOCIAL UTILITY——

A legal system is an institution of utility to society, conducting its regulatory impulses. But if a system is overloaded, the regulatory transmission can break down, leaving two choices: to throttle down for more efficiency but more limited social enjoyment or to expand the system.

We are now witnessing an increasing overload in our criminal justice system, in which the input of marginal crimes is becoming so high as to threaten breakdown. Take the phenomenon called "victimless crime" as an example. While the very label is controversial, it is plain enough that many "crimes" of prostitution, gambling, drunkenness, and the possession of soft drugs are part of acceptable social conduct to a significant portion of our population. When court costs and capacity factors were insignificant, a popular indifference could stand as to crimes we might term "marginal." But now, their undeniably extensive role in court congestion compels attention. Crimes of greater magnitude become subordinated to their volume. Both the dollars and the room compel fresh attention to their policy bases and the relative social priorities.

Victimless crime is only a part of a much broader bolt of social cloth. The very ability of our society to contain crime, to provide a stable order generally, is in doubt today. To complain that light punishment or no punishment at all is the weakness undermining the criminal-justice system is to ignore the reality that it is the entire system that is at stake. Crime floods society for reasons deeper than its criminal-justice system; the amount of chargeable crime exceeds the capacity of the entire legal establishment to deal fully with all of it. But, once this is said, are we certain that we are maximizing the enormous facilities we do have? I doubt it.

Infinitely fewer people go to jail than are actually arrested for felonies in urban areas, largely because of police budgets, increasing shortages of effective prosecuting facilities and problems of proof. In an effort to build conviction records of important offenders, some prosecuting offices have taken to "screening" criminals and to devoting extra effort to so-called career criminals. This is fine so far as it goes, but what does that emphasis do for the bulk of the crimes committed by others? The performance record to be admired is not that of any prosecutor's conviction rate of those cases he chooses to prosecute, but the government's rate of successful apprehension, conviction, and rehabilitation of people who commit crimes.

Constitutional protections are now criticized as thwarting irresponsibly the arrest of "criminals." Many feel that an obvious solution for the prevalence of crime is the relaxation of constitutional safeguard and the jailing of apparent "criminals." In a way, this is to think the unthinkable, for without our basic liberties, we are not a free people.

At one time, I would not have believed that average Americans could seriously entertain police-state notions. I was disabused as much as fifteen years ago, when crime in the streets was much less of a problem than it is today. In speaking at suburban Rockville Centre, New York, surely no bed of Bolshevism, I found myself questioned whether safe streets and security in the home were not worth sacrifices of traditional constitutional values, whether survival was not now the issue. Several people recently returned from a commercial European tour found the Moscow streets noteworthy for their safety and thought perhaps we were doing something wrong. The implied trade-off was appalling to me. And over the years I have heard the refrain more, put with varying gentility and with an intent to improvement. Danger to free democratic society lurks everywhere people are overly eager to hand their rights and liberties to the state in the guise of fighting street crime.

"Constitution," for all its sanctity, is not a magic incantation;

and law enforcement officials and judges must hear its sound truly and not fall under a spell. There are obligations among law enforcers and judges to respect rights, but there are also obligations, particularly among judges, to understand that the object of criminal justice is not to free suspects through intellectual exercise in constitutional constructs. The object is to do justice. The genius of our Constitution has been its adaptability to the times. When today's city block can bulge with more and more different people than a whole state of our colonial era, when even the simplest technologies fly beyond any fantasy of that earlier period, and when social patterns and human and institutional values have altered so radically, the senses of justice should loom as large as life in constitutional interpretation. It is increasingly important to reassess civil-liberation roles in light of the vastly accelerated numbers of victims and criminal opportunities. The safeguards of less complicated times may work injustices today.

Justice entails, among other recognitions, reappraisal of such constitutional doctrines as dismissing criminal guilt plainly but largely established by illegal search and seizure, releasing accused criminals under speedy trial laws that ignore unprejudicial delays, unreasonable suppression of convincing evidence of guilt, permitting endless appeals, extending entrapment as a defense, and overreliance on magic words of warning and procedures. Overly generous criminal dispensations can be avoided consistent with basic constitutional safeguard. Fresh attention must be drawn to judicial conduct that unduly benefits offenders and the constitutional liberties of their victims, as well as those of the radiating pool of citizen observers who in turn feel threatened. Our constitutional rights of liberty and property are sacred, but every legal construction of them is not.

PAYING THE PRICE

In the end, the principal remedial inquiries as to the functioning of our legal system and its logistical needs turn to the philosophic and the normative. Is our society overlegalized? Overregulated? Do Americans reach for lawyers too fast?

Some devastating statistics appeared in a 1980 article in the *Atlantic Monthly* by Harvard Law Professor Lawrence H. Tribe, entitled "Too Much Law, Too Little Justice." According to Professor Tribe, in 1977 approximately 150,000 new laws were passed by legislatures across the country, each necessitating, on the average, ten new regulations. In a three-year period, the case load of the federal courts tripled. Taking federal and state courts together at the current and projected growth rates, the numbers of appeals will be in the millions at the turn of the century.

Clearly, something has got to give. The multiplication rate of lawsuits nationally is long past the alarming stage. In addition, the coming to age of increasing numbers of lawyers, population growth, and the extension of legal outreach into all segments of society will contribute to rampant inflation of the search for legal justice.

The fundamental policy issue of the legal justice system is now squarely on the table: Should access to the courts and to legal services be continually encouraged as a prime social value? Or should court access be limited to accord with cost factors and the minimization of undue opportunities for harassment?

The American people will not be changed overnight. Regardless of the speculation about why court actions are increasing, whether it be rupture of institutional ties, modern impersonality, growing frustrations, enhanced awareness of suing and being sued, cynicism, the greed of lawyers and everyone else, or governmental encouragement, it is at least plain that the increases are huge and continuing. The likelihood, I believe, is that legal access will continue to the saturation of disenchantment, and that only when people in sufficient numbers face the failure of their law expectations and seek other ways to satisfy their needs will fundamental change come about.

Governmental decisions addressed to court access are being made continuously. There seems now no sustained responsible articulation of any view that law court access should be limited as a matter of social value. Our tradition is completely contrary. Some people fear that reforms addressed to increasing nonjudicial or expedited dispute resolution threaten the quality of our justice. Their theories soundly question the utility of expedition, if justice is sacrificed in the process. Others counter that the legal system will simply collapse of its own weight unless it is made leaner and more popularly responsive, and if it collapses, such access as remains will be counterfeit.

Excessive law is in major part a direct function of how much regulating the governments choose to do. Unless there is a sufficient slowing of the seemingly infinite escalation of government regulation, a quantum leap must be anticipated in the legal establishment, with all it entails in cost and effort. Quite obviously, governmental policy goes off on broader planes of public good than that of saving legal costs, but it must also be remembered that there cannot be boundless regulation within a limited legal infrastructure. Part of the enhanced social cost of government regulation is the expense of keeping pace in court. There is a crossover point at which any excess of government regulation defeats itself by public disgust over increased taxes and pass-through costs to goods and services, and by the weakening of the fabric of willing compliance. Recognition of this will be a major act of government.

For how much justice is the American taxpayer prepared to pay? What, if anything, is the American public, in this age of population growth, technological leaps, and increased social expectations, willing to yield of its traditional system?

These are the questions.

────READING MATERIALS────

There is no shortage of books in and around the law. For anyone wishing to explore further any aspect of *Law, Lawyers, and Laymen*, all good general libraries offer a wide range of materials. The best law libraries are in law schools, in courthouses of courts of record, and in a number of bar associations.

I share with you here some of my own favorites.

The Legal Profession Overall

The grandfather of today's progeny of lawyer "debunkers" is the most serious and articulate of the lot: *"Woe Unto You, Lawyers!"* (NY: Reynal & Hitchcock, 1939), by Professor Fred Rodell of the Yale University School of Law. If you are thinking of becoming a lawyer, or if you simply do not like lawyers, this classic is "must" reading.

Martin Mayer, *The Lawyers* (NY: Harper & Row, 1966, 1967), written by an able lay observer in a sure literary style, surveys the profession in absorbing fashion. Recently, I came across Joseph W. Bartlett, *The Law Business: A Tired Monopoly* (Littleton, CO: Rothman, 1982), which I can also recommend.

The most scholarly and comprehensive treatment of the legal profession with which I am familiar is L. Ray Patterson and Elliott E. Cheatham, *The Profession of the Law* (NY: Foundation Press, 1971). This is heavy reading, by law professors of reputation, but worth the effort.

From the Social Science Side

If you have time for only one book on the law organized as a socially scientific and philosophic phenomenon, your choice should be Edwin W. Patterson, *Jurisprudence: Men and Ideas of the Law* (NY: Foundation Press, 1953). I must confess to considerable prejudice here, since Professor Patterson, for whom I once worked as a research assistant, was my original legal mentor at the Columbia University School of Law. I admired him and I liked him. A man with a forbidding exterior but gentle insides, he started me on the path of legal scholarship and afforded me many personal kindnesses. He would have preferred any reference to him to be here, for he was uneasy with thanks and most comfortable among the books.

History, I predict, will classify Professor John Rawls as a legal philosopher of the ilk of the British philosophers of the seventeenth and eighteenth centuries. In his *A Theory of Justice* (Cambridge: Harvard University Press, 1971), Professor Rawls, who is a philosopher and not a lawyer, has sought to rationalize justice into an organized logical scheme built around two principles of justice which he postulates and a hypothetical "Original Position" from which all legal value judgments proceed. In the end, this remarkable synthesis breaks down, both from the weight of its own structure and from its failure to account sufficiently for the role of personality and the hardnesses of political, social, and economic reality. Nonetheless, it affords a strenuous intellectual exercise for law thinkers. Robert Paul Wolff, *Understanding Rawls* (Princeton: Princeton University Press, 1977), described as *A Reconstruction and Critique of A Theory of Justice*, is a good companion piece for this extraordinarily complex book, as is the more critical Brian Barry, *Liberal Theory of Justice: A Critical Examination of the Principal Doctrines in A Theory of Justice by John Rawls* (Oxford: Oxford University Press, 1973).

For popularized history of the development of law in this country, see Schwartz, *The Law in America* (NY: American Heritage, 1974). It provides a valuable overview, although it tends to oversimplification.

Of and by Judges

Jerome Frank, *Law and the Modern Mind* (NY: Brentano's, 1930, 1931) is discussed in the text. Judge Frank's foray into psychology and law was a pioneer work among the earlier American legal realists and has stood well the test of time. His subsequent *Courts on Trial, Myth and Reality in American Justice* (Princeton: Princeton University Press, 1949) is also important.

Two of the landmark books of the law are discussed in the text. They are O. W. Holmes, *The Common Law* (Boston: Little Brown 1881–Howe Edition 1963), and B. N. Cardozo, *The Nature of the Judicial Process* (New Haven: Yale University Press, 1921); the second is a series of four lectures delivered at Yale University by Mr. Justice Benjamin N. Cardozo.

Donald Dale Jackson's *Judges* (NY: Atheneum, 1974) is described on the jacket as "An inside view of the agonies and excesses of an American elite." This is a journalistic expedition that works despite its own excesses. An interesting study of the English system appears in Shimon Shetreet's *Judges on Trial, A Study of the Appointment and Accountability of the English Judiciary* (NY: North Holland, 1976).

Ethics

Read: John Hart Ely, *Democracy and Distrust* (Mass: Harvard University Press, 1981), for a literate discussion of the theories of judicial review.

The standard text in the field of legal ethics is Henry S. Drinker, *Legal Ethics* (NY: Columbia University Press, 1953). It is essentially a dry collation of the ethical code and judicial and bar association rulings.

Two commentaries on ethics written in a more popular and aggressive mode are Monroe H. Freedman, *Lawyers' Ethics in an Adversary System* (Indianapolis: Bobbs Merrill, 1975), and Jethro K. Lieberman, *Crisis at the Bar* (NY: Norton, 1978). Both are discussed in the text. Dealing with the need for the apparency of justice, John P. MacKenzie, *The Appearance of Justice* (NY: Scribners, 1974), focuses on judicial ethics.

The Pragmatism of Practice

James C. Freund, *Lawyering: A Realistic Approach to Private Practice* (NY: Law Journal Seminars Press, 1979), is a cracking good book for practicing lawyers, and sophisticated laymen will appreciate its insights into the lawyer at work.

Helene E. Schwartz, in *Lawyering* (NY: Farrer, Straus & Giroux, 1976), presents a warm account of her legal practice. Work with the poor and in the public interest are explored in Ann Fagan Ginger, *The Relevant Lawyers* (NY: Simon and Schuster, 1972).

The methodology of legal research is well covered in Morris L. Cohen's textbook, *How to Find the Law* (St. Paul: West, 1976).

An unusually good work, which is both too small and too fragmentary, lurks within the paper covers of Stephen Gillers, *The Rights of Lawyers and Clients* (NY: Avon, 1979). It meanders through a variety of lawyer-client relationships. Gregory White Smith and Steven Naifeh, *What Every Client Needs to Know about Using a*

Lawyer (NY: Putnam, 1982), offers useful reading, particularly in its discussion of finding and choosing lawyers.

Lloyd Paul Stryker was one of the best-known trial lawyers of his time. His *The Art of Advocacy* (Albany: Hughes Press, 1954) is a treat, complete with wisdom and anecdote.

Law School

There are a number of books that describe law schools by facilities description, enrollment size, and prerequisites. The best known are *The Pre-law Handbook* (Newtown, PA: Law School Admissions Services, 1982) and *Barron's Guide to Law Schools* (Elliott M. Epstein [ed.]), Woodbury, NY 1977. In a much more informal vein, Sally F. Goldfarb, *Inside the Law Schools: A Guide by Students for Students* (NY: Dutton, 1980), highlights the life styles of many law schools.

Professor Karl Llewellyn's *The Bramble Bush* (Dobbs Ferry, NY: Oceana Publications, 1960) is absolutely required reading for any would-be law student. A chucklesome relic of a past law school era is E. H. Warren, *Spartan Education* (Boston: Riverside Press, 1942).

A new work on the history of law schools, well worth reading, is Robert Stevens, *Law School* (NC: The University of North Carolina Press, 1983). The subtitle of the book is "Legal Education in America from the 1950s to the 1980s."

Two books based on the storied competitive environment of Harvard Law School offer amusing reading. They are John J. Osborne, *The Paper Chase* (NY: Popular Library, 1971), and Scott Turow, *One L* (NY: Putnam, 1977). *Paper Chase* is slicker and went on to television and movie fame, whereas *One L* is more a stream of consciousness. Neither is really representative of the majority of law schools, although competition on a lesser scale does apply to several high-ranking law schools. Of course, there are fiercely competitive individuals everywhere.

Social Justice

The works by Holmes, Frank, Patterson/Cheatham, Ely, and Rawls address themselves in differing degrees to questions of "social" as well as "legal" justice.

Jerrold S. Auerbach, *Unequal Justice: Lawyers and Social Change in Modern America* (London: Oxford University Press, 1976, 1977), written in crisp style, is a superior work when it is not beating dead horses.

Elizabeth Levy, *Lawyers for the People* (NY: Dell, 1974), contains a series of nine interviews with lawyers pursuing within their profession their own conceptions of social and legal justice.

The punishment factors of the criminal law are treated in Ernest van den Haag, *Punishing Criminals* (NY: Basic Books, 1975). Its subtitle, "Concerning a Very Old and Painful Question," is very apt.

The role of the United States Supreme Court was examined in the inimitable intellectual manner of Adolph A. Berle in his *The Three Faces of Power* (NY: Harcourt, Brace and World, 1967), which is a series of lectures given at Columbia University. Although the events in the book are dated and lapsed in novelty, the analytical technique of Professor Berle is still something to behold.

Joseph Goldstein, Anna Freud, Albert J. Solnit, *Beyond the Best Interests of the Child* (NY: Free Press, 1973), is a small and controversial gem about adoption.

American Bar Association

The American Bar Association is a veritable fount of legal publication and information. Its current address is 1155 East 60 Street, Chicago, Illinois 60637. The Association is extremely cooperative in its services and affords a good starting point for a broad spectrum of inquiries into the legal profession. Committees and Commissions of the Association prepare publications, as does the American Bar Foundation, the association's research arm.

Publications I used for reference in *Law, Lawyers, and Laymen* include commission work on standards relating to *The Prosecution Function and the Defense Function*, *Trial Courts* and *The Administration of Criminal Justice and Probation*.

I also found informative the following publications of the American Bar Foundation: *The Legal Profession in the United States* (1970); Olavi Maur, *Research on the Legal Profession, A Review of Work Done* (1972); F. B. MacKinnon, *Contingent Fees for Legal Services* (1964); F. Raymond Marks, Kirk Leswing, Barbara A. Fortinsky, *The Lawyer, the Public and Professional Responsibility*

(1972); Barbara A. Curran and Francis O. Spalding, *The Legal Needs of the Public* (1974); William Thomas Braithwaite, *Who Judges the Judges?* (1971); Barlow F. Christensen, *Lawyers for People of Moderate Means* (1970); T. Finman, *Legal Services for the Poor* (1972); Barry B. Royer and Roger C. Cramton, *American Legal Education: An Agenda For Research and Reform* (1974); Robert L. Rabin, *Lawyers for Social Change: Perspectives on Public Interest Law* (reprinted from 28 *Stanford Law Review* 1976); and Werner Pfennigstorf, *Legal Expense Insurance* (1975).

General Reading

Two grand books for legal buffs come quickly to mind, both by the redoubtable Catherine Drinker Bowen. They are *Yankee from Olympus* (Boston: Little, Brown, 1944) and *The Lion and the Throne* (Boston: Little, Brown, 1957). The *Yankee*, who is Oliver Wendell Holmes, Jr., highlights the life of the man who at age 65, after a distinguished career, went on to the U.S. Supreme Court for what was then the longest tenure in history. It is poignantly highlighted by the description of his father's (the Autocrat of the Breakfast Table) search for him during the Civil War when he was wounded, immortalized in "The Search for My Captain." The "Lion" is Lord Coke (pronounced "Cook"), perhaps the most familiar of the ancient common law judicial eminences.

Fictitious as the law may often seem, we cannot rest only on nonfiction. There are admirable works of popular fiction that light up the law and its inherently most dramatic aspect—the trial. Overlook neither Agatha Christie's *Witness for the Prosecution* (NY: S. French, 1954) nor Judge Robert Traver's *Anatomy of a Murder* (NY: Green Hill, 1953). You will also want to try George V. Higgins', *Friends of Eddie Coyle* (NY: Ballantine, 1981), and Barry C. Reed, *The Verdict* (NY: Bantam, 1981), both straight from the Boston Bar. For views of Wall Street practice, pick up Louis Auchincloss, *The Partners* (Boston: Houghton-Mifflin, 1974).

INDEX

AALS. *See* Association of American Law Schools

ABA. *See* American Bar Association

Advertising (of lawyers' services): ethics of, 87–91

"Affirmance," 64

Alabama Code of Ethics, 81

Allen, Frances A., 34

"Ambulance chasers," 40

America in Search of Itself (White), 17–18

American Bar Association: ethical standards, 81–84, 87, 94; lawyer referral handbook, 186; sponsorship of "merit selection" of judges, 229; ref: 29–30. *See also* Model Code of Professional Responsibility; Model Rules of Professional Conduct; Code of Judicial Ethics

American Bar Association Journal, 230

American Digest System: how to use, 75

American Judicature Society, 229

American Lawyer, 132

Anatomy of a Murder (Traver), 314

Anatomy of Melancholy (Burton), 4

Appeals process, 163–66

Appearance of Justice, The (MacKenzie), 311

"Appellant," "Appellee," 164

Appellate courts, 63, 163–66, 164; ref: 155

Appellate decisions, 64, 241

Appellate reversal: judges' views of, 251

Art of Advocacy, The (Stryker), 312

Associates. *See* Law Associates

Association of American Law Schools (AALS), 29–30

Attorney, 39. *See also* Lawyers

Auchincloss, Louis, 314

Auerbach, Jerrold S., 313

Authority, legal, 65–66

Bail: purpose and abuses of, 278–79

Bar, the, 35–36, 40–41

Bar associations: role in enforcing professional ethics, 83, 85; role in judicial selection, 226–30; services to the poor, 298. *See also* American Bar Association

Bar examination, 47. *See also* Multistate Bar Examination

Barrister, 36; ref: 81

Barron's Guide to Law Schools (Epstein), 312

Barry, Brian, 310

Bartlett, Joseph W., 309

Bates v. State Bar of Arizona, 87

Berle, Adolph A., 313

Beyond the Best Interests of the Child (Goldstein et al.), 313

Bible, 4

"Binding" (of precedents on a court), 66

"Black horse cases," 65

Blackmun, Harry A., 64

Black's Law Dictionary, 82

Boswell, James, 4

Bowen, Catherine Drinker, 314

Braithwaite, William Thomas, 314

Bramble Bush, The (Llewellyn), 312

Brandeis, Louis D., 222–23

Brant, Sebastian, 36

Brennan, William J., Jr., 64

Brotherhood RR Trainmen v. Virginia State Bar, 89–90

Burger, Warren E.: on trial lawyer incompetency, 171, 175, 178; ref: 64
Burton, Robert, 4
"Buying the business," 116

Canons of Professional Ethics, 81
Cardozo, Benjamin Nathan, 246–47, 310
Carswell, Harrold, 222–23
Case law, 18
Cases: precedent value of, 65; unwinnable, 248
Charges (of judges to the jury), 155, 157–59, 161
Cheatham, Elliott C., 309
Child custody proceedings, 256
Christensen, Barlow F., 314
Christie, Agatha, 314
Circuit Courts of Appeal: admission to, 41; selection of judges for, 224; ref: 67, 150–51, 165
Citations: understanding, in legal research, 69–72, 74–77
Civil disobedience, 287
Civil trials: mistrials and deadlocks in, 161–62
Clark, David S., 17
"Clearing the court calendar," 263
Code of Judicial Ethics, 218–20
Code of Responsibility. See Model Code of Professional Responsibility
Cohen, Morris L., 311
Commercial matters: fees for, compared with litigation, 104–7
Common law, 16, 65. See also Precedent
Common Law, The (Holmes), 22, 310
"Common law rights," 16
Computer systems for legal research, 76
Concurring opinions, 64, 77

Confidentiality: ethics of lawyer-client, 91–95
Constitutional rights: and criminals, 303–5
Construing statutes. See Statutory construction
Contingent fees: described, 102–3; business people's preference for, 107–8; types of, 127–29; conflicts of interest in, 129–30; ethics of, 130–46; restrictions on, 133; author's position on, 134–44; "no-fault" auto liability a result of excessive, 137–40. See also Fee restoration
Contingent Fees for Legal Services (MacKinnon), 313
Continuing education and recertification proposals, 175–76
Corbin, Arthur Linton, 62
"Counselor," 39. See also Lawyers
Court decisions, 16
Court reform: involving lawyers, 175–76; involving judges, 215–38; involving efficiency in justice, 263–68; involving juries, 269–70
Court reporters, 153
Courtroom monitoring, 263–64
"Courts of limited jurisdiction," 152
Courts on Trial (Frank), 310
Court system in the U.S., 149–66
Cramton, Roger C., 314
Criminal justice system: overload in, 303
Criminals: and constitutional rights, 303–5
Criminal trials: mistrials and deadlocks in, 161–62
Crisis at the Bar (Lieberman), 93, 311
Cross-examination: description of, 252–56; reasons for, 258–59
"Curbstone opinions," 61

Curran, Barbara A., 314
Custody proceedings, 256

Deadlocks, 161–62
Decisions, judicial, 16, 244–48
"Defendant," 157
Delay, deliberate: as an ethical
   question, 95
Democracy and Distrust (Ely),
   311
"Demonstrative" evidence, 173
"Demurrer," 154
"*De novo*," 163
Depositions, 180
Dictum, 65
Digests: use of, in legal research,
   74, 75
Diploma privilege: question of, as
   admission to the bar, 47–49
Disadvantaged, the. *See* Poor, the.
Disbursements: billing for, 117–18
Dissenting opinions, 63–64, 77
District Court: admission to, 40;
   selection of judges for, 224; ref:
   67, 150–51
Divorce. *See* Matrimonial litigation
"Divorce, poor man's," 199
Douglas, William O., 64
Drinker, Henry S., 81, 82, 311
Dual representation: problems
   with, 190–91
Dunne, Finley Peter, 233
"Dynamite" charge (of a judge to
   a jury), 161

Efficiency, judicial: problems with,
   263–68
Ely, John Hart, 311
English system of justice: compared
   with American, 36, 81, 131–32,
   134–35, 178, 271
Epstein, Elliott M., 312
Equal Access to Justice Act
   (proposed), 141

"Esquire": proper use of term, 39
Ethics. *See* Legal ethics
Ethics in an Adversary System
   (Freedman), 91–92
Evidence: lawyers' misunderstand-
   ing of rules of, 172–75; rulings
   on admission of, 269
Expediting justice: problems with,
   263–68
"Exposure," 119–20

Fact-finding, 12
Federal court officials: their role
   in making law, 17–18
Federal courts: hierarchy of, 67,
   150–51; specialized, 150; juris-
   diction of, 150–51
Federal judges: selection of, 223–26
Federal Reporter: how to use. *See*
   Law case reporters
Fee restoration (from troublemak-
   ing losers to winners), 140–44
Fees, legal. *See* Legal fees; Fee
   restoration
"Fifty percenters," 193
Finman, T., 314
"First-party insurance," 138
Fortinsky, Barbara A., 313
"Forum shopping," 245
Foundation, 173, 257
Frank, Jerome, 19, 22, 310
Frank, Leo: role of confidentiality
   in his murder case, 93
Freedman, Monroe, 91, 311
Freud, Anna, 313
Freund, James C., 311
Friends of Eddie Coyle (Higgins),
   314
Friess, Alan I., 274
Frontiero v. Richardson, 64

Gideon v. Wainwright, 298
Gillers, Stephen, 311

Ginger, Ann Fagan, 311
Goddess of justice, 36–37
"Goingness," 120–21
Goldfarb, Sally F., 312
Goldfarb v. *Virginia State Bar*, 90
Goldstein, Joseph, 313
Grand juries: purpose of, 155
"Grinding down" the other side (in a legal dispute), 95–96
Gulliver's Travels (Swift), 4

Hamilton, Andrew, 40
Harnett, Andrea, 222
Harnett, David, 42
Harnett, James, 42
Harnett, Joel, 242
Harassment of the other side (in a legal dispute), 95–96
"Harvard Citator," 72
"Hearsay" testimony: use of, 172–73
Higgins, George V., 314
"Holding" (of a case), 64–65; ref: 77
"Hold-outs" (on a jury), 160
Hollister, Burr: requiem to, 279–80
Holmes, Oliver Wendell, Jr., 22, 259, 310
"Hornbook law," 63
"Horseback" opinions, 60
"Hot bench," 165
How to Find the Law (Cohen), 311
"Hung jury," 161

"Immaterial" (as an objection), 173
"Incompetent" (as an objection), 173
Index to Legal Periodicals, 75
Induction (to the bar), 36
"Inferior courts," 152
Inns of Court, 81

Inside the Law Schools (Goldfarb), 312
"Irrelevant" (as an objection), 173

Jackson, Donald Dale, 310
Judges: their role in making law, 17–18; their ineffectiveness in monitoring lawyers, 177–79; politics a threat to quality of, 215–30; impediments to selecting qualified, 231–35; pros and cons of career, 235–38; key to order in the courtroom, 242–44; power of, 249–51; personalities of, 259–62; erroneously blamed for treating criminals too softly, 272–76. *See also* Courtroom monitoring; Decisions, judicial; Efficiency, judicial; Federal judges; Judicial campaigning; Lawyer-judge relations; State judges; Trial judges
Judges (Jackson), 310
Judges on Trial (Shetreet), 311
Judicial campaigning, 218–21, 249–50
Judicial selection: need for reform in, 215–38; role of bar associations in, 226–30. *See also* Merit selection
"Jumbos," 132
Juries: entitlement to, and waiver of, 154; selection of, 155–56; role in trial, 157–63; unpredictability of, 179–81; importance and purpose of, 269–72. *See also* Grand juries
Jurisprudence: Men and Ideas of the Law (Patterson), 309
Jury. *See* Juries
Justice: its relation to law, 13–16; its relation to economics, 14; legal definition of, 16; goddess of, described, 36–37; question of

equal opportunity for, 296–301; slow pace of trials necessary to serve, 263–65. *See also* Social justice

Justice Department: problems with its role in selecting federal judges, 224–25

"Key system": use of, in legal research, 75–76

King, Martin Luther, Jr., 287

Law: popular perceptions of, 1–7; nature of, 2–3; as a process, 11–13, 19–22; kinds of, 16–19; variations in applications of, 19–22

Law and the Modern Mind (Frank), 19, 310

Law associates, 104, 110–12, 118–19, 121–22

Law Business, The: A Tired Monopoly (Bartlett), 309

Law case reporters: understanding, in legal research, 63–64, 69–70

Law Digest (of *Martindale-Hubbell* law directory), 77

Law firms: as a business, 101, 108–13, 118–23

Law in America, The (Schwartz), 310

Law libraries: how to use materials in, 60–77

Law partnerships: economics of, 101, 108–13, 118–19, 121–22. *See also* Law associates

Law reporters. *See* Law case reporters

Law review articles: understanding citations for, 71–72, 75

Law school: admission to, 29–31; choosing a, 31–32; prerequisites for, 32–33; teaching methods in, 33–34; pros and cons of more

open admission at, 49–50. *See also* Continuing education and recertification proposals

Law School (Stevens), 312

Law School Admissions Test (LSAT). *See* LSAT

"Law's Delays, The" (Dunne), 233

Law specialties, 188–89

Lawyer, the Public and Professional Responsibility, The (Marks et al.), 313

Lawyer-client relations, 185–212

Lawyering: as a business, 101–23

Lawyering (Schwartz), 311

Lawyering: A Realistic Approach to Private Practice (Freund), 311

"Lawyering presence," 119

Lawyer-judge relations, 245–46

Lawyers: popular perceptions of, 3–7, causes of, 19–20; first step in legal redress hierarchy, 23; roles played by, 24–25; licensing of, 29–36, 41, 46–48, 50; demographic characteristics of, 37–38; locales in which they practice, 40–42; their work, 42–45; personality and professional characteristics of, 50–55; incomes of, 101, 108, 121–23; faults of, 171–75; choosing, 186–200; alternatives to, 196–99; social values of, 283–86, 289–96. *See also* Political lawyers; Trial lawyers

Lawyers, The (Mayer), 309

Lawyers' Ethics in an Adversary System (Freedman), 311

Lawyers for People of Moderate Means (Christensen), 314

Lawyers for Social Change (Rabin), 314

Lawyers for the People (Levy), 313

"Laying a foundation," 257
"Leading the witness" (as objection), 173–74
Legal aid: lack of funding for, 176; societies, 298–99. *See also* Legal services
Legal Clinic of Bates and O'Steen, 87
Legal clinics: fees of, 115
Legal ethics: history of, 81–86; defined, 82; enforcement of, 83–85; issues in, 87–98. *See also* Code of Judicial Ethics; Model Rules of Professional Conduct
Legal Ethics (Drinker), 81, 311
Legal Expense Insurance (Pfenningstorf), 314
Legal fees: discussed, 102–23; fixed by court, 113–15, proposal concerning, 142–44; who pays, 127–46; forwarding, 128; prepaid, 300–1. *See also* Contingent fees
Legal harassment (by utilities, corporations, and the government), 144–46
Legal Needs of the Public, The (Curran and Spalding), 314
Legal process: undermined by social disorder, 243–44, 287–88
Legal Profession in the U.S. (ABA), 313
Legal proof: uncertainty of, 167–69
Legal redress: description of steps of, 22–23
Legal reform. *See* Court reform; Legal-system reform. *See also* Continuing education and recertification proposals
Legal research, 59–77
Legal services: need to increase availability of, 83–84, 87–91, 297–301, 283–84, 306–7

Legal Services for the Poor (Finman), 314
Legal-system reform, 301–3. *See also* Court reform
Leswig, Kirk, 313
Levy, Elizabeth, 313
Lexis, 76
Liberal Theory of Justice (Barry), 310
Libraries, law. *See* Law libraries
Licensing of lawyers. *See* Lawyers: licensing of
Lieberman, Jethro K., 93, 311
Life of Johnson, The (Boswell), 4
Lion and the Throne, The (Bowen), 314
Litigation: fees for, 104–7. *See also* Personal-injury cases
Llewellyn, Karl, 312
Losers: fees of. *See* Fee restoration
Loss, Louis, 62
"Loss leaders," 116
"Low ball," 116
LSAT, 30–31

MacKenzie, John P., 311
MacKinnon, F. B., 313
McLuhan, Marshall, 11
"Majority" views (in a court decision), 67
Marital litigation. *See* Matrimonial litigation
Marks, F. Raymond, 313
Marshall, Thurgood, 64
"Marshalling the evidence," 158
Martindale-Hubbell law directory, 77, 186
Matrimonial litigation: lawyer-client relations in, 201–5; responsibility for fees in, 201–4; ref: 256, 264–65
Maur, Olavi, 313
Mayer, Martin, 309

MBE. *See* Multistate Bar Examination
Mead Data Central, Inc., 76
Merit selection (of judges): 228–31, 274
Milton, John, 4
Minority groups. *See also* Law school: pros and cons of more open admission at; Lawyers: demographic characteristics of; Poor, the
"Minority" views (in a court decision), 67
Missouri Non-Partisan Court Plan (1940), 229–30
Mistrials: in civil and criminal cases, 161–62
Model Code of Professional Responsibility, 81–82, 87
Model Rules of Professional Conduct; history of, 81–84; described, 84–86
"Modified" opinions, 64
More, Thomas, 4
Motion practice, 154
Multistate Bar Examination (MBE): description of, 47–48; alternatives to, 47–50

NAACP v. *Button*, 89
Naifeh, Steven, 311
Nassau County Supreme Courthouse, 242
National Legal Services Corporation, 299
Nature of the Judicial Process (Cardozo), 246–47, 310
Negligence cases: author's distaste for, 134–36; terminology, 168
Negligence lawyers: description of their work, 127–28
New York Law Journal, 224
Nixon, Richard M., 223
"No-fault" auto liability, 137–40

"Obiter dictum," 65
Objections: definitions of, 173–74
"Of Education" (Milton), 4
Official reporters. *See* Law case reporters
"On all fours," 65
One L (Turow), 312
"Opinions," 166. *See also* Dissenting; Concurring; Appellate decisions; "Horseback"; "Curbstone"; Court decisions
Osborne, John J., 312
"Over-ruling," 64

"P.A.," 101
Paper Chase, The (Osborne), 312
Paralegals: work and qualifications of, 145
Partners, The (Auchincloss), 314
Partnerships, law. *See* Law partnerships
Patterson, Edwin W., 309
Patterson, L. Ray, 309
"P. C.," 101
Percentage fees, 114–15
Percentage of recovery. *See* Contingent fees
Perjury, 93–95
Personal-injury cases: charges for, 132–33. *See also* Contingent fees
"Petitioner," 164
Petty juries. *See* Trial juries
Pfennigstorf, Werner, 314
Phagan, Mary, 93
"Philadelphia lawyer," 39–40; ref: 81–82
"Plain meaning" (of a statute), 68
"Plaintiff," 157
Plea-bargaining: economics of, 144, 265
Political lawyers, 193–94
Political trials: dangers of, 243–44
"Polling the jury," 162

Poor, the: question of availability
of legal services for, 14, 45,
298–301. *See also* Legal services
"Poor man's divorce," 199
Poverty lawyers. *See* Legal services
Powell, Arthur, 93
Powell, Lewis Franklin, Jr., 64
"Practicing law," 42–45
"Practicing lawyer," 38
"Precedent," 17, 18, 19, 65
Pre-Law Handbook, The, 312
Prepaid legal service, 300–1
Pretrial conferences: settlement
issues at, 267
"Pretrial discovery," 180
Preventive detention: its associa-
tion with bail, 278–79
Price-fixing (in the legal
profession), 90
Prior representation: problems
with, 190
"Private practice," 38
Pro bono service, 291–92, 299
Profession of the Law, The
(Patterson and Cheatham), 309
Property-injury cases, fees for. *See*
Contingent fees
Pro se court appearances: problems
with, 197–99
Prosecution offices. *See* Public-
prosecution offices
Prosser, William Lloyd, 62
"Public interest" law firms, 14
Public-prosecution offices: polit-
icization of, 176
Punishing Criminals (van den
Haag), 313

Rabin, Robert L., 314
Rawls, John, 310
"Real" evidence, 173
Recertification: proposals for
lawyers', 175–76

"Record" (of a trial): how it is
created, 152–53
Redlich, Norman, 84
Reed, Barry C., 314
Referral fees, 128
Regulations. *See* Rules and
regulations
Rehnquist, William H., 64
Relevant Lawyers, The (Ginger),
311
"Remand," 64
Reporters. *See* Law case reporters
Research on the Legal Profession
(Maur), 313
"Respondent," 164
Retainers: as a fee-charging
method, 113
"Retaining a lawyer," 102
"Reversal," 64. *See also* Appellate
reversal
Rights of Lawyers and Clients, The
(Gillers), 311
Rockefeller, Nelson, 221
Rodell, Fred, 309
Royer, Barry B., 314
Rule of law. *See* Law
Rules and regulations, governmen-
tal, 16–17, 71, 76–77; ref: 69
"Runners": example of offensive
solicitation, 90

Schwartz, Bernard, 310
Schwartz, Helene C., 311
Self-representation in a lawsuit:
problems of, 197–99
Sentencing, 162, 276–78
Settlements: defined, 264; lawyer-
client problems in, 200–1; ethics
of judicial, 264–68
Sharswood, George, 81
Shepard, 77
Shepard Citator: use of, in legal
research, 75
"Shepardizing," 75

Shetreet, Shimon, 311
Ship of Fools (Brant), 36
"Shyster," 39–40
Simmonds, Andrew, 36
Smith, Gregory White, 311
Social disorder: its relation to legal process. *See* Legal process
Social justice: its relation to legal justice, 284–85, 287–88
Soliciting (of law business): ethics of, 87–91
Solicitors, 36, 81. *See also* English system of justice
Solnit, Albert J., 313
Spalding, Francis O., 314
Spartan Education (Warren), 312
Standardized charges, 114–15
Stare decisis, 66
State court system: jurisdiction and hierarchy of courts in, 151–52; "limited" courts in, 152
State judges: selection of, 216–23
State reports. *See* Law case reporters
Statutes, 16, 67–71, 76–77
Statutory construction, 67–69
Stevens, Robert, 312
Stewart, Potter, 64
"Strike" suits, 114
Stryker, Lloyd Paul, 312
Summation, 157
Super Lawyers, The, 189
Supreme Court (U.S.). *See* U.S. Supreme Court
Swift, Jonathan, 4

Testimony, perjured: ethics of using, 93–95
Textbooks: their role in legal research, 62–63, 71, 74–75
Theory of Justice, A (Rawls), 310
"Third-party insurance," 138
Three Faces of Power, The (Berle), 313

"Time charging": described, 103–13; role of disbursements in, 117–18
Tocqueville, Alexis de, 52
"Too Much Law, Too Little Justice" (Tribe), 305–6
"Touts": example of offensive solicitation, 90
Traver, Robert, 314
Trial courts: order in, 241–44, 261–62; ref: 155
Trial judge: role in legal redress hierarchy, 23; functions of, 155–63
Trial juries. *See* Juries
Trial lawyers; choosing, 170–71; question of their competency, 171–79; question of licensing of, 175–79; ref: 188–89
Trial procedures: described, 256; reason for question-and-answer routine in, 258–59
Trials: description of, 152–63; purposes of, 155; reasons for slow pace of, 257–59. *See also* Criminal trials; Civil trials
Trials, political. *See* Political trials
Tribe, Lawrence H., 305–6
Truman, Harry, 4
Turow, Scott, 312

Understanding Rawls (Wolff), 310
Unequal Justice: Lawyers and Social Change in Modern America (Auerbach), 313
"Uniform Citator," 72
Uniform System of Citation, A, 72
United Mine Workers v. Illinois Bar Association, 90
United States Code, 71
United States Code Annotated, 71
U.S. Constitution, 17. *See also* Constitutional rights

U.S. Supreme Court: its role in making law, 21; admission to, 41; its position in *Frontiero v. Richardson*, 64; its role in promoting legal ethics, 84; its role in increasing availability of legal services, 87–91; selection of judges for, 224; ref: 18, 67, 150–51

United Transp. Union v. State Bar Michigan, 90

Utopia (More), 4

Van den Haag, Ernest, 313
"Venue": importance of, 169
Verdict, 159, 160
Verdict, The (Reed), 314
Victim-less crime, 303

Warren, E. H., 312
Watson, Tom, 93
Weinstein, Jack B., 62
Westlaw, 76
West Publishing Co., 63, 71, 76, 77

West System, 75
What Every Client Needs to Know about Using a Lawyer (Smith and Naifeh), 311–12
White, Byron R., 64
White, Theodore, 17–18
Who Judges the Judges? (Braithwaite), 314
Wigmore, John H., 62
Williston, Samuel, 62
Winners: fees of. See Fee restoration
Witnesses: preparation of, versus coaching of, 94–95; role in trial, 157, 207–8; variability of, 169; a judge's view of, 251–57
Witness for the Prosecution (Christie), 314
"*Woe Unto You, Lawyers!*" (Rodell), 309
Wolff, Robert Paul, 310

Yankee from Olympus (Bowen), 314

Zenger, John Peter, 40